Dear Carolyian, Thanks so much for your support.

Hannah Blue Heron

10-2-05

THAT
STRANGE INTIMACY

BY

HANNAH BLUE HERON

This tells a portion of my life as I remember it. The names of some people and
places have been changed.

Note for Librarians: A cataloguing record for this book is available from Library
and Archives Canada at www.collectionscanada.ca/amicus/index-e.html

ISBN 1-4120-5803-1

Printed in Victoria, BC, Canada. Printed on paper with minimum 30% recycled
fibre. Trafford's print shop runs on "green energy" from solar, wind and other
environmentally-friendly power sources.

TRAFFORD
PUBLISHING

Offices in Canada, USA, Ireland and UK
This book was published on-demand in cooperation with Trafford Publishing.
On-demand publishing is a unique process and service of making a book
available for retail sale to the public taking advantage of on-demand
manufacturing and Internet marketing. On-demand publishing includes
promotions, retail sales, manufacturing, order fulfilment, accounting and
collecting royalties on behalf of the author.

Book sales for North America and international:
Trafford Publishing, 6E–2333 Government St.,
Victoria, BC v8t 4p4 CANADA
phone 250 383 6864 (toll-free 1 888 232 4444)
fax 250 383 6804; email to orders@trafford.com
Book sales in Europe:
Trafford Publishing (uk) Ltd., Enterprise House, Wistaston Road Business
Centre,
Wistaston Road, Crewe, Cheshire cw2 7rp UNITED KINGDOM
phone 01270 251 396 (local rate 0845 230 9601)
facsimile 01270 254 983; orders.uk@trafford.com
Order online at:
trafford.com/05-0703

10 9 8 7 6 5 4 3 2

ACKNOWLEDGEMENTS

MANY THANKS TO the Southern Oregon Women's Writers Group, Gourmet Eating Society and Chorus for giving suggestions on the first draft many years ago, especially Tangren Pearl TimesChild.

Thanks also to the Desert Women's Writers Group for their many helpful suggestions on this last draft, especially Margaret Moore and Lois Lockhart. Also thanks to Wind Euler for editing the first ten chapters and to Pat Murphy for an excellent job of editing and proofreading the entire text.

I dedicate this book to my beloved life companion Margaret Moore for her constant encouragement and support and for writing an excellent Afterward.

CHAPTER ONE

I WAS LYING in the porch swing at the back of our house, staring up at the familiar blue of the Colorado sky, when my mind began to go over the events of my first year at college at the Colorado State College of Education in Greeley.

I had been popular among the Independents and among some of the young and inexperienced Greeks (sorority girls), because I knew how to have fun even *without* the boys. The older, more sophisticated Greeks apparently knew I didn't know how to have fun *with* boys. I wasn't even rushed. Because I was as tall or taller than most of them, boys didn't give me a second look. Since my older sister, Margaret, had been a sorority woman at the University of Denver, I felt slighted at first, though I soon realized the Independents were more my type. I hated dressing up, going to teas and being proper. I had made a lot of 'barbarian' friends, but no one I was close to, as I had been with my high school friend Betty Bernsen. A twinge of sorrow seized me, as I realized that Betty and I had grown apart. Betty had begun attending a business college in Denver at the same time I had left for Greeley. She had come for a visit one weekend early in the first quarter, had written me a thank you note, which I answered but we hadn't communicated since. We both realized, at least subconsciously, that out lives were taking very different paths.

During the second quarter I had gotten a job reading for Gerry Gonzales. She had been born blind and the state paid for someone to read the assigned texts for her courses. We also compared our class notes and had become close friends in the process. This continued during the spring quarter, but even though we had both attended the summer session, we were not taking any of the same classes, which was to be true for the rest of our time in college.

The summer had been most rewarding academically. A music scholarship had given me the opportunity to be in a summer orchestra and chorus enhanced by the presence of experienced teachers returning for advanced degrees as well as talented guest conductors.

As a new freshman, I had had the good fortune to be assigned to Leslie Lindau as my advisor and my instructor in humanities. When he learned I played the violin, he graciously invited me to his home to participate in a string quartet of other students. He was a very gifted pianist and a fairly good 'cello player and I had many enjoyable hours with the group. But the lack of a close friend continued to haunt me. An event the following day, at least temporarily dispelled these thoughts.

The strident voice bellowing over the loud speaker system in the brand new super market, in which I was shopping for the first time, filled me with horror at President Truman's command to drop an atomic bomb on Hiroshima, Japan. This was a rapid switch from my feelings of pleasant surprise at the solidly stacked shelves of supplies which had been rationed during the war. The announcer excused the atrocity of killing Japanese civilians (mostly women and children) in Hiroshima by reminding us listeners that many lives of U. S. servicemen would be saved. I agreed that this was a good thing, but I was not convinced that the loss of so many innocent lives was justified by such an argument. In a shocked daze, I left the store without buying a thing. It was August 6, 1945.

During the days that immediately followed, there were many commentators who agreed with my assessment of the situation. Yet a few days later another bombing was carried out on Nagasaki. In spite of the fact that this caused the Japanese warlords to capitulate and the United States was at peace for the first time in over four years, I was left feeling helpless and depressed. However, as time went on and service men and women began to return home, the bombing incidents gradually receded from from the minds of most, including my own.

Although my sister Margaret had been married the previous January, sometimes her husband, John, would be gone hunting on weekends and Margaret would come home to enjoy Mama's and my company. We three women had been very close and it seemed like old times.

Margaret had been learning the art of fortune telling from our mother Julia, and was eager to try out her skills. Of course Mama had advised us not to take such things seriously, but we did. So did Mama.

One afternoon when Margaret came over, I was wondering what the new school year would bring and I asked her to do a card reading. I had a strong premonition that it was going to be significant.

"Hmm," murmured Margaret, as she pondered the cards, "It looks like you are going to meet someone soon, who will play a very important part in your life."

"I am?" My interest level rose significantly. "Tell me more!"

"Well, let's see," Margaret responded, still studying the cards. "Huh! It looks like it's a woman. See? Here she is, the Queen of Hearts." I heard the disappointment in Margaret's voice, that it was a woman instead of Prince Charming. In contrast, my heart began beating with excitement.

"She's light complexioned, but not blond," Margaret continued. "Probably her hair is lighter than yours and she wouldn't have brown eyes." I hardly heard this latter remark, I was so intrigued by the symbolism of the Queen of Hearts.

Back at school later that month, my two dorm roommates and I were apprehensive when we discovered our *triple* had been changed into a *quad* and that the college had already assigned a new woman to share our room.

"Gosh," said Patty, as she read the notice, "she's twenty-four!" To the nineteen year olds, twenty-four sounded ancient.

"Wow, she's even been teaching already," I exclaimed, as I looked over Patty's shoulder. "She's probably coming back to school to finish getting her degree."

When the interloper arrived, I didn't recognize her as the Queen, although her hazel eyes and light brown hair matched the coloring signified by the Queen of Hearts. In spite of the fact that Lynn was older and an experienced teacher, I sensed her discomfort at being the only person in the room who didn't know anyone.

"How would you like to take a tour of the campus?" I invited.

"Why, I 'd like that very much, thank you," Lynn quickly replied.

We grabbed our sweaters and hurried out of the dormitory. As we crossed the street, I pointed out the Women's Physical Education Building, surrounded by ball fields and tennis courts.

"That's where I tend to spend too much time," I said, pointing to the tennis courts. "Do you play?"

"No, I never have," Lynn confessed, "but I am going to major in Phys. Ed. That's a pretty impressive building, isn't it? Must have been built just shortly before the war."

You're probably right," I agreed. "It's certainly better than the music building. Music is my major,"I announced proudly.

"Really!" Lynn sounded impressed over hearing this.

"Do you play an instrument or sing?" I asked.

"Oh, heavens no!" Lynn exclaimed. "I can't even carry a simple tune! But I love to listen."

"Well, we musicians certainly need listeners," I assured her.

"So, I…I wonder if you would be able to teach me to play tennis," Lynn asked hesitantly. "I want to major in Physical Education to teach people to be more fit and healthy. I really hardly ever had time to play any sports. My father owns a horse ranch in Wyoming and the whole family is pretty much involved in keeping the business going, that is, we were before the war. I used to go out with my father and brothers on round ups to do the cooking. I have ten brothers and sisters."

So there's eleven of you all together?" I asked. When Lynn nodded in the affirmative, I continued, "Gosh, I only have one sister and she's seven and a half years older than I. It must have been great, when you were all kids, to have so many playmates."

"Well, we were never lonely, even though we lived on a ranch in the boonies. Like other circumstances, there were good times and times not so good," Lynn said. "My father primarily raised polo ponies for the army, so sometimes the gleanings were slim, but we did grow a lot of our own food."

My admiration for this new friend grew by leaps and bounds. "I'd love to show you how to play tennis. We can probably find a pretty good second hand racket at Joe Cook's Sporting Goods in Denver. I'll be going home sometime in October and in the meantime, maybe they'd let you borrow one from the P. E. department. Denver's where I live, by the way.

"The building on your right is the library. It's the newest building on the campus, I understand. It is really nice and they have comfortable seats and couches to sit on while you study. See that tall old house far over to the left? That's the other end of the campus and is the music building. It's mostly practice rooms, with a practice hall in the attic for band, orchestra and chorus rehearsals. Classrooms are mainly in other buildings on the campus."

"What instrument do you play – or are you a singer?" Lynn inquired.

"Mainly, I play the violin – have since I was six years old. I chose to come here, because Henry Trustman Ginsberg is the violin teacher here. I heard him play in Denver and knew at once I wanted to study under him. As it turns out, he is a good teacher as well as a fine violinist."

"I'd love to hear you play sometime," Lynn said.

The sincerity in her voice led me to promise to play for her soon.

On Saturdays, the two of us began taking long walks in the country together. At that time, Greeley was a small town made up primarily of students, professors and retired farmers. A fairly short walk would find us in the country side where I thrilled at the saucy song of a meadow lark or was pleasantly assailed by the aroma of a freshly plowed field. I liked to guess the approximate temperature by the pitch of the cicadas' buzzing. Lynn enjoyed these outings, because it reminded her of the days when she rode the range with her father and brothers. We often found some trees to sit under and would speak of our dreams of the future. Nevertheless, Lynn was always careful to be back in time to go to confession, late in the afternoon. She was Catholic and, I discovered, took her religion seriously.

Toward the end of October, I was in a methods class in elementary school music, when I received the message that my father had died and my uncle would be coming for me within the hour. My father had been ill with cancer for the past six months and had been in a coma for several weeks. I was not surprised, but the irreversibility of suddenly being fatherless was still a shock.

As I walked across the campus towards my dorm, the grass seemed unbearably green against the intensely blue sky. The brilliance of the golden leaves of the cottonwoods and the red of the sumacs seemed to pierce my eyes. I saw Lynn coaching a game of soccer in the field behind the gym and wanted desperately to run over and tell her what had happened. Then I realized how much I wanted to be spending this beautiful day with her.

"My gosh!" I exclaimed to myself. "Do I love her more than I loved Daddy?"

Since I could hardly interrupt Lynn in her duties as a student teacher, I resolutely walked by, hoping that Lynn would at least see me and come home before I left, so I could tell her of the turmoil of my thoughts and feelings. But Lynn hadn't come by the time my uncle arrived.

When I returned from the funeral, I was feeling guilty about not having loved my father as he had wanted. "He always said that I was his favorite – that he loved me most," I explained to Lynn. "But I don't think he loved any of us very much. He just said this to torment Margaret. It was as if he were getting back at her for something! But what could she have done to him? We were just little kids when he started doing that. That's why I never could really love him. I couldn't even respect him, because of what he did to Margaret."

Lynn was listening attentively and I could feel her sympathy, so I continued. "After he retired from the railroad, I think he really did want to become close with me, but it was too late. By that time my mom and I were really close and he wasn't nice to her either." Lynn held me close, while I was crying, comforting me, while my tears washed away my feelings of guilt.

Mr. Lindau came by that weekend to take me to his home for a music fest and after he expressed his sympathy for my having lost my father, surprised me by giving me a copy of the complete Beethoven Sonatas for violin and piano, suggesting that I begin with the fifth one, called the Spring Sonata, because of its joyful nature. Later I would play it at the spring recital of the Delta Omicron honorary music sorority, which I had pledged at the end of my freshmen year.

Two or three days later, Lynn confided to me that the real reason she had come down to Colorado to finish college was to get away from the man who had broken their engagement the previous spring.

"He had bought me a beautiful ring and everything. He was ten years older than I and had been working in the same hardware store for a number of years, so he seemed pretty steady. Even though he wasn't Catholic, my family really liked him. My father isn't Catholic, either."

"Really?" I interrupted. I didn't know that."

Lynn held fast to the subject at hand. "You can imagine my shock when he told me that he had met someone he loved more. He felt bad and said I could keep the ring, but of course that was the last thing I wanted."

"I can understand that," I readily agreed.

"The worst thing was when he brought her over to my apartment to meet me. I have to admit she is much prettier than I. She had just graduated from high school and was absolutely thrilled to have a mature man with a job fall in love with her. I telephoned him afterwards and told him I didn't want to see him anymore. He was sorry that I didn't want to remain friends, but that was not an option for me. I felt betrayed by him, as well as rejected."

"Maybe you were lucky, after all," I said.

"Maybe so, but it was really embarrassing to have to tell my family and close friends. They were all very understanding, but I guess in my pride, I didn't like people feeling sorry for me. I just had to get away!" Again, Lynn began to cry and I put my arms around her and assured her that he didn't sound worthy of her anyway.

Christmas vacation came and Lynn went home to Laramie and I returned to Denver. Never before had I missed a person as I did Lynn. I could hardly wait to get back to school so that I could tell her how I felt.

The evening of our first day back found Lynn and I alone in our dorm room right around sunset. The sky was brilliant in golds, reds and purples. We were standing at the window admiring it, when I stammered, "I...I sure did miss you!"

"I missed you, too," Lynn replied.

"I've...I've never felt like this before, though," I continued. "I think...I think I love you very much!" I looked very carefully into her eyes, so I could see how these words affected her. Lynn showed surprise and then she seemed to be pleased. I took her in my arms and kissed her gently on the forehead. She didn't resist the embrace nor refuse the kiss. Then I kissed her fully on the lips, at first tentatively, then tenderly and finally, with passion. Lynn pushed me away, exclaiming, "The others will be coming back any minute!" I immediately released her. I had forgotten that there was anyone else in the world.

It wasn't long before we were making passionate love during the hours when our roommates were in class and we were free. Everything became beautiful, as Eros bloomed in me.

I loved Lynn's huge, floppy, soft breasts. None of the women in my family were so endowed. I named one of them Augusta and the other Abusta. I celebrated with them, when Lynn released her breasts from a very confining bra'; they would plunge into my hands, overflowing my long fingers. Then I gently nuzzled them with my nose and began to kiss and caress them with my tongue, sucking the nipples which, by then, were more than ready. Lynn moaned and her back began to arch. It seemed there was a direct connection between her nipples and her vulva. I held her as she thrust against me.

I embraced her with one arm and with my free hand found her pulsing labia and entered her. I did not know about the clitoris, but just from the shape of my hand, my thumb was rubbing her there as my fingers slid in and out from her thrustings. Neither of us had heard of orgasm and were blessedly ignorant of the goal we were supposed to achieve. What became the culmination for me was the ecstasy of peace, light and fulfillment I felt after the excitement of the love making.

One afternoon, Lynn pushed away my trembling body, exclaiming, "What we're doing is a mortal sin and if we don't stop, I'm going to have to ask to be assigned to another room!"

Shock stopped the trembling. Having been raised a Christian Scientist, I was unfamiliar with the term *mortal* sin. Sin was a product of mortal mind, as was sickness and I certainly did not want to be cured of this by saying the Scientific Statement of Being. I hadn't read the definition of sex, if there was one, in the glossary of the *Science and Health with Key to the Scriptures* by Mary Baker Eddy. I guessed that it was probably another product of mortal mind and, therefore, unreal.

I had quit going to Sunday School during my junior year in high school.

A few days later, the story of Ruth and Naomi vaguely came to my mind. I was sure it was in the Old Testament. I borrowed Lynn's Bible and became very excited when I found the Book of Ruth. Upon reading the first section, I was so impressed with its beauty, I called out, "Lynn, listen to this. It's from the Old Testament...the Book of Ruth."

"Naomi said, "See your sister-in-law has gone back to her people and to her gods. Return after your sister-in-law."
But Ruth said, "Entreat me not to leave you
or to turn from following you,
For where you go, I will go
and where you live, I will live.
Your people shall be my people
and your God my God.
Where you die, I will die
and there will I be buried.
May the Lord punish me severely
if I allow anything but death
to separate us."

"Now, isn't that beautiful and doesn't it sound like us?" I was jubilant.

"Well, yes, it does," admitted Lynn reluctantly.

"Why don't you tell the priest about it at your next confession?" I suggested.

When Lynn presented this new evidence in our favor at her next Saturday afternoon confession, the priest quickly retorted, "That certainly does not mean that they made love! Of course not! You'd better go home and read the Old Testament stories of Sodom and Gomorrah. Making love with a person of your own sex is a MORTAL SIN! Now, if you're truly sorry for offending Jesus in such a way, for your penance, I want you to make the Stations of the Cross, with much sorrow for the way you have offended your Lord. God bless you, now, and go in peace."

Later, back in the dorm, Lynn faced me again with the ultimatum, "If we don't stop doing this, I'm going to have to get switched to another dorm!"

I was immediately aware that Lynn was very serious, but it was hard for me to believe that something so beautiful as our love making was wrong. "Why is Lynn's face so beautiful afterwards, if it's a sin?" I asked myself. However, by then, I was so in love with Lynn, I couldn't stand the thought of being apart from her and quickly decided our friendship was worth the celibacy. We kept sleeping together when we had the chance, and even hugged and kissed, but very carefully kept our hands above our waists. It wasn't easy. In fact, it was extremely frustrating.

In the meantime, since religion seemed so important to Lynn, I began to initiate long discussions about it. These were very metaphysical, because of my Christian Science background. I started, once again, to attend Christian Science services to see if they had anything to say about sex. Assiduously, I studied Mary Baker Eddy's writings, but wasn't enlightened at all. I ultimately made an appointment with our family practitioner, terrified at the thought of telling Mrs. Thompson about my feelings for Lynn. As I sat in the reception room waiting to be called, I couldn't help but overhear Mrs. Thompson counseling someone over the telephone.

"Remember that God is Love and is All in All. Nothing else really matters." Such advice was very familiar to me, but I felt that something was missing. I was tempted to get up and leave, when Mrs. Thompson appeared in the doorway and beckoned me in.

I wasn't able to speak directly of Lynn, but blurted out, "Can't we love people, too, besides God, that is?"

"Of course, child, but in as spiritual a way as possible."

I didn't like being called a child, but my mind quickly skipped over that as I wondered if that meant loving without love making. I remained silent, but I did look directly into the older woman's eyes, letting my pain show.

"Georgette, I think if you continue attending Sunday services and study your lessons each week, you will finally find the answers to your problems," the practitioner said, thus terminating the session.

On the streetcar ride home, I realized I was no longer a Christian Scientist. I knew Mrs. Thompson wouldn't have approved of my love making with Lynn either.

Shortly after that experience, Lynn got our discussions off the metaphysical plane and told me about the Real Presence of God on the altars of Catholic Churches and that if you were in the state of grace, you could receive Him into your heart every morning at Holy Communion. I was impressed with this daily contact with such a concrete God. I decided that I wanted to learn more about that religion.

For me, it was like falling in love all over again, this time with Jesus in the Blessed Sacrament. Lynn had rarely gone to Mass except on Sundays and Holy Days of Obligation, but in the joy of my discovery, we started getting up at six o'clock in order to attend Mass at seven. Since both of us had eight o'clock classes, that meant going without breakfast, so Lynn could receive the Body of Christ in Communion. At that time, it seemed to me that both of us were being rewarded for our fasting. I wouldn't be able to receive until after I had taken instructions and had been baptized.

In May, Lynn went home for a week, because several of her brothers and one sister had furloughs from various branches of the Service. The family would be all together for the first time in several years.

After Lynn left, I wasn't as lonely as I had been at Christmas. It seemed as if all the love I had for Lynn, which I was forced to repress in many ways, welled up in me and poured itself out on Jesus.

As I walked alone to Mass each morning, all the creatures I met were drawn to me, because of the love emanating from me. One little dog insisted on following me to church and would be waiting there when I came out. As soon as we returned to its yard, it ceased following me. Even the birds seemed to fly lower to join their songs with those of my bursting heart. I began writing poetry and soon filled the little blank book Lynn had made for me in a book binding class. I continued to go to Mass, to cry tears of longing to receive Holy Communion and to carefully watch the nuns up in the front of the Church, wondering what their lives must be like.

At summer school, Lynn and I were able to obtain a double room in another dorm. However, we were thoroughly dismayed when the Methodist dorm mother confronted us with the fact that she had entered our room early one morning and had found us together in one of the single beds…and in the nude!

"Here you two are, piously going to Mass each morning, and you," she said, thrusting a finger in my face, "taking instructions to become a Catholic, while at night…" The sentence ended in sputtering. "I've never, in all my born days, I have never known such hypocrites!"

I was speechless with shock but somehow Lynn was able to convince Mrs. Hausman that we were only sleeping together – in the nude because of the heat. Nothing more came of it, except that I fully realized that two women making love was not approved of by Catholics, Protestants…the entire world!

Nonetheless, I was duly baptised at the end of the summer and joyously received Holy Communion the very next morning.

At the end of my sophomore year, the savings Mama had toward my college education were exhausted. Mama had to admit that the varicose veins in her legs had progressed to the point that it was getting difficult for her to continue working as the manager of the student union cafeteria at Denver University. I was very aware that she would probably try to keep working until she dropped dead, because she felt that a college education was of primary importance for her daughters.

I had already given up my major in music, so I could work more. There were so few credits given for music courses that I was in school from eight in the morning until six in the evening. It was somewhat of a compensation when I was counseled to go for a triple major, in which I would major in music, English and Spanish with fewer credits in each than required for a full major, but more credits than for a minor. Now I decided to quit college temporarily. I was determined to find a job of some kind and finish on my own so Mama could quit working.

Because Lynn's savings were also getting low, she made a similar decision.

CHAPTER TWO

BECAUSE THE MEN and women of the Armed Forces were not yet back from the war, in the spring of 1946, Lynn and I were able to obtain well-paid teaching positions at a little farming community fifty miles east of Denver for the year to come. Lynn would teach the first, second and third grades, while I would teach the fourth, fifth and sixth grades.

For the summer, we were able to obtain jobs counseling at the Flying 'G' Ranch, the Girl Scout Camp nearest Denver. I had been an enthusiastic Brownie Scout, Intermediate Scout and Senior Scout. I had also attended the camp during my thirteenth and fourteenth summers. I was quite excited to be a counselor. Somehow it felt like a homecoming.

Lynn was assigned to the oldest group of campers, who were thirteen and fourteen. Each unit was composed of sixteen girls, four to a tent. Lynn's was called the Wranglers, since they would be working a lot with the horses. Because of Lynn's experience with horses and camping, they felt she would be most able to manage the three day camping trip these older campers were offered.

I would be in charge of the youngest group of seven, eight and nine year olds, whose unit name was the Pine Cones. In the meantime, June, Lynn's older sister, was released from the Navy, and since she intended to go to college in the fall, when she heard what Lynn and I were doing for the summer, she applied and also got a counselor's job at the Flying 'G'. She was assigned to the middle group, the Chipmunks, who were ten, eleven and twelve years old.

After buying our camp uniforms of light blue denim trousers and white, short sleeved shirts, the three of us caught a ride to the camp with Scotty, the program director, who had also interviewed us for our jobs. She explained that the camp director had gone up a few days ahead to familiarize herself with the setting. Amy Freeman was a professional camp director, who was not directly affiliated with the Denver Girl Scouts and had never seen the Flying 'G'. June, Lynn and I were surprised to meet a woman in her fifties, since Scotty was only a little older than Lynn. We soon realized that Amy was a proficient leader, who would have a way with the young campers.

Many of the girls in my unit had not only ever been to camp before, but this was their first time away from home. At the first meeting, right after lunch, I began by having them sing some camp songs to make them feel as at home as possible. Then I went over the camp directives with them, making sure they understood them.

A few days after they were there, we all went down to the wash house to do a little laundry together. Even though I had warned them not to put colored clothing in with white, while I was busy supervising them, a pair of red socks got in with the whites, leaving pink socks, panties and blouses. I felt responsible, but Amy assured me that it wasn't the first time such a thing had happened.

At night, after the evening camp fire, I went to each tent to see that the girls were ready and in bed before lights out. I found some of them were very homesick, crying for their mothers. I would hold them in my arms, trying to comfort them, which worked for awhile, but after a few days the parents of three of them had to be called to come and get their daughters. Again, Amy reassured me this often happened with such young campers.

The counselors were given one day off (a full twenty-four hours) each two week session, when they could go anywhere and do as they wished. Lynn and I were able to get our day off together and decided to go fishing. The stream running through the camp was posted, so we were able to catch a mess of small rainbow trout, six to eight inches long, with poles improvised from willow switches, ordinary string and bent pins. The very real worms from the barn helped, too.

"Let's clean and cook them right away," Lynn suggested. "You can't imagine how much better they taste when you do that."

"I…I've never cleaned fish before," I gulped.

"No time like the present to learn," Lynn chuckled. "Get out your trusty Girl Scout knife and we'll do it together." After she got a firm grip by putting a finger in each gill, she skillfully slit a fish's belly, then reached in and pulled out the entrails in one swoop. "May as well leave the bones in. After they're cooked, it's easy just to suck off the meat."

"Okay, then," I said, as I gritted my teeth and, inserting my fingers into the gills, carefully slit the first belly. It took me two tries to get out all the guts, but I could honestly say, "This isn't so bad," as I picked up another fish.

"Some people just throw the entrails back in the stream, but I prefer burying them for the sake of the folks down stream," Lynn instructed. "We can do that when we've finished."

Since the youngest group of girls didn't have an overnight planned, I was glad to get the chance to camp out with Lynn. We hadn't brought a tent, but simply rolled out our sleeping bags on a bed of pine needles and prepared to watch the stars until we went to sleep. When it got pretty cold towards morning (the Flying 'G' was at 8000 feet) we managed to unfold our separate bed rolls, leaving half the blankets for a cushion and the other half to cover ourselves. By cuddling together we were able to keep warm, as well as feeling comforted.

I immediately decided that my campers would like to learn to fish, too, since it was so easy. I spoke to Scotty about it, since she was the program director. She couldn't believe that they hadn't thought of taking the campers fishing before, but hesitated doing it for the first time with the thirteen youngest girls.

"I thought we could collect the willow switches, string and pins and put the poles together the day before," I explained. "Then we could catch the worms in the morning right before we go."

"Well, yes," Scotty agreed, "it might work that way. It's the cleaning of the fish that concerns me, though."

"I see what you mean," I agreed, frowning as I sought a solution.

"I know what we can do," Scotty exclaimed. "I'll go with you and you and I can probably do most of it. Maybe some of the nine year olds could do a fish or two. We can have the kitchen pack some peanut butter sandwiches, apples and cookies to round out the meal. It would be their lunch for the day. In fact, I bet Amy would like to come along. She could teach your campers how to set a fire."

"That would be great, Scotty!" I was grateful for the solution.

The campers were more than pleased about the opportunity, especially when they learned they were the first campers to go fishing. Of course some of them didn't want to handle the worms and just left them in the cans filled with dirt and horse dung – although most of them joined in when they saw the others enjoying themselves.

Only three or four of them wanted to learn how to clean the fish, while the majority learned how to set fires in pits and prepare for cooking the catch. There were others who really did not enjoy the flavor of the fish, but were satisfied with the rest of the lunch and on the whole were happy with the outing.

By the time Lynn and I were ready to take our twenty four hours during the second session, Lynn had become friends with the horse counselor, Julie. The girls in Lynn's unit not only learned to ride, but also learned to put on the saddles and bridles and were expected to muck out the stalls and provide their mounts with fresh food and water. Because of her experience with her father's horses, Lynn was an invaluable aid to Julie.

I had learned the fundamentals of riding during my experiences as a camper and had gone riding a few times on rented horses since then. I was thrilled when Lynn and I were invited to go riding along with the older campers, even though it was Lynn's day off. There was a beautiful sorrel horse named Cassandra, sixteen hands high, who would suit my long legs to a tee. In fact, there were two such horses and no one besides the wrangler, the title bestowed on the horse counselor, was tall enough to ride them. She definitely encouraged me to join them at every opportunity, so that Cassandra would get the necessary work outs. Julie's own favorite was a piebald named Jeremy, who was laid back enough that she felt safer riding him, while at the same time instructing the campers.

It wasn't much of a holiday for Lynn to go riding with her campers, but she knew how much I would enjoy and appreciate the experience. How proud I was when Julie came up to me after the ride and told me I was a natural. This was to be the first of many wonderful rides.

Lynn also enjoyed my enthusiasm at learning to saddle and bridle my mount and was proud of my being just as enthusiastic about mucking out Cassandra's stall and providing her with fresh hay and water.

Later in the summer, when we three went out for a ride, Julie suggested that we ride bareback, definitely a first for me. I was ecstatic feeling the muscles of my horse as they moved beneath my buttocks and legs. I quickly became aware of Cassandra's unique gait between her trot and canter. Her trot was smooth and her canter even smoother, but the gait in between was absolutely jolting. I learned to quickly kick her into the canter, when I was ensconced in the saddle and my feet were firmly in the stirrups, but without that support, the first time we rode bareback, I suddenly found myself on the ground. Fortunately I wasn't dragged as I might have been had a foot been caught in a stirrup. Also there was a nearby fence to help me remount.

The only other liability of riding in that way was a sore tailbone for a few days, but the feeling of freedom drove me on to ignore the pain until I formed a protective callous.

It was during the final session of camp that the three of us found an opportunity to go out bareback riding for the last time. Our mounts seemed fresh and eager to get a good workout. Up until that day, we had never gone beyond a canter. While I wondered what it would be like to actually gallop, I was pretty much satisfied with cantering, but was Cassandra? Shortly after we had begun our return to the corral, Cassandra decided, on her own, that she would like to gallop and gallop, faster and faster. I automatically tightened my long legs around her girth and with that grip managed to stay on, but nothing I did persuaded Cassandra to go back to a canter. While I was thrilled to feel those huge muscles expanding and contracting beneath me, as I noticed the hills seeming to speed by in a haze, I was filled with terror as to the outcome of this adventure. We approached the gate leading to the barn and corral and Cassandra didn't slow down one bit. I wondered if she would "jump it" or "stop on a dime" in which case I would be thrown over Cassandra's head. Neither possibility was consoling to me, since I had never jumped with a horse, even in a saddle, much less bareback, I wasn't at all certain that my already aching legs could grip hard enough to remain on the horse should she suddenly stop.

Cassandra chose to stop and my legs proved strong enough to withstand the shock, but just for an instant. As the big horse stood there panting, I somehow swung one leg over and slid down her side to the ground, where my tired legs buckled under. I was barely able to swing aside to keep from falling into Cassandra's legs.

In the meantime Julie and Lynn came galloping up, but in full control of their horses. They leaped off and ran over to see if I was all right. I laughed and cried at the same time, as I tried to describe the exhilaration I had felt, at the same time being totally terrified.

"Believe me," Julie exclaimed, "I know what you mean. I've been through it myself," she confessed. "You did really well, though, and I'm proud of you." I couldn't help but wonder if she was just saying that to make me feel better, but then I grinned as I realized Julie hadn't been born on a horse either.

"Thanks, Julie." I murmured. "That makes me feel better."

The summer came to an end and Lynn and I began to prepare for our teaching positions. We went out to Hibbings and got our respective classrooms prepared, decorating the bulletin boards and making sure our supplies were there. We were surprised, as was Mr. Clifford, the principal, to discover that the first and second grades numbered thirty children, which was a handful even for an experienced teacher like Lynn. So he moved the third grade up into my room, which was larger. The third, fourth, fifth and sixth grades numbered forty-five and extra desks had to be rounded up to seat them all. The room was crowded, but I, in the innocence of my inexperience, was sure I could manage all right. I did well enough, but going through that many workbooks for each subject and each grade, was a daunting task.

Fortunately, Mr. Clifford was aware that this would not be a good thing for very long and told me they were looking for another teacher to take the third and fourth grades.

"But that would leave me with just the eleven children in the small fifth and sixth!" I exclaimed.

"Well, I noticed all those courses you have in music education, so I thought you could teach music to all of the grades, but not all at once," he quickly assured me. "Besides that, the only other room in the building will only hold twelve desks."

The thought of actually teaching music was exciting to me. After the transfer, I discovered that a sixth grade boy played the saxophone, a girl the clarinet and one of my fifth grade students wanted to learn the French Horn. It just so happened that the school owned one, as well as a big bass drum. Another fifth grade girl was more than willing to play the drum.

Shortly thereafter, I was approached by a mother of a student in the fourth grade to see if I would have time to give him private lessons on the violin. I was most enthusiastic to take him on as well as earn a little extra money. Before long I was making an arrangement for my little band to play an accompaniment to *Meadowlands,* while the grade school chorus sang the words.

The first day I went into Lynn's room to teach the first and second graders music, all went well until I noticed it was time to collect the books before the bell rang. "This was a really fun class," I said, "but now it's time to pass your books up to the front."

I was amazed when they all simply looked up at me, but did nothing. I realized they weren't being naughty, and then wondered, "How can I say that any simpler?" Aloud, I tried again, "Please pass your books up to the front." The palms of my hands began to perspire as, again, they just looked at me or at each other. Finally, a second grader raised his hand and informed me, "Miss Deming has the monitors collect the books."

I could see, at once, the wisdom of this and breathed a sigh of relief. I quickly rephrased my command, "Will the monitors please collect the books." Almost as one, the monitors arose and dutifully collected the books, just as the bell rang.

Because Mass was celebrated in Hibbings only once a month, Lynn and I spent most of our weekends in Denver with Mama, so we could go to Mass on Sundays. Everyone in town thought we had boy friends in Denver. They were totally unsuspecting of the moral struggles we were having, sharing a room and a bed, albeit a double one. Finally, I felt obliged to speak of my temptations in confession, not because we had made love, but because of my imaginings. This time I got the full social conditioning on homosexuality. I was advised that it was not only a mortal sin, but a psychological illness, as well. I was told that if Lynn and I couldn't stop on our own, we should get professional help, and, of course, not live together. By then, I felt I couldn't live without Lynn, so a new resolve squelched the thoughts as well as the actions.

Because my father had been a railroader and had often been away from home, I had been raised in a woman-ruled household. My mother, sister and I would put up with his being the boss when he was home, but when he left, it would be as if a heavy fog lifted and the sun came out once more. We would celebrate until he came home again. Since by this time, Margaret was married, these weekends with Lynn and my mother were like old times.

With both of her daughters out of town, Mama was delighted to have Lynn and me stay with her on the weekends. She would cook up fabulous meals, which we really appreciated, often being too tired to cook much after a day of teaching and stacks of workbooks to correct before the next day.

Lynn and my mother quickly grew to like each other and when Mama found out how much Lynn had to pay for new brassieres, she suggested, "Why don't you give me one of your old ones that I could cut up and use for a pattern. I could make you some fine bras from Indian head cloth, that would be much sturdier than the ones you've got now, and wouldn't cost nearly as much."

"Really?" Lynn gasped. "How much would you have to charge?"

"Just the price of the material. It wouldn't take long at all," Mama assured her. Thus, Lynn got six new brassieres for the price of one of her former ones.

When Lynn and I returned to college for our final year, we were surprised to find an increase in the student population, from a little over three hundred students to nearly a thousand, precipitated by the recently returning service men and women taking advantage of the new GI bill. Lynn and I got a room in a private home and, again, were sleeping together in a single bed, although the room had a second bed. The bonds of our relationship grew tighter in spite of our continuing celibacy. Luckily, the elderly couple who ran the place were not snoopy.

I continued to earn a little extra money playing my violin at banquets, receptions and weddings, through the auspices of the music department, and was often told how much people enjoyed listening to me play.

A young boy, who was also studying under Mr. Ginsberg, although he was not yet a college student, played the *Symphonie Espagnole* of Eduard Lalo in a concert with the college orchestra. After the concert, I saw him being congratulated by an older couple, who turned out to be his sponsors. I wondered briefly if Mr. Ginsberg couldn't find a sponsor for me, but realized it was too late. I definitely had to finish school and not be dependent on Mama.

One day during a private lesson with Mr. Ginsberg, he began to question me about what I planned to do after graduation. I suddenly realized that I had never told him I had given up my full major in music.

"Oh, I'll be teaching high school English and Spanish. I had to drop my full music major, because I had to work some to get through college and I wasn't able to do that and take all the extra classes a music major needs. I probably won't teach music, since I only took methods for the elementary grades and I never took conducting."

"So your parents weren't able to help you much?" Mr. Ginsberg asked.

"Well, my father died during my sophomore year in college. He was already retired by then and they didn't have much money anyway."

Mr. Ginsberg seemed a little embarrassed by this information and said, "Well, you can probably have some private violin students and maybe find some people to play with for pleasure."

"Oh, I certainly plan to do that, thanks, Mr. Ginsberg," I responded. But I wondered, nevertheless, if I had told him of my financial hardships earlier if he might have offered to find a sponsor for me.

The following year, because of her teaching experience, Lynn was able to obtain a job in Colorado Springs. I had to be satisfied with a position in a little town just inside the Colorado/Nebraska border, where I would be teaching English to the ninth and tenth grades. Since Mama was no longer working, I asked if she would like to come and live with me. Pleased, she rented out her home in Denver and we found a small apartment within walking distance of the school.

Mama was of French descent and had black hair, deep brown eyes and dark skin. One day, Mama and I were grocery shopping. When we arrived at the check stand, the owner suddenly blurted out, "Well, now, I'll tell ya' somethin', ladies. Our little town is really for white folks only. Always has been," he added.

My mouth dropped and Mama quickly walked out of the store. I was so shocked, I couldn't think of a thing to say in return. I paid the bill, picked up the packages and followed after Mama.

After we arrived home, Mama shared an unpleasant experience she had had as a young woman working in a department store in San Diego. A Mexican man had come up to her and began speaking in Spanish. When she told him she only spoke English and didn't understand what he was saying, he began yelling at her for being ashamed of her Mexican heritage. Nothing she said convinced him otherwise. She ended her story with the remark that it was really hard to be so dark complexioned. Suddenly I understood why Mama always wore a heavy coat of powder on her face.

"Mama," I cried out. "I love your beautiful, dark skin. I wish mine was as pretty as yours."

"No, no, Georgette," Mama maintained. "You don't know all the trouble it has brought me!" We cried together some and then the subject was dropped. I was chagrined to think I hadn't realized this about Mama before.

In my classes at the high school, the boys began to set me up by asking me what good it did to go to school. When I tried to enumerate the benefits of an education, they laughed at me, saying that their fathers, who had very little education, were making much more money than I was. One boy's father had a combine that reached from one side of a street to the other. Another bragged that his father bought a new truck every year. Another family traveled to Florida every winter and now that the war was over, they were planning to go to Europe. They didn't seem to remember the drouth and depression of the thirties, even though this was only 1948 and there were still burnt out buildings standing on their lands to remind them. When I reminded them that they still had to go to school by law and tried to ignore their disparaging remarks, they would put their feet up on their desks and blow bubbles with their gum. As soon as I turned my back to write something on the chalk board, the air was filled with folded paper air planes and spit wads. I was bitterly embarrassed by the mess on the floor at the end of a day, wondering what the janitor must think.

I was ashamed to ask for help from the vice-principal, although I had sent some of the culprits to him several times. When Lynn came to visit one weekend, I tried to appear happy and took her to see my classroom. Looking over my bulletin board, Lynn said, " Georgette, come here and look at this."

I apologized at once, because I hadn't put anything new on it since the second week of school. I hadn't even admitted to myself that I simply didn't have the energy. When I stepped up by Lynn, I saw the words *blue nose* scribbled over the pictures I had put up. At the bottom someone had written, "Miss Benton is a blue nose."

"What does it mean, Lynn?" I asked with a trembling voice.

"I don't know," Lynn stated, " but I doubt if it's complimentary. I think you should take them down." She started taking them down herself. "I know what a pain boys this age can be. You ought to go to your vice-principal and get some help," she suggested.

"Well, the girls are almost as bad. They keep laughing at everything the boys do." I tried to be fair, even in my pain.

Later that week, I spoke to the vice-principal about it and he told me to send the culprits to his office. I couldn't admit that sometimes it seemed as if the whole class was against me.

Mama soon noticed that my usually hearty appetite was on the wane. I would stay up until one or two in the mornings, trying to think up lesson plans that would get the students' interest, but they only seemed to inspire them to more ridicule.

Finally, one Friday night, I pushed away my supper plate and began crying hysterically. "I hate this job! No matter what I do they just make fun of me! It's not like teaching in Hibbings, at all! I can't go back another day!"

"Well, I agree, you certainly can't go on like this. You'd better go call the principal and tell him how you're feeling," Mama advised.

The principal was surprised to learn I had been having so much trouble and promised to come to my class room to see if he could give me some help. By then, I was sobbing. I was finally able to blurt out, "I'm afraid it's too late! I just can't make myself go into that room again! I did talk to Mr. Bloomquist about it," I added.

"I wish he had told me you were having so much trouble," Mr. Thornton said. I guess he took in the extent of my distress and acquiesced. "Well, all right, then, we won't expect you on Monday. Send me your address so we can mail what we still owe you." He thanked me for telling him and wished me well.

Since Mama had rented her house in Denver, we decided to move to Colorado Springs to be near Lynn. When I telephoned Lynn to tell her, she expressed sorrow for my pain, but assured me it would be nice living close to each other again.

For economic reasons, Mama and I rented a one bedroom apartment, and shared the big double bed. I was stunned, one night, when I woke myself in the midst of masturbating, lying next to Mama. I quickly froze and listened to see if she was breathing as if she were asleep. It was absolutely still. Neither of us said anything. After an interminable amount of time, I heard Mama breathing as she did when sleeping. Then I worried about how to confess such a sin! It had been the first time I had done such a thing since I had been baptized. I didn't even consider that it might be a warning, but Mama did.

Several days later, in a rather clumsy way, Mama said, "You know, dear, you ought to think about meeting some man and getting married. The older you get, the harder it is not...not to...have someone to love." Mama hadn't married until she was thirty.

I quickly responded, "But, Mama, I'm just not interested in any men."

Mama was just as quick to respond, "Well, Lynn may not be around forever."

That ended the conversation, but not without leaving me fearful as to my feelings for Lynn. I knew that I loved her more than I had loved anyone else and that being near her was all important. But I had to wonder if Lynn felt the same way. Lynn had never talked about men in *that* way since we had become close, but, I reminded myself, we were no longer lovers, and never would be. Besides that, I was very shy because of my height and was also disdainful of the way girls seemed to have to act in order to be sought after.

Even though I saw Lynn rarely, since we were living on opposite sides of town, I nevertheless knew we were still close, which took away the urgency to "find a man" which I might have felt otherwise.

I had always been very close to Mama, but the four months we lived together in Colorado Springs were very hard on both of us. I could not obtain a job. Shortly after we were settled in our new apartment, I signed up with an employment agency. I also answered ads in the newspaper and one of these really appealed to me. I would be trained to do research for lawyers. I got an interview and was told that I was overqualified. They were certain that I would ultimately find the job uninteresting and would finally quit. They didn't want to spend money training me, only to have me leave. I wondered how they could know this, but I also knew I couldn't promise to do otherwise.

The agency told me of a position teaching in a one room school house, first through eighth grades, but I had to remind them that my training was for secondary and, at all events, I didn't have the confidence to try teaching again.

In January, I was hired temporarily by the electric power company to help with their annual inventory. It was the most boring, tedious task I had ever encountered. Besides that, the man in charge of the temporary help was always accusing one or another of us of talking about him behind his back. Sometimes, he would come to our table and, after putting one foot up on an empty chair, he would continuously scratch his crotch, while he told us stories about his home life. Naturally all us, (most of the others were just out of high school), were trying not to look, but at the same time, we were sneaking glances at each other to see if the others were noticing. I saw that some of them were blushing, others were smirking, and I, myself, desperately wanted to laugh and cry at the same time. When the month was up, I had no desire to apply for the permanent position which had opened up.

Shortly after this, I went back to the employment agency where they felt they had just the job for me. It was as a receptionist with only a small amount of typing. Most of my job would be meeting people or talking with them over the telephone. It sounded promising. When I showed interest, the counselor telephoned to make an appointment for an interview. Suddenly she put the telephone aside and said, "You aren't Catholic, are you?"

"Why, yes, I am," I stammered.

The counselor informed the person on the other end of the line and after asking what difference that would make, finally hung up and told me that my would be employer was a group of Christian Science practitioners and they absolutely refused to hire a Catholic. She apologized profusely, but was powerless. I was stunned. I had been unaware of any such prejudice when I had been attending Christian Science Sunday School all those years. Later when I told Lynn about it, we laughed and wondered if it would have made any difference had they known I had been raised a Christian Scientist.

★ ★ ★ ★ ★

One of the most difficult things for me at this time was not to have the solace of daily Mass. Our apartment was within walking distance of a Church, but the order of priests there took pride in the fact that they could say a weekday Mass, including distributing Communion, in less than twenty minutes. This lack of reverence for something so important to me, became so painful, that I finally gave up going, except on Sundays. One Sunday, I went to Lynn's Church on the opposite side of town. The pastor there obviously loved the Mass and said it with care, but I couldn't have afforded to make the bus trip every day and it would also have impeded my search for a job.

In February, Mama gave notice to her renters in Denver. "I want to be in my own home," she explained firmly. I noticed that her eyes were wet. "Besides, there are probably more jobs in Denver. Maybe I could get you on at the cafeteria at D. U." She took it for granted that I would return to Denver with her.

"I…I s'pose so," I agreed, but at the same time I felt my stomach lurch. How could I ever explain to Mama how I felt about Lynn? A huge weight seemed to surround my heart. The college education I had received through much sacrifice on Mama's part seemed to be of no use now. Mama had never hinted that she was disappointed in me, but I felt she must be. Nonetheless, my need to be with Lynn was such that a few days later I was ready to share my immediate plans with Mama.

"Mama…I…I've decided to stay in Colorado Springs. I've found a little room for rent a couple blocks from Lynn's. It has a hot plate, so I can cook my meals, and it's only twenty dollars a month. Besides that I've got a job at a carnation factory beginning next week and it's within walking distance from my room.

"Well, if that's what you really want to do, I guess there's nothing for me to say," Mama replied. I saw tears misting her eyes, but I was driven to continue.

"If you could possibly lend me money for the room and a little for food, I'll pay it all back." My face was burning and I was also on the verge of tears. Mama agreed to lend me the money.

Lynn seemed pleased with my decision to remain in Colorado Springs, although she told me that she didn't feel she could move out on her room mate before the end of the school year. The inference that we would then live together was enough for me.

At the carnation factory, I was a cultivator and de-budder at minimum wage. They didn't even ask about my background. They didn't care if I was over qualified or not.

Shortly after this, one of the teachers at Lynn's school asked me to play my violin at a reception they were having for their son, who was returning from the Pacific war zone. They were so pleased with my playing that when Lynn told them I was having a hard time finding a suitable job, Mr. Benson, who had worked for the telephone company for a long time, offered to be a reference for me.

After three weeks at the carnation factory, I obtained a new job as a telephone operator, at much better pay, and in June, Lynn and I found a two bedroom apartment – to live happily ever after?

I was happy to be living with Lynn again, but after a month or so, my job as a telephone operator was simply something I did for money with no challenge or feeling of accomplishment. I worked night hours and split shifts, which paid better, but kept me from doing things with Lynn.

In the meantime, Lynn had become active in a parish organization called the Legion of Mary. The Legion helped the pastor keep in touch with his parishioners by making house calls and learning about problems the parishioners might be having. If they were unable to help directly, they would tell the pastor, who would follow up.

In return, the members were given spiritual guidance for their personal lives through little homilies the pastor would give at their monthly meetings and through the confessional. I became an auxiliary member right away, but was unable to join actively, because of my irregular hours.

Lynn brought home some of the books in the Legion's library, which I read avidly. These included the voluminous *Life of St. Teresa of Avila* by Thomas Walsh and Teresa's own *Way of Perfection* and *The Interior Castle*. Once more purpose came into my life, as I began to imagine herself as a contemplative nun. With St. Teresa as my model, I began meditating daily and practicing acts of asceticism.

In August of that year, Lynn attended a three day retreat for lay women at a location just outside Colorado Springs. During it, Lynn spoke to the retreat master about her homosexual experiences with me. He was very understanding, commending the two of us for our celibacy and giving Lynn peace of mind about our living together. As soon as she returned home, she shared this with me.

As Lynn described the retreat, I felt a desire to attend one myself and saved up enough money to go to one a month or so later. The retreat was situated on very spacious and beautifully landscaped grounds. The Stations of the Cross were surrounded by a formal flower garden. I spent most of my free time outside, meditating, reading, making the Stations and reciting the Rosary. As the retreat progressed, my desire to become a contemplative nun became more urgent, but I wondered with dread, "How can I tell Lynn?"

At our final meal, we retreatants were permitted to talk and one of the women looked me directly in the eyes and said, "You ought to become a nun. I think you have a vocation." I blushed, but conceded that I was seriously thinking about it.

That night, when I returned home, as soon as Lynn greeted me, I began to cry. Lynn took me in her arms, which only accentuated my conflicting feelings. I finally stopped crying and blurted out, "I…I think I want to become a nun, but I don't see how I can leave you!"

Lynn held me silently for a time and finally said, "It's all right. I want to be a nun, too."

Because I owed Mama money from our time in Colorado Springs and also wanted to have her old coal furnace changed over to gas so that she wouldn't have to shovel coal and carry out ashes during the winter, it would be at least another year of working for the telephone company before I could think of entering a religious order.

Most of that year I went around in a state of euphoria at the thought of becoming one with Jesus as His bride. As Lynn and I walked to Mass every morning, I was captivated by the beauty of Pike's Peak as the rising sun suffused it with varieties of colors. Each day the mountain seemed to be more beautiful than the one before. I felt that this was the way Jesus spoke to me of His love, preparing me to receive Him in Communion with a fully open heart. In this way, I almost completed the process of sublimating my illicit love for Lynn into love and adoration for the Son of God. Almost, but not quite.

In spite of the fact that our apartment had two bedrooms, Lynn and I continued to sleep together in the larger one. Although we no longer slept in the nude and allowed ourselves only a chaste good night kiss, we still enjoyed snuggling together, feeling our love for one another.

Nevertheless, I was inspired by St. Teresa's life and dreamed of becoming a Carmelite. The Carmelite Order is a strictly contemplative order, where the women spend the bulk of their days in meditation and chanting the Divine Office. They grow most of their own food and earn some of the money they need by baking the little breads that would be transformed into the Body of Christ at Mass.

When I approached my pastor about becoming a Carmelite, he quickly expressed his pleasure that God had blessed me with a vocation. Then he used a New Testament parable to buttress his opinion as to the kind of order I should choose.

"You don't want to hide your light under a bushel, you know. Your musical talents and college education would be more useful in an active order." At Christmas that year, I had not only added my strong alto voice to the choir, but had played an *Ave Maria* on my violin.

Surmising that I still preferred my own choice, he wisely suggested, "Say, I have an idea! Why don't you write the Sisters of the Good Shepherd in Denver? They're a semi-contemplative order which helps to rehabilitate delinquent girls." "I think I might like that," I conceded. The apostolate of working with young troubled girls especially appealed to me. "Maybe I could write to the Carmelites at the same time?" I added.

"Why don't you do that," Father agreed.

About two weeks after I had sent my letters to the two orders, I received an informative, but distant letter from the Carmelites. A future visit was not suggested. Two or three days later, I received a very warm and encouraging letter from the eighty-three year old Good Shepherd Provincial, who suggested I visit the Denver convent. I was most disappointed with the letter from St. Teresa's daughters, but went ahead and made an appointment with the Good Shepherd Sisters in Denver. During that visit I was as much impressed by the 'delinquent' girls, as I was by the sisters in their beautiful and ancient white habits. I was eager to have a hand in helping these troubled girls turn their lives around. I joyfully realized I had finally found my true calling. No further correspondence with the Carmelites seemed necessary. Having made this decision, it was time for me to tell Mama about entering the convent. Mama was totally surprised and realizing that our close relationship would be irrevocably changed, she burst into tears. I was astonished at Mama's response, but quickly took her into my arms. As she quieted down, I tried to explain why I wanted to do this, but without much success, as far as Mama was concerned.

I was again surprised, when two days later, I received a letter from Mama telling me that she wanted nothing more than for me to be happy, and assured me that it would make her happy, too. if entering the Good Shepherd Order was what I truly wished to do.

Thus, in August of 1950, I prepared to leave for the novitiate in St. Paul, Minnesota. Even though, by then, Margaret and her husband, John, were living in Yampa, Colorado, where John was teaching, they had come down to Denver for a week so that Margaret could have some visits with me before I left. On the appointed day, Margaret drove Mama, Lynn and me to the railroad station to see me off. After kissing each of them good-bye, I boarded the train, filled with the excitement of beginning an entirely new life. I was shocked, however, when I looked out the window and saw that Margaret was sobbing unrestrainedly. When I looked over at Mama and Lynn, only Lynn had a smile on her face. Mama was not outwardly crying, but I knew that she would have liked to. When Lynn and Mama saw me looking, they waved. Margaret turned and stumbled away. That was the last I was to see Margaret for over fifteen years.

I was stunned. I hadn't realized how much my leaving had hurt Margaret. Only then did I understand how my new life would draw me apart from my family, from the three women I loved most in the world. Nonetheless, my intention remained firm and I spent most of the time on my trip dreaming of my life to be.

CHAPTER THREE

THE CONGREGATION OF the Good Shepherd is world wide with Provinces on six of the seven continents. The main Mother House is in Angers, France, where the Order was founded. Each Province has a Mother House, in which to train young women, in that particular area of the world, for the religious life. In 1950, in the United States, there were Provinces in Peekskill, New York, Cincinnati, Ohio, St. Louis, Missouri, St. Paul, Minnesota and Los Angeles, California.

The St. Paul Province had Missions in Demoines and Dubuque, Iowa, Omaha, Nebraska, Denver, Colorado, Helena, Montana, Portland, Oregon and Spokane and Seattle, Washington. In the St. Paul Mother House, besides the Provincial and the Prioress (both called Mother by the rest of the Sisters) and a Sister Assistant, there were approximately twenty other professed sisters, five novices and an unusually large band of nine postulants, of which I was to be one.

When I arrived at the mother house, I was taken right up to the visitor's gallery to see the three-fold chapel, which characterized Good Shepherd convents. The visitor's gallery over the Sacristy gave a bird's-eye-view of the entire Church. I recognized the habits of two Good Shepherd nuns in the chapel directly facing the altar. To my right, the contemplative Sisters Magdaline were chanting. Because the chapel to my left had pews instead of choir stalls, I easily discerned that was the chapel for the girls. I was flooded with the feeling of having come home at last.

I was given the long, black skirt, long-sleeved black blouse and short cape with a starched white collar of the postulant, signifying my interest in becoming a Religious of the Good Shepherd. The postulancy of most orders was six months long, but the provincial in St. Paul felt that because of the difficulty of our specific vocation, they should extend it to nine. It isn't easy to help young women, who have been told that they are bad, to discover the good in themselves.

My loneliness for Lynn gradually subsided as I was kept occupied with an intensely busy schedule. I was constantly learning new things. It was like being introduced into an entirely different culture. Even much of the language was strange, e.g. the small snack after Vespers, called *collation* in the *refectory* (dining hall). In the refectory were long narrow tables with places on one side for about eight sisters. Probably to protect the white habits of the sisters, each sister had a large linen piece or *serviette*, folded in thirds; one end was pinned to her *guimpe* (collar), the other end remained on the table stabilized by her plate.

While we postulants took college classes in psychology and sociology to help prepare for our future work, we had little contact with the delinquents. Actually, most of us were not much older than the girls. At twenty-four, I was considered a *late* vocation.

After I had been there for a couple weeks, I found that at times I would feel a burning ache in my back and ribs. When I could, I would stretch my arms to get some relief. My Christian Science training helped me deny this, at least enough so I didn't worry about it too much and didn't relay this to Mother Mechtilde, the Directress of Novices.

One morning, while I was sitting in a desk chair just outside Mother Mechtilde's office waiting to see her, I found myself fantasizing being stretched out in a nice old overstuffed chair, as I had done many times before entering the convent. Then I realized that there was no such furniture anywhere in the novitiate. We sat in straight chairs and kept ourselves sitting upright all of the time. It slowly dawned on me that this was the reason for the burning pain in my back. My muscles were simply being asked to do something they were unused to. What otherwise might have been an annoyance, getting up at 5:30 a.m. and retiring by 9:30 seemed nothing by comparison.

There was another postulant, Sister Nancy, with a late vocation, and also with an abundance of energy. The two of us always seemed to end up together in our assigned places in the chapel, dormitory and refectory. Sister Nancy loved to find things to laugh about as did I. We remained in the good graces of Mother Mechtilde because neither of us minded working hard.

On October 20, the Feast of the Divine Heart of Jesus, a principal feast of our order, we postulants had the privilege of attending Matins and Lauds of the Divine Office★ for the first time. Because we were a semi-contemplative order, we sang Matins and Lauds before retiring rather than at dawn. This would last for two hours, quite a long session for already tired beginners. Sister Nancy and I had been washing down the high walls of the novitiate for most of the day.

At the beginning of Matins, there is a place where the sisters turn towards the altar, genuflect (bend the knee in worship), then rise and turn back to face each other in the choir. At this point Sister Nancy whacked into her choir stall with a resounding thud. This sent the two of us off into what would have been gales of laughter had we not been in the chapel. As it was, we had to stifle our natural impulses with muffled giggling. We could each feel the other tremble as new waves of suppressed laughter welled up. Thus, we continued for the entire two hours, with aching ribs, burning faces and fearful hearts.

Afterwards, in spite of the strict silence demanded in the dormitory, Sister Nancy whispered to me. "If we're sent away, you can come home with me to Minneapolis."

"Gosh, do you really think we'll be sent home? Yah, well...thanks a lot," I gulped.

Because of the observance of strict modesty of the eyes in the chapel, no one had even noticed us. Nothing was ever said about it.

My love for music is one of my earliest memories. Even before I went to school, Mama could leave me inside listening to music on our old fashioned Victrola with a large horn for a speaker, while she went out to hang clothes. She would invariably find me still listening, when she returned.

My sister, Margaret, taught me to sing *When Its Springtime in the Rockies* and *Jeanine, My Queen of Lilac Time* before I went to school. I made my stage debut the summer before I went to kindergarten singing *A Bicycle Built for Two* with a little red-headed boy who lived in the neighborhood. This turned out to be the favorite event at a circus put on by my sister Margaret and a friend.

During the first grade I began taking violin lessons, which I continued through college. It had been a heart break to have to discontinue my full

---

★The Office is made up primarily of psalms, which are sung antiphonally (first one side sings a verse, then the other side takes up the next verse). They are designated to the hours of the day. Matins and Lauds are sung first, just before dawn in contemplative Orders, followed by Prime, terce, Sext and None, corresponding to the morning hours, then Vespers in the mid afternoon and finally, Compline, sung just before retiring for the night.

music major for financial reasons, but I continued my violin lessons and played in the college orchestra and in the Greeley Philharmonic. Every summer I received a scholarship for participating in the summer orchestra and chorus. Filled with teachers coming back for advanced degrees, these two organizations were larger and more professional than they were during the year and I always looked forward to them.

It wasn't surprising, therefore, that my introduction to Gregorian Chant was love at first sound. When the young professed sister first handed out the *Liber Usualis* (a rather large tome containing the music for the many Masses and Offices) and I saw the medieval notations known as neums, I thought that because of the vow of poverty, the order had never purchased updated hymnals. I vaguely remembered having seen pictures of these strangely shaped notes in my music history class. I thought I was being pretty clever when I asked the sister what a *square* note sounded like. Everyone had a good laugh, but within the week I had fallen in love with this modal music and was eager to learn the meanings behind the odd symbols.

I literally blossomed in the all-woman environment of the convent. For the first time in my life my talents were fully appreciated and put to use. Mother Mechtilde had me tutor several other postulants, who were having trouble with spelling and reading. I was often asked to write the little verses of celebration, set to some familiar tune, for the feast days of the various superiors. I always managed to include a bit of witticism, which made them well received.

I overheard Mother Mechtilde telling someone over the phone that if she put Sister Georgette on a cleaning project, she could depend that it would be done thoroughly and as quickly as possible. All this trust helped to heal the wounds to my pride from my recent failure at teaching. I loved the responsibility and responded by giving of myself unstintingly.

Towards the end of the nine months of postulancy, Sister Nancy and I were up in the dormitory being fitted for bridal gowns and veils in preparation for receiving the habit. The sister *robier* had finished with her tuggings and pinnings and had just left. We were all dressed except for our postulant veils, which were made of heavy black silk and covered our hair almost as efficiently as the veils of the habit, leaving only a narrow fringe of hair exposed across the top. I glanced over at Sister Nancy and for the first time saw her luxuriant red curls.

Without thinking, I exclaimed, "Why, Sister, your hair is beautiful. Wow!

I'm getting out of here." I could hear Sister Nancy's pleased laughter as I pulled on my veil, while running down the stairs with a racing heart.

"Am I in love with her?" I asked myself. I joined the others at recreation out-of-doors, but continued the questioning in my mind. "Yes, I do have fun with her and yes, her hair amazed me, but my feelings for her are nothing like how I felt about Lynn!" I sighed with relief and joined fully in the conversation with the others.

Finally, the day came to receive the habit. The Good Shepherd Order was one of the few which still adhered to the custom of wearing bridal gowns and veils at the beginning of the ceremony to signify the young women's desires of becoming brides of Christ. As we stood in line waiting for the cue to enter the chapel, I felt self conscious and half angry in my makeshift gown with a large ruffle added to the bottom to make up for my extra inches. Although a few of the women had beautiful gowns, heirlooms provided by their families, the majority of us were wearing hand-me-downs as I was. Still I couldn't help but be aware that I looked even stranger than the others after the necessary alterations to make up for my *unwomanly* size.

"Well," I assured myself, "this will be the last time!" It brought back memories of those years in my early teens, after my father had lost all his savings in a business venture, just before he retired. Overnight, we were desperately poor, just at the time clothes were beginning to be important to me. Hand-me-downs from cousins twenty years older became the order of the day. Mama put in a great deal of time and effort into making them fit well, as well as to make them look more youthful, but it was next to impossible to make professional business women's clothes into something appropriate for a teen-ager.

I quickly returned my attention to the present, as the organ drew us into the chapel. There, we were given each piece of the habit with an explanation of its symbolism. We left the chapel as *worldly* brides and returned transformed by the beautifully gracious white habits, which had remained the same for three hundred years.

I loved the feel of the ankle length robe, which was a huge sack with wide flowing sleeves. It was carefully pleated in the front and back, held in place by a cincture (belt), symbolizing our adherance to Christ. Over the belt we wore a teal blue cord ending in tassels, which each of us had woven with yarn through a spool, during our postulancy. The blue symbolized our dedication to Our Lady of Charity, one of the many titles given to Mary, the mother of Jesus. Also symbolizing this dedication was the long narrow scapular of the same color and material as the robe, under which we were directed to modestly hide our hands when walking about the cloisters (halls).

The first piece we put on for our head covering was a skull cap. To this we pinned the white, unstarched guimpe or collar, which had a piece on each side fitting closely under the chin and up each side of our jaws, where we pinned it to the skull cap. Then we placed a narrow linen *bandeau* over most of our forehead, which went on around to the back where we tied it in place. Finally, we were ready to put on the soft veil, shaped by a small piece of hidden cardboard where it went over the head. We pinned it with a large hat pin through the cardboard to the skull cap. It draped down over our shoulders, where we secured it with more pins. The sole purpose of the veil was modesty. We novices did not shave our heads, because without having taken vows, we would be ready to leave at any time.

I received the name Sister Mary of St. Teresa of Avila, which was my first of three choices. I still loved this contemplative nun, who had had the courage to stand up to bishops who hadn't fulfilled their promises of providing suitable housing when they requested the presence of her order in their dioceses.

St. Teresa even wrote little antiphonal verses for her sisters to sing about the fleas that they had inherited from the old barns in which they were expected to live. Nonetheless, later, this patriarchal Church had to recognize Teresa as a Doctor of Divinity, because of her astute writings on mysticism.

Besides Mama, my former pastor came for the ceremony, a pleasant surprise, as I knew how busy he was. I was glad he could have a little respite from his many parish duties. Another surprise was the presence of Pauline Sorbesky, a close friend of Lynn's and mine from our days in Colorado Springs. Since Lynn felt unable to take time off from her teaching, Pauline came in her place.

A not so favorable incident took place when Mama unwittingly asked Mother Luke, the Provincial, if she would see to it that I would finish getting my Bachelor's degree, since I only had twelve more quarter hours to go. The Provincial chillingly informed her that that was not the reason one entered a convent. Mama quickly stammered that she was certain that wasn't why I had entered.

Mama was crying when she related the incident to me that evening, fearful that it might endanger my position with the Provincial. I was primarily concerned with the hurt my mother had received and spent the rest of the evening trying to assure her that everything would be fine. I was relieved that Mother Mechtilde wasn't as ascerbic as the Provincial.

During our first canonical year, Good Shepherd novices were not permitted visits with family or friends. However, about two months after I had received the habit, I obtained permission for Lynn to visit with me. Lynn was entering the Sisters of Charity that summer, so this might well be the last time we would see each other. Besides, Lynn had been the catalyst to my conversion and since she was also called to a religious vocation, she wasn't considered a danger to my vocation.

After Mother Mechtilde left us alone in the parlor, Lynn embraced me warmly. "Oh, I've missed you so much this past year!"

I felt the old rush of passion rise up and in fear, pushed Lynn away, stammering, "Gosh, I don't feel very much like a nun!" I saw guilt flood Lynn's face and hated myself for what I had done, but my terror held firm.

"It's okay," I quickly assured Lynn, as I led her over to one of the chairs in the room. "How's your mom and how is June?" I asked as I sat down in a chair opposite her. We spent the rest of the evening updating each other on our respective families and friends.

Just a few hours before the visit, I had attended a very graphic lecture on the dangers of homosexuality in convents and other women-only institutions. It had been torture for me, sitting there listening to a description of a chapter in my own life. As I listened, I again firmly repudiated my old feelings for Lynn. When Lynn had embraced me, I discovered the feelings were still there. At once, I realized Lynn's fervor was from loneliness. I knew, for certain, that Lynn's own vocation to the religious life was still quite intact. It was the flooding of my own feelings that had terrified me.

As I knelt in the chapel, the next day, tears filled my eyes as I recalled the pained expression on Lynn's face when I had pushed her away. I came to the rather disconcerting realization that my heart had indeed been opened to love being with Lynn. I knew that probably my love for Jesus would not be as joyful nor as deep, had I not been with Lynn first, in that forbidden lover relationship. I was very aware, even then, that not all of the sisters' hearts had been opened by love.

Then I realized that perhaps my mating with Lynn had not been as totally evil as the term *mortal sin* led one to believe. I was certain that I was a stronger, better person for it and surely God knew that, too. I looked intently at the tabernacle feeling that my Spouse had led me to this understanding. It was to be our secret.

Shortly after receiving the habit, I was, again, assailed by a burning sensation, this time in my ears. Again, I went into denial, but would find myself surreptitiously reaching a finger up under my guimpe and massaging first one ear and then the other. At night, as soon as I had undressed I would give each ear a long and relieving massage. It finally dawned on me that the pain came from the guimpe being tied tightly enough to pull my ears back closer to my head. I hadn't realized that they had poked out that much. After a time, my ears finally gave up complaining and gradually adjusted themselves to their new position.

★ ★ ★ ★ ★

In the Good Shepherd Order, one remained a novice for a second year in order to get a taste of the unusual and difficult work of the apostolate. This gave us novices the opportunity to make a more knowledgeable choice about wanting to dedicate our lives to this work. It also gave the order the chance to evaluate us as to whether to permit us to take our vows. For me, this taste included a two hour stint in the pressing room of the commercial laundry run by the sisters.

The first day that I went over, I knew that it was the custom for the girls to address us as *Mother* and that we sisters were, indeed, to try to take the place of the girls' mothers during their stay at the Home. But when I heard myself called *Mother* for the first time, I was surprised at the physical reaction I experienced. I actually felt a deep caring for them flush through my heart, at the same time that I came to a quick understanding of the responsibility that went with the title.

There were two young girls, each working a presser and an older woman, who worked two pressers. One of the girls developed a crush on me that was almost overwhelming. When I entered the room, Sally would return my smile and then blush furiously.

The first few days went by pleasantly enough. I hadn't been advised of the rule of silence in the laundry, and listened with interest to the girls' stories. Jane, the older woman, would greet me and then continue working in silence. She was one of ten older women, whom the order had taken in when they were still quite young, so that the state would not sterilize them.

We novices had been told that they were of low intelligence, so I thought that was why she didn't talk much.

The pressing room was off the main part of the laundry, but the girls on the mangles in the main section could see us chatting and laughing. Eventually, we were reported. I was chagrined and a little angry that I had not been advised of the rule before.

Keeping the rule of silence made the two hours seem endless for all of us. I would stand by with nothing to do, but to watch first one and then another. Finally, one busy day, Jane asked if I would mind shaking out the wet railroad uniform coats and pants and then hang them over a box, thus making the pressing go faster. I was most relieved to have something to do. Tension dropped at once. Later on, when one of the girls was absent, Jane taught me how to work her press. I enjoyed the challenge of learning how to press a nice looking piece.

One morning, I noticed that Sally was very pale and her eyes were red and swollen from much crying. When I greeted her, Sally began crying. A red spot appeared on each cheek, instead of the general blushing of previous days. Since she couldn't seem to regain control, I excused her and began to work her press. In a few minutes she came back and resumed her place, but started pouring out her story as she worked.

"One of the windows in my dorm had a hole smashed in it. Someone told Mother Divine Heart that they had seen me in the dorm after everyone else had left. It's true I was late leaving the dorm 'cuz I couldn't find a pair of socks that matched, but I didn't break the window! Why would I? Why would anyone? You still couldn't get out through the detention screen. Besides that, the window wasn't broken when I left. Someone must have *lost it* later and smashed it! But it wasn't me, honest, Mother Teresa!" She again burst into tears.

Sally finally regained control and continued, "Now, Mother Divine Heart is mad at me and who knows when I'll ever get to go home. I was s'posed to go this June…but now! Besides, Mother ought to know me better than that. I'm always helping her with little jobs…and, besides that, I like her! A lot! I wouldn't do anything to make it harder for her…or to hurt the Home!"

I knew that stopping her by reminding her of the rule of silence would not be wise. However, I was nervous that we would be reported again. Jane kept on working silently, but gave me a little smile that said she approved of what I was doing. Suddenly I knew who had reported us before. Although this made me feel a little strange, I became more at ease in listening to Sally's story.

"Sally, did you try to explain your situation to Mother Divine Heart?" I asked. "Can't you tell her that while it was true that you were the last one in the dorm yesterday, you didn't break the window. Also, it would help for her to know that it hadn't been broken yet when you did leave."

"Mother Divine Heart is so mad at me, she wouldn't even hear me if I tried. You don't know how it is!" Sally exclaimed.

"Maybe I don't," I conceded.

I left the laundry a little early, seeking Sister Divine Heart in her office, so that I could explain what had happened. Sister Divine Heart understood at once and queried, "Why couldn't Sally have told me this herself?"

She went back to her work without waiting for an anwer. She probably was aware that, at times, she must have come across as being angry, when she was really only very fatigued from trying to deal wih the problems of one hundred and fifty girls almost single handedly.

The next day when I returned to the pressing room, Sally was all smiles and adoration. Thanks to me, Sally was reinstated with Mother Divine Heart. Now her eyes followed my every move and she declared, "You're the only *real* Mother in this whole convent!"

I was aware that Sally was in need of real mothering, more than the overly busy Mother Divine Heart was able to give. I was grateful that I had been able to help in this, although I found the adulation a little hard to take.

Shortly after this incident, when I arrived at the pressing room one morning, I found that Jane was missing. The other two were very upset, explaining to me that Jane had fainted at her press. They quickly assured me that she hadn't burned herself, but they told me she had, nevertheless, looked very bad. Two of the maintenance men had come and carried her up to the girls' infirmary. I worked Jane's two presses the best I was able. The others and I usually only worked one press at a time.

When it was time to leave, I asked the sister in charge of the laundry if she knew how Jane was. She told me that Jane had suffered a major stroke and that she was so bad, they were afraid to send her to a hospital. Receiving permission to go up and see Jane, I was surprised to find her by herself.

"Jane! Jane, are you all right?" I asked.

Jane opened her eyes. They were filled with terror. I grasped her hand and felt Jane cling back. Understanding that Jane was unable to speak, I began praying the *Hail Mary* aloud. The terror in Jane's eyes diminished at once and tears started to roll down her cheeks. Her head fell back and at first I thought she had died, but her hand loosened its grip and a faint smile appeared on the good side of her mouth.

Just then, Sister Divine Heart came rushing in, exclaiming, "Thank God, you came, Sister! I had to answer a very important telephone call and there was no one around to relieve me. Could you possibly stay a while longer?"

I stayed until lunch time. Jane seemed to be resting easier when Sister Divine Heart returned, but she died about four hours later.

I cried a long time that night with an unspeakable grief thinking of Jane's hard and very limited life. I prayed that there truly was a heaven and that Jane was now happy and fulfilled.

It was during my second year as a novice that I was frequently put in charge of the choir, whenever Sister Michael was unable to make it, since she was also the principal of the girls' high school. I continued to love the Gregorian chant and was happy to be able to transfer my enthusiasm to the others.

It thus happened that I did the majority of the instruction and coaching in preparation for the long services of Holy Saturday. I had never attended these services before entering the convent, so this was only the second time for doing this. The responsibility for making the proper responses at the appropriate times was mine and was almost overwhelming. This realization didn't really come home to me until I was kneeling in my place in the chapel that morning. I carefully checked all the little pieces of paper marking the places of the choral responses, took a deep breath and focused on the task at hand.

I was able to bring this about without a glitch, but I surprised myself when tears of relief began running down my cheeks, when it was all over. As I joined the recession from the chapel, my legs felt like they would buckle under me, yet somehow I carried on.

Two months before our first profession of vows, we second year novices were relieved of our duties to go on an intense two month retreat. The confessor for the novitiate was a very fatherly person and a patient listener. I felt compelled to tell again of my experience with Lynn. Father O'Sullivan assured me that after seven years with no lapses, I had proven myself strong enough to commit myself to the religious life.

On April 24, 1953, the Feast of the Mother Foundress, I vowed to practice poverty, chastity, obedience and zeal for the salvation of souls for one year.

During the simple ceremony, we all received the black veil, crucifix and silver heart★ of the professed sister.

★The Religious of the Good Shepherd wore a silver locket shaped like the Sacred Heart of Jesus instead of the wedding band, worn by the sisters of many other congregations. Inside the locket they kept a miniature copy of their vows and a relic of a Saint.

CHAPTER FOUR

MAMA HAD MADE the trip to St. Paul in order to attend my first profession of annual vows. After the brief ceremony, the two of us were animatedly catching up on family news, when the Mother Provincial's secretary stopped by to tell me that all the young professed sisters were to meet with the Mother Provincial at four that afternoon. I was surprised that we would be receiving our *missions* (assignments) so soon. and as a group. I didn't even think of another reason for the gathering.

I took Mama to the guest room where she would be staying during the next few days and left to go to the Provincial's office for the meeting. I was very excited about learning what my first job would be, as well as what the others in my group would be doing.

Upon entering the office, I was surprised to see that the young professed in their second or third year of annual vows were also there. After everyone had arrived, Mother Luke had a surprise for us.

"Because we have been blessed with so many vocations since 1950, we feel there are enough sisters in temporary vows to establish a juniorate. The purpose of juniorates is to give young sisters the opportunity to finish their training for our work. Along with your college classes, each of you will be given a small assignment working with the girls. Those of you who already have your degrees will, of course, be given jobs with more responsibilities.

"I'm sure most of you have met Mother Francis of Assisi, who will be your juniorate directress. Mother Francis has had much valuable experience in our work and will be a great help to you in learning about it. You will meet with her individually once a week in order to get advice, as you did with your directress of novices. She will also conduct a chapter★ for all of you, once a week. Now I will give out your missions and then you can go

---

★spiritual instruction on the religious life

to your chapter room and get to know your new mother. She will be able to answer any questions you may have concerning the juniorate."

Although it was almost unheard of that a newly professed sister would be assigned to such a responsible position, Sister Louise, my red-headed friend, was named as the second directress of the large class, where the girls ranged in age from fourteen to eighteen years. She would be directly under Mother Divine Heart, taking the place of Mother Francis of Assisi, who had held that position for five years. However, Sister Louise had been working with the girls as a volunteer for several years before she entered the Order and was well qualified.

Then I heard Mother Luke announce my name, saying that I was to be the second directress of the smaller junior class, where the girls were from eleven to thirteen years old. I would also be teaching an eighth grade English class until the end of the school year, as well as continuing to direct the sisters' choir when Sister Michael was unable.

After the rest of the young professed had received their assignments, Mother Francis led the way to the room specified for us. I liked her right away. She had a warm and friendly smile. "I bet she's easy to talk to," I thought.

The following day I told Mama of our new assignments and introduced her to Mother Francis. Mama, who was often uncomfortable in the presence of the nuns, mellowed out right away with Mother Francis' easy manner.

"We're really happy to have Sister Teresa as a member of our order and thank you for your support of her vocation, especially when you aren't a Catholic yourself. I'm sure it was hard for you to let her go."

It was the first time any one in the Order had expressed such understanding and Mama's eyes filled with tears of gratitude and her concern for my welfare in the convent disappeared completely. My estimation of my new directress was raised by several degrees.

Soon I learned that Mother Francis was much less formal than the directress of novices had been. She encouraged me to speak of my family and of my life before entering the convent and even shared bits of her own personal life. This opened me up in numerous ways, making me feel free to speak of experiences that were enjoyable as well as of those that were difficult and with which I needed help. In this way, Mother Francis drew out my natural abilities, in order to see how they could fit in with the work of the order.

My love affair with Gregorian chant had flourished and I was very happy to get to direct the choir occasionally. A few weeks after the profession ceremony, a sister from the Mother House in Angers, France arrived with the duty to instruct us further in Gregorian chant. She, herself, had studied at the Benedictine monastery in Solesmes, France, where most of the restoration of the chant had begun during the last part of the nineteenth century. I was thrilled when I was given the chance for special tutoring on *chironomy.* ★

I delighted in Sister Gemma's wit and gladly helped her when her command of the English language failed.

"Do you know vat I tink are ze most beautiful words in ze English language?" she asked me, one day during a private lesson.

I smiled with anticipation as I waited to hear Sister Gemma's pronouncement.

"Well, ze meaning of zese words may not be so beautiful," Sister Gemma explained, "but eef you just leesten to zem, I tink you will see vat I mean," she continued. My grin broadened with the feeling of suspense. Sister Gemma was aware of this and enjoyed stretching out her story.

"Leesten carefully now, Seester Teresa. I believe ze mos' beautiful words in ze English language are…cellar door."

I burst out laughing, but I readily agreed that these two words did sound beautiful, especially when Sister Gemma said them. At recreation that night, I coaxed Sister Gemma into telling all the sisters. This pleased Sister Gemma as well as amusing everyone else.

While she was in St. Paul, Sister Gemma had an impacted wisdom tooth extracted. When I went up for her lesson in chironomy, the morning after the surgery, Sister Gemma was still in bed, recovering. I excused myself and began to leave, but Sister Gemma assured me she would be able to give me the lesson. Even though small night veils were a part of the general issue, Sister Gemma wasn't wearing one. I felt embarrassed seeing her short light brown locks, but was intrigued by them at the same time. Then Sister Gemma hung her legs over the side of the bed and bade me to sit beside her, while we went over the assignment from the previous lesson. Soon I became aware that Sister Gemma's night gown, which buttoned at the neck like my own, was unbuttoned low enough that the cleavage from her ample breasts was much in evidence. When Sister Gemma put an arm around my shoulder to guide my arm in the movements, I was very aware of a warm

★literally to rule by hand, describing the hand movements of the choir director

breast resting against my other arm. It became increasingly difficult for me
to concentrate on the music.

"Is she coming on to me?" I wondered to myself, but instantly I re-
buked myself for the thought. "A sister from the Mother House would not
do that!" Nevertheless, the proximity of Sister Gemma's soft, ample bosom
was more than I could handle and I quickly suggested, "You know, Sister, I
think I would get more from this if I actually stood as if I were directing the
choir and you could see better when I make a mistake." Having said this, I
got up from the bed, faced Sister Gemma, held the assignment in front with
my left hand and, while singing the chant, did the chironomy movements
with my right hand. Sister Gemma agreed, at once, that this was a better way
to do it.

In June, after school was out, I was sent to St. John's Abbey, in northern
Minnesota, to study Gregorian chant under the direction of a monk from the
Solesmes Abbey. I took a course in chironomy from him and another course
in Gregorian chant accompaniment from a French Canadian layman.

Dom Deroquettes impressed me deeply with his simplicity and the obvious pleasure he derived from the chant. The class was large, so he couldn't
help us individually with our hand motions, as Sister Gemma had helped me.
Some sisters from the Congregation of Perpetual Adoration of the Blessed
Sacrament had noticed that I seemed to know what I was doing in class.
They asked me to tutor them, as they were having difficulty transferring
their drawings over the notes to the movements they were to be making
with their hands.

After they had practiced for some time, one of them remarked how
young I was and when they discovered that I had just made my first profession of vows, one of them said, "Your Mother Superior must have a lot of
confidence in you to let you go away from home like this so soon."

"Well, I am twenty-seven," I explained. "I was a late vocation, you see."

Then they invited me to eat with them as there was no one with me
from my own order. I accepted promptly, and with relief, because I had been
snubbed by some Dominican Sisters when I told them I was a Good Shepherd Sister. Actually, I didn't understand why they had snubbed me until I
went home and asked Sister Michael about it.

"They probably thought you had been one of the girls and, therefore,
not a virgin. Some Orders make you have a doctor's statement certifying
your virginity before you can enter. They really believe they are superior to

anyone who isn't. Of course, we know that anyone who has been a Good Shepherd girl cannot enter our order, but it isn't because she might not be a virgin. Probably many of our girls are virgins and undoubtedly ninety-nine percent of the sisters are," Sister Michael explained, after she had heard the story. "These snobs really make me mad. They've never heard of Christian charity, I guess. And they call themselves Brides of Christ! He certainly can't think very much of them!"

I heartily agreed, and then began to wonder if I were a virgin. I knew my hyman was intact, because when I went to have the physical requested by the order before entering, the doctor took it for granted that they wanted proof of my virginity. Nonetheless, I had made love with Lynn. I finally decided I didn't have to worry since it wasn't a prerequisite of our order. In fact on some occasions, widows, who had been mothers, had entered the order.

It did stir up the discomfort I felt when I had learned, while still in the novitiate, that no girl who had been a resident in the Home was permitted to enter the Good Shepherd Order. If they felt a girl had a vocation to the religious life, she was advised to enter the penitential order of the Sisters Magdalene. They were a strictly contemplative order under the care of the Good Shepherd Sisters. Still, that meant that those who didn't have a vocation for the contemplative life had to try to get into another order. Most of them simply forgot about having a vocation, believing that once it was learned they had been Good Shepherd girls, they wouldn't be accepted. Now I realized they were probably right.

My job as the second directress of the Junior Class was the first quite difficult assignment I had encountered. The first directress, Sister Patrick, was directly from Ireland and although she had been in the United States since she was a young girl, she still had such a heavy brogue that half the time I couldn't understand her, or, worse yet, would misunderstand her, even after working with her for several months.

Our cultural differences didn't help either. I was scandalized the first time I heard Sister Patrick yell at one of the girls, "Get to work, you little scut, or I'll knock your head against the wall!"

In the eighteen months I was to work with her, I never saw this threat carried out. However, the first few times I heard Sister Patrick make the threat, I fully expected her to carry it out. The new girls felt the same way.

It seemed impossible for me to please Sister Patrick. According to Sister Patrick, I smiled too big and too often, wasn't tough enough and didn't even do as I was told. This last accusation had been true on a few occasions, because I had literally misunderstood what Sister Patrick had requested. On top of that, Sister Patrick would yell at me in front of the girls. Many were the times I would leave the class on the verge of tears, feeling both humiliated and angry. I would restore myself by a visit to the Blessed Sacrament, pleading for understanding and enlightenment.

The Junior Class was situated in the oldest building on the campus. The paint was flaking off the walls and the colors had been drab from the first. I asked Sister Patrick if she would like me to supervise the painting of the dormitory, the sewing room, the stairway, the parlor and the recreation room. Sister Patrick didn't think she would get permission from the Mother Prioress, because they were considering tearing down the building and replacing it with a new one. I approached the Mother Prioress about it anyway.

"Well, Sister, if you think you can do it, it would be a good idea. It is going to be years before we will be able to replace that building," the Mother Prioress assured me.

Sister Patrick was delighted when she heard this and chose to paint the walls a bright pink, set off by white trim on the wood work. Her estimation of me rose rapidly as she saw that I wasn't afraid to work hard and seemed to know how to help the girls enjoy making their living quarters easier on the eye. However, by the time we got the job finished, the girls were all thoroughly tired of the pink and said they never wanted to see anything that color again. I laughingly had to admit I felt the same way. Some of the girls who hadn't helped with the painting overheard our remarks and felt we were being disloyal to Sister Patrick. They were jubilant one evening when they saw a new, wide finned **pink** Chevrolet with a white stripe on the fins in a commercial on television.

"See!" they declared. "Mother Patrick's right in style with the times!" I could see Sister Patrick was enjoying this loyalty and heartily agreed with them. "You're right," I chortled. "Mother is really in step with the times."

Every Saturday morning five or six girls were assigned to scrub the large recreation room floor with brushes. This meant they did it on their hands and knees. The wood was totally without varnish and didn't look much better after the scrubbing. It couldn't be varnished, because it had been used for roller skating, which had totally ruined the soft wood.

One day, when I was helping Sister Patrick clean her office, I saw a Sears and Roebuck catalog on the desk advertising a sale on floor tiles.

"Look at this, Sister Patrick," I said as I took the catalog over to where

Sister was cleaning out a cupboard. "How would you like it if we tiled that ugly floor in the recreation room?"

"Do you really think you could do it?" Sister Patrick asked, wide-eyed with hope and doubt.

"Well, of course, I'd have to have some help," I answered, "but with Judy, Betty and Caroline helping, I'm positive we could do it. We could use the big lawn roller to press it down." Judy and Betty were the oldest girls in the class and had proven themselves as reliable workers during the painting. Caroline was a lay person who worked a few hours a day with Sister Patrick. She had also proven invaluable during the painting, being in charge when I wasn't there.

I was getting more excited at the prospect of it. Again, I received Mother Prioress's permission and the tiles were purchased.

In the meantime, I had been intrigued with the pattern of tiles on the floor of the classroom of the new novitiate. One block was begun with a single dark tile in the center, which was surrounded by light tiles. This was then framed by a row of dark tiles. The next block was formed oppositely with a light tile in the center, surrounded with dark tiles and then a light colored frame around it. The contrast was somehow pleasing to the eye and one's sense of order, yet was more interesting then a simple checkerboard pattern.

When I showed the pattern to Sister Patrick, she rolled her eyes in wonder and said, "If you can figure it out, go ahead!"

It meant that the girls would have to have recreation in the parlor, which was much smaller than the recreation room, but Sister Patrick wanted the new floor badly enough to agree to this. The three girls and I thought we could do it in five days, if Judy and Betty could be excused from their classes in school. We chose five school days, when the other girls didn't have as much time for recreating.

After two days, Sister Patrick couldn't stand supervising the recreations in the small parlor. Without consulting the work crew, she got permission for the girls and me to work all day the third day in order to finish. After ten hours of almost uninterrupted labor, the four of us finished, totally exhausted from heavy labor we were not used to. The Mother Prioress and Mother Francis of Assisi hadn't realized how heavy the work was, nor that it would take so long. The four of us were given permission to *sleep in* the next morning.

I didn't know if I was pleased with this turn of events. I hadn't missed daily Mass since the day I determined to become a nun. However, when Mother Francis arrived in the juniorate dormitory with a breakfast tray at nine a. m. the following day, I realized I hadn't even heard the others get up and get dressed. Only then did I come to know how very tired I had been.

That fall, I was given the full responsibility of the sisters' choir and also began teaching music theory and voice in the novitiate. These classes were mainly in the morning after the chanting of the Little Hours (Prime, Terce, Sext and None). I really enjoyed working with the postulants and novices and they, in turn, were inspired by my love of the chant, and my sense of humor. They loved it when I would stop in the middle of a sentence, bringing their attention to the call of a cardinal or some other bird, coming through the open window. "First things first!" I would exclaim and then return to the lesson. It had been Mother Francis who had initiated my love of recognizing birds by their calls, during the Junior Sisters' walks in the evening.

After my classes in the novitiate, I went over to the Junior Class to supervise the cleaning of the refectory and dormitory. I would stay on and take them to lunch and be with them for their period of recreation before they returned to school in the afternoon. This turned out to be a long period of time to be with girls needy for attention and the many varied ways they would go about obtaining it. My sensitive nature made getting used to their boisterousness and seeming rudeness like a baptism of blood.

Mother Francis advised me how to put my sensitivities to good use. I was quick to see when things weren't quite right with them and my compassion and sincere interest in their lives encouraged them to trust me and do as I suggested.

I was then able to be a good mediator between the girls and Sister Patrick, when things would be tense between them. After several months, Sister Patrick was able to appreciate this and she decided that she would make a three day retreat, leaving *her girls* in my hands full time.

The first night, I walked between the rows of beds in the dormitory reciting the rosary with the girls, following Sister Patrick's custom. After we finished, I started to go to Sister's sleeping room, when a little Chicana spoke up.

"Aren't you going to give me my *hog?*" she asked.

I realized the little girl wasn't asking for a pig, but what she did want remained a mystery. As if she could read my mind, Betty quickly explained that Sister Patrick gave them each a hug after the rosary, but she also said that the young Mothers weren't expected to do this. I remembered the warnings we had received as novices that we were not to touch the girls and was, at the same time, relieved that this rule was sometimes broken, but also aggravated at the seeming over-protection of young sisters.

Anita kept at me for a hug, because she claimed to like me better than Mother Patrick. I held firm, because I realized that part of the strain between Sister Patrick and myself was the older nun's fear that I would become more popular with the girls than she was. I had no desire for this to happen.

When Sister Patrick came back after this short retreat, she thanked me and then proceeded to have the girls do a heavy cleaning of the class, as if they hadn't done any cleaning while she was away. She was deaf to the girls' protests.

Several months later, when Sister Patrick decided to make the annual eight day retreat, the first for her in several years, I was amazed to be trusted to be in full charge of the girls for so long. Fortunately, I was able to live up to the trust, because no major catastrophes occurred while she was away.

Missing the nightly hugs and other signs of affection Sister Patrick gave them, they were sincerely looking forward to her return. Two days before she was due back, everyone worked very hard to clean things up to surprise her. They even thought to pick a bouquet of flowers to put in her room. Sister Patrick acknowledged the flowers, but still conducted the usual grand house cleaning, with the usual cries of protest. I discreetly stayed away as much as I could. Nevertheless, some of them made sure to be present when I came over to relieve Sister Patrick the next day.

"Mother Teresa, didn't I clean the sewing room the day before Mother Patrick came back?" Anita cried out.

"You sure did," I admitted. "I checked it out myself."

"See, Mother Patrick! I told you so!" and turning to me, she bellowed, "She made me clean it all over again this morning!"

I began to blush and laugh at the same time. "Well, that just goes to show who is the most particular about cleaning!" No further complaints were made.

Mama again made the trip to St. Paul for my second renewal of temporary vows. Lynn had left for the Sisters of Charity and my sister, Rose, was living in Sacramento, California with her husband and children. After Mother Francis of Assisi, again gave her a cordial welcome, Mama and I en-

joyed the hours when I could get away from work. Mama would always go
to the chapel when I was directing the choir.

"You know," she claimed later, "I can hear your voice over all the others."

"You can!" I exclaimed, not knowing whether or not it was a compliment. "How do you know it's mine?"

"Because it sounds like mine used to. I never told you I took voice lessons for awhile before I married your father, did I? My teacher said I had a
promising voice."

"Gosh, no! You never told me that before," I answered, absolutely astonished. "Well, thanks. I guess that means you like mine. But I can't ever
remember hearing you sing at home. Would you sing something for me
now?"

"Oh, no! I couldn't do that!" Mama firmly refused. " It has been too
long!"

"But you never even sang with Margaret and I when we were kids! How
come?" Then I noticed tears brimming the edges of Mama's eyes.

"Mama! What is it? What's wrong?" I put my arms around her, but she
quickly and uncharacteristically pushed me away, as she regained control.

"I…I really can't talk about it. It's all right! It really is! Please, let's drop
it. Anyway, I really love to hear you sing!" Mama assured me. "And I like the
way you move your hands when you direct the choir. It's…it's almost like
you're dancing."

"You know I've felt like that, too! I love to do it. It's one of the few times
I feel graceful," I admitted.

After Mama had left, one of the sisters asked, "What do you talk about
all that time in the parlor? I can hardly think of enough to say for the two
hours of my monthly visit! I'm sure glad my parents live close enough to
come every month. It would really be hard to visit for such long periods of
time. You always look like you're enjoying yourself, though."

I hardly knew how to reply. "I…I guess we've always been close," I
murmured.

CHAPTER FIVE

THE FOLLOWING AUGUST, I received my first assignment away from St. Paul.

"We're going to miss you directing the choir, Sister," the Mother Provincial said, after telling me I was being sent to the Home in Portland, Oregon to help with the girls. I hope to be able to send for you by Christmas. In the meantime, I want you to do everything you can to help Sister Joan of Arc. She is practically alone in that big class of girls in Portland. You will be her second."

On the day I was to leave for Portland, all the sisters who were free to do so came to the foyer of the Mother House to say goodbye, with promises of prayers for success on my first mission. For the occasion, we were permitted to grasp each other's arms and lightly kiss one another on each cheek, after the manner of the French. When it was Mother Francis of Assisi's turn to say goodbye, somehow our lips touched during the transfer from one cheek to the other. My entire body was inflamed. Mother Francis quickly dispatched me to the awaiting laywoman, who was driving me to the train. I couldn't help wondering if Mother Francis had felt such a reaction. During the ride to the station and even after I had settled in my compartment, the flame burned on.

Hot tears ran down my cheeks. I was extremely grateful for the privacy I could never have afforded when I had been working in the "world".

"Am I always going to be like this?" I asked myself angrily. I was terrified that I would have to leave a life where I had found more happiness than I had believed possible. This realization helped me, once again, to squelch my sexuality.

Fortunately, upon arrival at the understaffed mission in Portland, I didn't have time or energy to dwell on this dilemma. I soon found myself in a very difficult situation, which made any question about my sexuality pale by comparison.

Portland is called the City of Roses. The first night I was with the sisters for the evening recreation, I found out why. The cloister yard was pungent

with the odors of many and varied rose bushes. I had never before realized
there was such a variety. Besides that, at the far end of the yard was a small
orchard of fig trees. As we would walk by, we would pick the tree-ripened
fruit and munch on them. This was the first time I had tasted a fig that wasn't
dried or canned. I was amazed at the difference in flavor and enjoyed them
thoroughly, although being a young religious, I wondered about the injunction of the rule that the sisters not eat between meals.

The second night I was sent over to spend recreation with Sister Joan of
Arc in the girls' large combination gym and auditorium. Rhythm and Blues
played away on the sound system, while the girls danced together. After a
few dances, I couldn't believe what I was seeing. There were two different
couples dancing very close together. One of the girl's legs was thrust between her partner's while her partner rode it, obviously with much pleasure
– in time with the music, of course. On occasion they kissed quickly but
fervently. I looked over at Sister Joan of Arc, who seemed happily oblivious
to what was going on. I tried hard to be equally oblivious, but I wasn't too
successful.

"Well, it takes one to know one," I said to myself gritting my teeth, but
not at all comforted by the thought. "At least I'm not the one in charge!" I
sighed, keeping myself busy looking elsewhere.

When it was time for me to leave, Sister Naivete (I had already dubbed
her thus in my own mind) had two of her girls take me through the long
corridor leading to the convent. As we were walking along, I felt one of my
garters snap off the belt and the long white stocking it had been holding up
began its trip down my leg. Before we got to the door, the top of the stocking was dragging around my ankles and the garter was dragging behind on
the floor. Not even my voluminous, long skirt hid it. I wanted very much to
join in the giggling going on behind me, but instead, as we finally reached
the door, I quickly unlocked it and said, "Good night and God bless you!"
saving my own laughter until I was safely inside the cloister.

"Well, I guess that's what I get for practicing the vow of poverty to such
an extreme," I thought as I wiped away the tears from laughing. "I'll have to
request a new garter belt first thing in the morning."

By that time, the other sisters had sung Matins and Lauds and had retired. I had my meditation to make up, as well as saying Matins and Lauds. In
the dark chapel, I knelt a few minutes to begin my meditation and then sat
for the remainder. It wasn't long before my chin was bouncing on my collar
bone and as I lurched forward, I awoke as I struggled to regain my balance.

I wondered how long I had been sleeping. My room was right next to the Mother Superior's and I didn't want to disturb her. Forgetting Matins and Lauds, I hastily genuflected and hurried to the chapel door. I opened it and sped through, only to slam hard into a solid wall. I had mistakenly opened the door to the confessional, not the door to the hallway outside the chapel. Having been knocked down by the impact, it took me a few seconds to get my breath, a few more to figure out where I was, and some minutes to find my way to the real exit.

When I finally reached my room, I had to stuff a pillow into my mouth to keep the gales of nervous laughter from overflowing, the sound of which would certainly awaken Mother Anthony. The entire evening had been just too much!

Soon after this incident, I was called into the Mother Superior's office. After entering, I knelt down, as usual. I remained that way for the rest of the interview, as was expected.

"You probably don't know, Sister," Mother Anthony began, "but it has been way over a year since Sister Joan of Arc has made the annual retreat. They will be having an annual retreat in the Omaha convent, soon, and I would like to send her there, far away from her usual responsibilities, so she can have a good rest as well as a fine retreat."

Although I had to agree with the superior's assessment, I felt cold sweat running down from my arm pits. I had a good idea what was coming next.

"She won't be leaving for another week, but for the following two weeks you will be in complete charge of the girls. Sister Joan of Arc feels certain that you can do it. She says you are really good with the girls." I quickly kissed the floor to show my acceptance of the command, but I had to wonder how Sister Joan of Arc could make such a judgment of my abilities with the girls in such a short time, since I had arrived only a few short days before.

Another week was barely enough time for me to put all one hundred and fifty names with the right face, much less to absorb all of the duties of the first directress. Shortly after Sister Joan of Arc left, I met a girl whose name was also Georgette. I began to ask her to do some little tasks, often because she was the only one present whose name I remembered. Georgette responded to the trust shown her and became very helpful to me.

When Sister Joan of Arc returned, she was amazed at the trust I had shown Georgette, because the girl had entered the Home only a few days before Sister Joan had left for her retreat. Nonetheless, I continued to call upon Georgette, since by that time she had definitely proven herself as trust-worthy.

I had been in charge only a few days when Ginny, one of Sister Joan's helpers, came to me full of indignation and some fear. She reported that Bil-lie, one of the girls I had noticed dancing suggestively, had grabbed her and forced her to kiss her in one of the lavatories the night before. Several other girls attested to similar experiences with Billie. When I questioned Billie in their presence, the girl blushed furiously, but admitted her guilt. Because she had forced herself on the others, I had her back in the juvenile holding hall before the day was over. Actually, I discovered later that I had probably fallen for Billie's ploy to get herself out of the Good Shepherd Home. Billie had heard that she probably wouldn't have to stay as long in the state reformatory and that such overt sexual activity was somewhat ignored there.

The day after Billie had been sent away, two other girls, Lisa and Monica, asked to see me privately. After they had arrived at my office and seated themselves, Lisa asked, "Are you going to send us away, too, Mother?"

"We really like it here, Mother," Monica assured me.

I was somewhat surprised at the question until I remembered that they had been one of the couples dancing so suggestively. However, they had very much modified their behavior, at least in public, so that I hadn't connected them with Billie. I observed Lisa's closely cropped, blond, curly hair in con-trast to Monica's dark hair falling about her shoulders, but failed to take in the significance.

"No one has come to me complaining about either of you," I assured them. "You know that Billie forced several girls to kiss her in the lavatories. We just can't have that kind of thing happening in the class." I paused and then continued, "If you start acting like that....well, yes, I would have to send you away as well." I looked at each of them straight in the eyes and they quickly assured me that they would never do anything like that.

After they had left, I wondered if I was being as naive as Sister Joan of Arc. I would certainly have to take notice of these two. However, their behavior, at least in public, was exemplary and other serious problems soon took all of my attention.

The next morning Ginny informed me that she and Sister Joan did locker checks in one of the dormitories each week, so that each dormitory was thus supervised at least once a month. Sister Joan hadn't mentioned such a task to me, but there had been many other tasks she hadn't mentioned either. I went with Ginny to the designated dormitory and followed her suggestions as to the method of going through the lockers. I began to feel more and more uncomfortable about opening notebooks and reading notes Ginny pointed out to me as having suspicious material in them. Because of the incident with Billie, I, too, began to see sexual implications in remarks like, "Will you be with me tomorrow?"

After a half hour or so, I could see that it would take hours to thoroughly conduct such a search. "Ginny," I asked, "did Mother Joan go through everybody's note-books like this?"

Ginny blushed and admitted that she hadn't.

"Well, you put those books back where you got them," I commanded.

Then we quickly looked for obvious contraband like cigarettes, food, matches etc. and went on to other tasks. I felt put out with myself for falling for Ginny's ploy to snoop into the others girls' business, but I also realized Ginny might have done it to gain praise from me. I ultimately chalked it up as another learning experience and let it rest, not without acknowledging my own naivete.

I presided over the girls' meals. In this way the girls could get permissions, make complaints or simply share with me some incident of the day. I became so occupied with this that I didn't take much notice of the food being served. One day a girl came up with her plate full of food and asked me to look at it. I saw right away that it was most unappetizing. The potatoes were watery and everything else looked overcooked. I admitted that it didn't look very good. I got up and went to look at the food in the steam tables. The food was hot, but that was about all you could say for it. One of the girls, who worked in the kitchen, came up and defensively declared that that was the way Mother Imelda made them cook it.

I wondered why this would be. The Portland Home received funds from the United Way and had more money to spend on the girls than the convent in St. Paul. Jeanine, the girl who helped in the kitchen, asked me to visit the kitchen the next day. I went over about eleven the following morning on the pretext of taking a tour. The girls were going about their tasks in silence. Sister Imelda looked sullen, too, but I had noticed that was the way she looked at the sisters' recreations, as well. Jeanine then asked me to go out to the store room with her. There I saw fresh fruits and vegetables, much of it spoiling from not being used soon enough.

For the next few days, I carefully observed the meals being served and found that they were all poorly prepared and sometimes were not even adequate. Being the youngest sister in the house and being only temporarily in charge of the class, I didn't feel I should approach Sister Imelda directly. Still, I didn't want things to continue as they were. I finally approached Mother Anthony.

"Mother, I hate to say this, but the meals the girls are being served are sometimes inadequate and are prepared in a most unappetizing manner. When I went out to the store room I saw fruits and vegetables spoiling and going to waste from not being used. I . . .I wonder if Sister Imelda is feeling well. She even looks pale at times and always seems to be fatigued."

"Sister, I think you're right," Mother Anthony quickly agreed. "She's been working in that kitchen for years, probably for too long. The woman who has been cooking for the sisters has quit, and Sister Imelda would probably love to cook for the few of us. I even think I know who would like to take her place. Sister Joseph loves to cook and she loves the girls, too. She does have bad asthma attacks, at times, but I'll ask her if she feels up to it. You could see to it that she has plenty of help, right?"

I was delighted. "I surely will, Mother," I promised. "Oh, thank you so much!"

"Well, you had better pray that Sister Joseph will feel that she is able."

Apparently Sister Joseph felt up to the task, because the next morning I found her in the kitchen and the meal served that noon was both tasty and attractive. The girls were amazed and vociferous in expressing their pleasure. They didn't even come up to ask for permissions or to talk to me until they were finished eating.

That very afternoon, I went over to the kitchen to make certain that Sister Joseph had enough help. I noted right away that the spirit in the kitchen was totally transformed. The girls were busy cleaning and organizing the food, giving suggestions as to how the girls would like the food prepared. Sister Joseph was listening attentively. The meals continued to be in top form.

The meals in the sisters' dining room were much improved, also, as were Sister Imelda's spirits.

Just a few days before Sister Joan was to return from her retreat, I received an urgent telephone call from Sister Eileen in the laundry.

"Sister Teresa, can you come right over?" she requested. "I really have a bad situation here." She hung up before I could even answer.

I went right over, although I was somewhat fearful, not having any idea what to expect. As soon as I walked into the laundry I sought out Sister Eileen. Everything seemed in good order.

"Don't turn around and look right away, Sister," I was warned. "The girls at the mangle doing pillow slips are acting very suspiciously. Would you mind finding out what they're up to?"

I walked around the laundry making favorable comments about the girls' work, leaving the girls at the mangle in question to last. In the meantime I had noted their discontented looks, flushed faces and nervous giggling. I finally walked up to the mangle and asked them directly if something was wrong.

One of the girls blurted out. "Nadine's sick and shouldn't have to work. When she asked Mother Eileen to leave, Mother said she didn't have anyone to replace her. She shouldn't be here, Mother! It isn't fair!"

I saw, at once, that Nadine's face was quite flushed and her skin felt unusually warm. "You go right up to the infirmary, Nadine. I'll take your place at the mangle," I said. The other girls were surprised to find me asking them what they were pressing and falling right into Nadine's place. They could see that this wasn't my first time at a mangle. They tried hard to show me how efficient they were. After about a half hour, Sister Eileen sent a girl over to replace me. On my way out, Sister Eileen stopped me, explaining, "You understand, don't you, Sister, that I can't work at a mangle and watch over the laundry at the same time." I readily agreed.

When Sister Joan returned, I was most relieved to have my responsibilities lessened, but that didn't turn out to mean quite what I had expected. Sister Joan of Arc would spend hours talking with the social workers, or designing new school uniforms for the girls, leaving me alone in the class for much of the day. She often didn't appear until time to take the girls for supper and then to supervise the evening recreation. Girls began coming to me for counseling, while I was supervising the cleaning of the dormitories, the recreation hall or going over the mail. I would be exhausted by the end of the day, finding myself with all of my prayers to make up. After spending only a few minutes at the nun's evening recreation, I would excuse myself, in order to begin making up my prayers.

The girls were complaining that Sister Joan of Arc was not available for counseling and giving them permissions, which only she had the power to give. I dismissed the complaints by taking care of their problems the best I could, but I did wonder why Sister Joan was never in class during the day.

Gradually, I began to realize that because of the incident with Billie and the disorder in the girls' kitchen and refectory, Sister Joan had been reprimanded by Mother Anthony. Sister Joan's way of responding was to leave me in charge all day, but without the necessary authority. I began to hear rumors that the girls were saying that Mother Teresa should be in charge, rather than Mother Joan. The sisters, on the other hand, were divided in their opinion. Some of them felt I was trying to get the job away from Sister Joan.

I finally faced Mother Anthony with my dilemma. "Mother, some of the girls are saying that I should be in charge of the class, because I am over there all of the time. Some of the sisters think I am trying to take Sister Joan's job away from her." Tears brimmed on the edges of my eyes. "I certainly do not want Sister Joan's position, but it is getting to be impossible to be over in the class by myself all day, and be left with all of my prayers to say after supper and then to be accused of taking over. I don't understand why Sister Joan stays away all day. The girls need her. I can't take her place, even if I wanted to!"

"Dear Sister, I am certain it has been very hard for you. Actually I did ask Mother Provincial if I could name you as the directress of the class, but she is adamant that you will return to the Mother House in January. Sister Joan can do better, I know. I will talk to her about being over in the class more. In the meantime, you must stop counseling the girls. It is the prerogative of the first directress, you know."

I was shocked to hear that the Mother Superior had made such a request of Mother Provincial, and was also surprised that it was only two months from when I would be returning to the Mother House. Life at the Mother House seemed like an entirely different life from this one. I had totally forgotten about my training in the chant, my work with the young sisters and that Mother Provincial had told me that I was on loan to Portland only for a brief time. However, I was relieved that Sister Joan would be in class more often.

Again events did not happen the way they had been described. Sister Joan continued to be away from class most of the day. I began telling the girls I was too busy to talk with them, in order to obey Mother Anthony's injunction that I not counsel them. The girls became quite upset when they found there was no one to listen to them. When I understood that Sister Joan was still avoiding the issue, I was overcome with a feeling of helplessness and resentment. I felt it wouldn't do any good to go to Mother Anthony again.

One noon, after supervising the midday recreation of the girls, just as I was locking the door, Patty and Julie came running into the yard. "Mother Teresa! Betty Jo and Mary just went over the fence down by the wash house. If you let us out through the gate, we could get them for you! We really could!"

I felt chagrined for having let Mary and Betty Jo escape my surveillance, and while I trusted Patty and Julie, I wondered at the advisability of letting them go after the runaways. I knew I had to act quickly, if at all, and finally walked over to the gate and let the two girls out. When Betty Jo and Mary saw that they were being pursued, they wisely broke up and Patty and Julie were able to apprehend only Betty Jo.

Betty Jo's clothing had been torn from going over the barbed wire at the top of the fence and all three of them were dirty from the struggle. Betty Jo was small, but hard and tough and undoubtedly had given Patty and Julie a challenge in bringing her back.

"Betty Jo, go with Patty and Julie to your dormitory and all three of you get cleaned up. Betty Jo, you come back down to my office and Patty and Julie, return to your classes," I commanded.

I then went into the office and called the juvenile authorities to report Mary's escape. I became sharply aware that this was really Sister Joan of Arc's office, that I didn't even have an office. I realized I better try to contact Sister Joan and tell her what had happened. When I reached the main switchboard of the convent, I was informed that Sister Joan was with some social workers and was not to be disturbed. I promptly told the sister at the switchboard that this was an emergency and that she should either get in touch with Sister Joan or Mother Anthony as soon as possible.

Then I settled back in Sister Joan's chair, hoping that she would turn up before Betty Jo did. If she didn't, what could I say to Betty Jo that wouldn't be counseling? Then the telephone rang with Mother Anthony on the line wanting to know what had happened. After I told her, Mother Anthony praised me for what I had done and promised to get Sister Joan there as soon as possible.

In the meantime, Betty Jo had slouched into the office. I nodded at the chair on the other side of the desk. Betty Jo threw herself in it, glaring hard at me. I suspected that Betty Jo's tough airs were not from her core being. After hanging up the telephone, I looked deeply into the girl's eyes, letting her see my compassion and caring. Betty Jo's own eyes suddenly filled with tears.

"So maybe this girl isn't so big and bad after all," I said to her with a smile. Betty Jo's toughness cracked wide open as she began to shed copious tears. I pushed a box of Kleenex towards her and waited for her to gain control. Finally she looked up at me as if to confirm that the compassion she had heard in my voice was sincere. When she was satisfied with what she saw, she began to pour out her story as to how she came to be sent to the Home and how hard it was not to have any freedom.

"Well, Betty Jo, it certainly wasn't all your fault that you were sent here, and I do understand your hating not being able to do what you want most of the time. But don't you think that the best way for you to regain your freedom is to do your best to learn what you can while you're here, so you can really be free when you leave. We have several programs in the high school that could do a lot to help you be financially independent then. Are you taking advantage of any of them?"

"No, not really," Betty Jo admitted.

"Well, I suggest you try to see Mother Benigna as soon as possible and get yourself set up for one," I advised. "It doesn't seem that returning home would be a good idea for you, not that you would want to very much."

Betty Jo agreed readily and promised to see the principal the next day.

"Can…can I come and tell you what we plan?" she asked

"Why, of course I'll want to know," I assured her. Then I sent her to her next class with an excuse for being late.

I sat in the chair a few more minutes, thinking over the conversation and then arose to go back to my duties. Just at that moment, Sister Joan came bursting in.

"What's this about Betty Jo and Mary getting over the fence?" she wanted to know.

I acknowledged the fact and went on to explain how Betty Jo had been returned and that I had reported Mary to the juvenile authorities.

"Why didn't you get me?" Sister Joan yelled.

"I tried to, but they said you were seeing a social worker and weren't to be disturbed. I told them that this was an emergency and that if they couldn't get you, they better get Mother Superior, which is what they did. She said I had done the right thing. I guess she told you as soon as you were finished," I replied, staying as calm as I could.

This quieted Sister Joan a little. "Did you put Betty Jo in isolation?" she wanted to know.

That was the first time that I had ever heard that there was such a place. "I didn't know we had an isolation," I said. "Actually, after Betty Jo got cleaned up, I had a talk with her and felt she was ready to return to school."

"You're not supposed to be talking with the girls, now that I'm back!" Sister Joan was yelling again.

My calm vanished. "If you were over in class more, I wouldn't have to!" I yelled back. Then tears came to my eyes. "We shouldn't be yelling at each other," I said. Tears came to Sister Joan's eyes, as well, but we didn't fall into each other's arms, even figuratively. Sister Joan pointed me out of the office and slammed the door behind me.

I walked miserably towards the girls' kitchen to see how things were going there. I heard the convent bell ringing for Vespers and decided to go there, instead, to join the Sisters singing, something I hadn't done for days.

Not long after this incident, while I was supervising the floor polishing in one of the school corridors, I suddenly heard a girl crying out my name. From the sounds of it, the girl was evidently in some distress and I automatically started going towards the sound. I was quickly intercepted by Sister Benigna, the school principal.

"You're the last one we want around here," Sister Benigna said, shoving me into the opposite direction. "Nadine slashed her wrists and is calling out for you!" Her tone of voice was full of disdain, as if I was somehow responsible for the situation. I felt enough concern for the girl that I started again in the direction of the voice. Sister Benigna grabbed me by the arm and told me that the doctor was with Nadine and that I was not to go near her. "Some of them will do anything to get attention!" she spat out.

Since I had felt it necessary to refuse Nadine's request to speak with her the evening before, I felt guilty. "Well, maybe she needs some attention." I replied.

"We don't have time for such things. We're far too busy to give in to their whims," Sister Benigna sputtered, her hand by then, digging into my arm. The doctor's taking care of her. You go on about your business!" she cried out and again gave me a shove.

I was furious, but knew a big scene would only exacerbate matters. I returned to the floor polishing, but was trembling with rage and confusion.

That evening Sister Joan of Arc didn't even return in time to take the girls to supper. After about twenty minutes, she rushed in, apologizing for being late. As I was leaving the dining room, I found Sister Therese of Lisieux waiting for me in the hall. Sister Therese had preceded Sister Joan in being in charge of the girls, before poor health had forced her to resign. She was teaching a couple of classes in the high school and was well aware of the tension building up among the girls.

"Sister Teresa, go tell Mother Anthony why you weren't at supper and then meet me in the Sisters' kitchen. I think I can help you," she promised.

Tears came to my eyes. "Well, yes, I could surely use some help, Sister. Thanks a lot!"

When I arrived at the kitchen and found Sister Therese waiting, I eagerly poured out my story, telling the older woman how difficult it was being the only one over in class all day without the authority to make decisions and the injunction not to offer advice or support to the girls, when no one else was doing it.

"Sister, I know the situation has become intolerable for you and for the girls, too. Sister Joan's pride has been wounded, but she is going to have to put it aside and start seeing the girls again. You see, Mother Superior told her she was replacing her with you, before she found out that Mother Provincial wouldn't let her. Then she was told she would be continuing in the position, since you were not staying. You can imagine how she feels, can't you?"

"I sure can." I readily replied.

"Also, Sister was put in this position while she was still too young. Did you know she was raised in Catholic boarding schools all of her life? Her mother was always too ill to take care of her. She entered our order right after graduating from high school. We've all come from protected backgrounds, but she was more naive than most of us," Sister Therese continued.

"Gosh, Sister, I had no idea." I exclaimed.

"But I think she will make a good directress, given time and a lot of support. I had a talk with her and told her she had to start seeing the girls again. That's why she was late to relieve you tonight."

"I see, "I said, flooded with new understanding. "I'll do all I can to help," I promised.

Then, to my amazement, Sister Therese made us each a big ham and cheese sandwich, which we ate with huge glasses of milk. Neither of us had had supper, but I would never have thought of "raiding the icebox" as it were. Then Sister Therese began planning a big Christmas party for the girls with me. This would take me out of the class more and help Sister Joan return to her duties.

As we were preparing to go to our rooms for the night, Sister Therese said with a big grin, "Why don't you call me Tessie and I'll call you Terry so we won't mix each other up?"

I laughed and said, "Well, then, good night, Tessie." I would never forget this woman's kindness and wisdom.

I began spending much time in the gym with various girls putting the very elaborate decorations for the Christmas party together. One afternoon I was working with a girl who was very conscientious and a hard worker. The girl decided to take advantage of the situation, being alone with me.

"You know, Mother Teresa, I thought you were going to really pull this class together and now you hardly have anything to do with us. Let me tell you, most of the girls are really disappointed in you. And here, I thought you were really different!" She ended her tirade glaring at me.

I looked hard at her, struggling to keep my tears back and to keep from defending myself. Finally I said, "I can understand why you feel that way. I'm sorry, but I am not the one in control and that's that!" The two of us continued to work in silence for a very long hour afterwards. I wanted out of the situation as soon as possible.

Shortly after Christmas, Mother Anthony called me into her office to tell me that I wouldn't be returning to St. Paul, after all. Instead I would be going to the Home in Helena, Montana, where they were very understaffed and would need my help for a time.

My stomach lurched. It sounded like the same song, second verse. I was certainly not ready to take on another frustrating situation.

CHAPTER SIX

When I saw Mother Francis approaching me from the other end of the hall, my eyes filled and I was afraid I was going to burst out sobbing with relief. I quickly stifled this urge and ran up to greet her.

"Mother, it's so good to see you! It has been quite an experience here." I couldn't help smiling at the understatement.

"So I've heard," Mother Francis said, returning the smile. "Well, we'll have plenty of time to talk about it on the train tomorrow."

I immediately understood that this wasn't the best time or place to begin my story, yet was assured that I would be heard. I was light-hearted as I finished my packing and was most grateful to Mother Provincial for sending Mother Francis to make the trip with me to Helena. In the meantime, I had learned that Sister Clothilde, who had been in her last year of temporary vows when I was a novice, was the first directress of the girls in Helena. I was fairly certain that no one ever put much over on her. This assured me that Helena would not be at all like Portland, and I breathed a sigh of relief.

On the train the following day, while we were traveling through the beautiful Glacier National Park in Montana, Mother Francis and I were both oblivious to the scenery being so absorbed with the sharing of my experiences in Portland.

Mother Francis held herself to a few comments. "When the laundry sister called for you to come over to right a situation, you could have called back and insisted that she give you more information as to the problem, but when you did go over, you certainly did the right thing."

"You're right, Mother. I didn't even think of calling her back, but if anything like that happens again, I'll certainly do just that."

"And you yourself have already realized that you really shouldn't have let the two girls who offered to go after the runaways do that, but, again, I can see you have learned from the experience and we can both be grateful that it turned out as well as it did.

I would call some of the decisions you made as coming from inexperience rather than naivete. You have already learned from your mistakes. I don't know if Sister Joan will ever realize her naivete. Hopefully, she will learn to be more observant as to what is going on around her."

"Sister Therese thinks she will," I said. " She is going to take my place as second in the class and if anyone can teach Sister Joan how to deal with the girls, it's her."

"I think you're right," Mother Francis agreed readily and also expressed her gratitude for the help the older nun had given me.

As we approached the convent in Helena, I saw that it was at the very base of the mountain from which the town derived its name. In fact its ascent began right behind the girls' yard. Having been raised in Denver, which is situated in sight of the Rocky Mountains, I hadn't realized how much I had missed their proximity and my spirit rejoiced that I would have this opportunity.

Shortly after we had arrived at the convent, I learned that I would be the principal of the high school as well as the second directress of the girls. It was a much smaller class than the one in Portland, consisting of about sixty girls. Right away Sister Clothilde told me that she wanted me to counsel as many girls as I was able, since she was very aware that she didn't have time to reach every girl by herself.

"I trust that you will not countermand any of my wishes, and if you're in doubt, you'll find out," she advised me.

I felt clear about what was expected of me and thus felt more certain of myself in my dealings with the girls. As principal, I was to see that the teachers and girls had any supplies they needed and would mediate if any problem came up between a girl and a teacher.

There were two lay teachers who taught academic and business classes and Sister Clement, one of the older nuns, taught sewing and cooking. She was also in charge of the girls' kitchen and clothing room.

I supervised the student who was assigned to take care of the library as well as the cleaning of the two classrooms. I oversaw the upkeep of the large hall where meetings were held, entertainments were given and the girls recreated when the weather was inclement. In addition I taught two religion classes to the girls who were Catholic.

My only duties as second directress were to take the girls to supper and supervise their evening recreations until Sister Clothilde came back from her own supper and making up her prayers. Compared to my duties in Portland, I felt I was being helpful without having to worry about impinging on another's responsibilities.

I soon became friends with Sister Immaculata, a semi-retired nun. It was obvious to me that this elderly nun had been opened up to love. Her love of God and for the sisters emanated from her. She took care of the guest dining room, where the priest, who celebrated the daily Mass, had breakfast each morning and she also supervised the cleaning of the hallways and lavatories in the convent. One Saturday morning, when I was helping her clean the guest dining room, Sister Immaculata told me she had never had a girl run away on her. She explained that this was because she showed the girls that she trusted and respected them and they didn't want to break that trust. This reminded me of my experience with Georgette in Portland and I greatly appreciated the wisdom behind Sister Immaculata's philosophy. Before I had arrived, it was Sister Immaculata who had sometimes supervised the girls' evening recreations.

"I'm afraid that I sometimes dozed off on them, but they never did anything to take advantage of me," she explained. Sister Clothilde was quick to corroborate her story.

Ruth Ann cleaned the school rooms in the morning. I was to check her cleaning as well as seeing that she had the necessary supplies. Since the girls were only in school during the afternoons, it was during the mornings that I made up my own lesson plans and corrected any religion assignments I had given as well as to aid Sister Clothilde by censoring some of the outgoing mail.

Soon, Ruth Ann began hanging around my office after she had finished cleaning, although she was supposed to go over to the laundry for the remainder of the morning.

Because she was so conscientious about her cleaning, I felt she wasn't trying to get out of her work in the laundry, but was trying to tell me something. After several mornings of this, I began asking about her family. Compared with many of the other girls' families, hers didn't seem too bad, boring perhaps, but no violence, incest or anything that seemed serious. We talked for only a few minutes, when suddenly Ruth Ann got up and left for the laundry.

The next morning Ruth Ann walked into my office crying. "There's something I need to tell you, but...but I'm so sc-scared! I...I don't know what you'll think of me!"

"Well," I replied honestly, "I don't either and I won't be able to know until you tell me. From what I know of you now, I will probably still like you, though."

"I'm doing something really terrible, though, and I can't seem to stop it! I can't seem to do anything about it!" She continued crying disconsolately.

"Maybe I could help you," I offered. "Why don't you try me out?"

"I'm receiving Our Lord in Holy Communion every day," she blurted out, "but I...I'm in the state of mortal sin." Ruth Ann's tears became a steady sobbing.

"Well, maybe you are, but then again, maybe you aren't," I said. "Anyway, Our Lord is very understanding."

"Oh, I know I am!" Ruth Ann declared with vehemence.

"In that case, you need to talk about it with Father O'Leary in the confessional," I advised. "I hear he is very understanding, too."

"Oh, Mother, I've tried! Every week I go in all ready to tell him...and then, I just can't! I can't! Then I tell myself I can't keep receiving Jesus, but, Mother, I want to so much. It helps somehow. I don't just do it to impress Mother Clothilde or even you." The girl continued sobbing.

"Well, I'm really glad about that," I said to encourage her. "You know I can't absolve you, only a priest can do that, but maybe if you tell me about it, it will make it easier to tell Father."

"Yah, maybe it will," the girl agreed. "I used to baby sit for these people. They only had one little boy, four years old and he was real easy to take care of. He always did what I asked." Here she paused.

"So what happened?" I prompted.

"Well...the woman got pregnant again and...and...she didn't want to *do it* with her husband because she said it hurt when she was pregnant." Again, Ruth Ann stopped.

"Did he tell you this?" I guessed.

"Yah, he did," Ruth Ann admitted. " It was when he would take me home afterwards that he would tell me these things. Then, when we would get to my house, he would turn off the car lights and engine and...and...at first he just put his arms around me. Oh, Mother, it felt so nice! I have to admit that I liked it! Even when he started to kiss me. In fact, I liked it even more! I...I had never had anyone be that nice to me before!"

"I think I understand," I said.

Ruth Ann looked up quickly. "Do you? Do you really?"

"Well, in some ways," I said, not wanting her to think the same thing had happened to me.

"And, and Mother, we finally started *doing it* ! You know! Making love!"

I nodded, showing I understood.

"At first it hurt, but he was real nice! He even helped me clean myself when it was over, from the blood and all! He apologized for having hurt me but promised it wouldn't hurt the next time. Well, I told myself there wasn't going to be a next time. After all, he was married!" Again, Ruth Ann commenced sobbing.

"But there was a next time?" I asked.

"Yah…yah, and he was right. It didn't hurt the next time. In fact it was the most wonderful thing that had ever happened to me. He kept telling me that he loved me, but that he loved his wife, too! Then he began asking me if I wanted to stop, but it was too late! I…I couldn't resist! Oh, Mother, it was all I could think about…at home, at school, even at the movies! I could hardly wait until they would call for me again. But I started hating myself, too. We weren't being fair to his wife. I knew that, but I just couldn't help it! Then his wife had their little girl and they stopped calling for me. I don't know why, but actually, I was relieved. But still, I've never been able to confess it. Maybe because I liked it so much, I'm not sure I'm really sorry."

"Well, for one thing, he was not only being unfair to his wife, he was being very selfish and entirely unfair to you getting you started," I said as firmly as I could, purposely letting my anger be heard.

Ruth Ann raised her head, looking directly at me. "You know, I never thought of that. But, yah, you're right. You're right!" she exclaimed.

"So it sounds to me that you really are sorry," I continued, "and he was taking advantage of a very young person. I'm sure Our Lord understands. However, you will still have to tell Father. I just can't say that none of it was your fault. Really, only Our Lord knows that. How about if I kneel by you during confession next Friday, maybe that would help you go in."

"Oh, would you really, Mother? Yes. Yes, I'd like that. Thanks a lot!"

Ruth Ann stopped receiving Communion and the following Friday, I was kneeling beside her as she was preparing for her confession. The line dwindled down until we were the last ones in the chapel. Father always waited a few minutes before leaving.

"Go on!" I whispered. "I'll wait here for you."

Ruth Ann became absolutely pale with bright red spots on each cheek. She emphatically shook her head negatively. She just couldn't go in. Finally the priest left.

"Listen, Ruth Ann," I offered. "Father always stops for a bite to eat before he leaves. How about if I go and tell him what happened to you so that all you will have to do is go in and tell him you were the girl Mother Teresa had told him about." I was somewhat fearful, not being positive that the confessor would agree to such an arrangement. However, Ruth Ann nodded in the affirmative.

"Now you'll be sure to wait here," I said.

Again, Ruth Ann nodded affirmatively. I rushed out of the chapel and over to the guest dining room so I wouldn't miss him. He was still there when I arrived and after apologizing for disturbing him during his repast, I told him Ruth Ann's story.

"Oh, Sister, you'd be surprised how often this sort of thing happens," he said sadly. "Sure, I'll go back up as soon as I finish this delicious cake."

I was most relieved to find Ruth Ann was still kneeling in the chapel and knelt by her to tell her that Father would do as I had requested. After a short time, we heard him enter the confessional. Again Ruth Ann's face went white and I was afraid she wouldn't go in. Suddenly she stood up and rushed over and into the confessional. A few minutes later she came out and knelt by me to say her penance. I could hear her tears of relief and remained until she was finished. Afterwards we left together and as we were ready to go our separate ways, I gave her a quick hug. Ruth Ann was all smiles.

The following day, I wondered why I had never looked up Ruth Ann's record. I discovered that she had been transferred directly from the Florence Crittendon Home for Unwed Mothers to the Good Shepherd Home, because her mother felt she was out of control. I was amazed that Ruth Ann hadn't shared the pregnancy with me. I wondered if the man by whom she had the baby even realized he had fathered another child. My eyes filled as I realized that Ruth Ann had been only fifteen when she had given birth to a boy, whom she had given up for adoption.

"Well," I mused, "I just have to presume that the people in the Crittendon Home helped her over that hurdle. She may tell me about it yet, but unless she does, I'm not going to bring it up."

A few days later Ruth Ann did tell me about the baby. I looked deeply into her eyes and asked, "Was it difficult to give up the baby?"

"Not really, Mother," the girl answered. "When I was told it was a boy, I didn't even want to see him. For some reason, if I had had a daughter, it would have been really hard to give her up. "

I didn't say anything, but felt under those circumstances I might have felt the same. I gave Ruth Ann a hug and told her I was actually proud of the way she had handled the situation.

About a month later, I was in my office straightening things up after a busy day in school. Suddenly I heard someone screaming in anger. It seemed to be coming from the second or third floor landing. I leaped out of my chair and ran through the assembly hall to the bottom of the stairs, when I recognized that it was Sister Clothilde screaming. I stood still, listening carefully to see if it was something I should concern myself with.

"Don't keep following me around like a lost puppy, Bette! You're not the only girl in this class! I've given you more than enough of my time, as it is! Go! Go to your dorm and study or get ready for supper or something! Just leave me alone!" I wasn't as surprised at the words as I was at the rage with which they were spoken. Still I could surmise how it had come about. When a girl got a crush on you, it *was* hard to manage. Nonetheless, it seemed to me that rejecting the girl was not the answer, although I could understand feeling that way. The screaming stopped and I decided I should not intervene, although I was deeply concerned.

As I walked towards the chapel for meditation, I thought about the time Sally had a crush on me when I was still a novice working in the laundry. But I realized I only saw her for an hour or two in the morning. I wouldn't run into her four or five times a day. There had also been Ginny and Betty Jo when I had been in Portland. I had found that it was best to ignore their fawning as much as possible, and make certain that I was fair with the other girls in the attention I gave them. I had to be aware of this because sometimes I did feel closer to them simply because they had confided in me more. That way, these girls came to realize that they couldn't expect favors from me over the other girls. They actually admired me for being fair. At the same time, by remaining friends with them, they often aided me in my relationships with others, who were difficult to discipline.

Some time after that, I was supervising the girls' evening recreation, when Jeanette asked me if she could talk to me that night, while I was supervising the dormitories. While the girls were getting ready for bed, Sister Clothilde sat in the hall between the two dormitories on the third floor, while I did the same on the second floor. Actually one of the dorms on the second floor was only used for disciplinary purposes and was often empty. It was off this dorm that I slept. Both Sister Clothilde and I used this time to talk with the girls, if it wasn't too personal.

Perhaps this wasn't a clear distinction for the girls, because as soon as Jeanette approached me on the landing, she pulled a chair up close by and I knew what she was going to say something personal.

"Mother, can you keep a secret?" she asked in a way that was almost seductive. She even had a little smile on her face. The smile led me to hope it was going to be some kind of a joke, and not be a serious conversation after all, but right away, Jeanette's demeanor was very serious. "Sometimes Mother Clement sends me up to the attic to get supplies for the sewing room. Have you ever been up there, Mother?"

"Why, no, I can't say that I have ever been up there," I answered, wondering where this was going to lead.

"Well…well, maybe you'd like to come up there with me sometime. It's really quite an interesting place," Jeanette continued.

I was immediately on my guard and gave an evasive answer. "Well, maybe, if I can ever find the time." I was quite certain that I wouldn't be able to find the time.

Jeanette put her face right up by mine. I pulled back as much as I could. "Mother, mother, listen to me. I…oh, you're never going to believe this, but…but I've seen the Blessed Mother up there…twice now." Jeanette whispered this in a very dramatic way.

"What…what did she say to you?" I asked with reluctance.

"Nothing. Nothing!" the girl cried out. "But…but I just knew that she loved me very, very much."

"Well, yes, the Blessed Mother does love us all very much," I agreed with some relief. At least Jeanette didn't believe that the Blessed Mother had some task for her to accomplish.

"Even if you're not Catholic?" Jeanette asked. I hadn't been aware that Jeanette wasn't Catholic, although I quickly realized that she wasn't in either of my religion classes.

"Why, of course," I replied. "Jesus came to save everyone and the Blessed Mother loves everyone, too." I was getting more and more uncomfortable with the conversation. Miracles and visions were not my *forte*.

"Listen, Jeanette, you should talk to Father O'Leary about this, not me. You can go and talk with him in the confessional even if you're not Catholic. Many of the non-Catholic girls do."

"Oh, Mother, I know that. Mother Clothilde tells us that all of the time," she assured me. "Well, if you think I should…"

"I definitely think you should," I said, wanting very much to be let off the hook.

"I…I thought you might want to come up with me sometime and see if you see her, too." Jeanette persisted.

But I remained firm. "Well, you talk to Father O'Leary about it first and then we'll see." Jeanette finally left the hall and went to get ready for bed. I breathed a sigh of relief and then, I felt somewhat chagrined, having given her such a hard time.

Then it came to me, "Maybe she's another Bernadette★ and I am like all the Bishops who gave her such a hard time! Well thank God, it wouldn't be up to me to confirm her visions, at any rate. And she could just be trying to get me up there for who knows what reasons. Yes, it's good that I resisted her," I praised myself, hoping this would be the end of the whole thing.

The following Friday after the girls' confessions, Jeanette again approached me. I saw her coming and braced myself.

"Mother!" Jeanette exclaimed, "I talked to Father O'Leary about seeing the Blessed Mother in the attic and he said I should get someone to go to the attic with me and find out if they saw her, too," she stated with triumph.

"Oh, thanks, Father O'Leary," I groaned to myself. Out loud I said, "You know, Jeanette, I think you ought to ask Mother Clothilde to go with you."

At once tears came to Jeanette's eyes. "I did, Mother, even before I told Father O'Leary about it, but she just laughed at me. She doesn't believe me and…and I guess you don't either."

"To be honest with you, Jeanette, I don't know what I believe. Well, if I can find the time some day, I'll go up with you," I conceded, much against my better judgment. "If she is hallucinating," I continued inwardly, "then I can get help for her all the sooner." I refused to consider if the girl was, indeed, having a vision, but I couldn't entirely disregard the euphoria I had seen on her face.

After several weeks of procrastinating, I finally found time to go up to the attic with Jeanette. The girl took me way in the back, where she claimed

---

★St. Bernadette, who saw Our Lady at Lourdes, France during the nineteenth century. After a long time, her visions were finally approved and after her death, Bernadette was canonized by the Church to have seen the Blessed Mother. I could see, at once, that the dim light would be conducive to having a vision, if that was what a person was seeking. The two of us knelt and quietly waited for the appearance.

Finally, I whispered, "Tell me if you see her." Nothing occurred and we finally returned to our respective tasks.

I didn't tell Jeanette that she hadn't seen the Blessed Mother, but in fact she persuaded me to go up again the following week. This time Jeanette claimed to see the Blessed Mother, but dimly. I peered into the place Jeanette was looking, but saw nothing. Again, I didn't repudiate the girl, but simply spoke the truth. "I really don't see her, Jeanette. Maybe you should ask her to say something to you," I suggested, cold sweat running down my sides.

"She's…she's gone now," Jeanette said. "Maybe I didn't really see her," she admitted.

By that time, I had read Jeanette's case history and found that her mother had been very rejecting of her, being somewhat jealous of her daughter's beauty. I could readily understand that the girl's need for a caring mother could cause her to imagine one, especially one that would gain another's attention.

A few days before Easter, which was early that year, there was a sudden turn in the weather. Helena received a huge blizzard and the temperature dropped to a record low for that time of year. Some birds, not quite as large as pigeons, but larger than doves, had begun to return. Their feathers were basically gray, like a dove's, but had a pinkish cast to them. The girls said they were snow birds. In their need to get protection from the cold, many of them broke through a number of windows in the convent. Most of them died right away from cuts and from being nearly frozen. I helped find boxes for the few who were still breathing, but none of them survived.

I remembered how on Christmas day in Portland, Betty Jo had brought in a couple of roses for me. Although they were among the last of the roses, the day had been balmy and there was no sign of it becoming a White Christmas. Now, here, in Helena, we would be having a White Easter. Well, it had truly been a topsy turvy year for me!

One morning while I was giving out cleaning supplies to Ruth Ann, I heard Sister Clothilde screaming again from upstairs. I quickly handed the last of the supplies to Ruth Ann, who was looking acutely embarrassed, and hurried over to the stair case to see if I could help in any way. This time Sister

Clothilde was upbraiding someone for not cleaning a dormitory in the way that she desired.

Then I heard Sister Clothilde yell, "You're nothing but a lazy little slut with nothing on your mind but making out with boys!" On hearing this, I cringed, realizing that Sister Clothilde must be referring to Bette's life before she was sent to the Home and probably had little to do with the girl's cleaning of the dormitory. Without further delay, I hurried up the stairs to the dormitory from where the screaming came.

"Is there something wrong?" I asked as I hurried in.

Sister Clothilde, whose back was to me, swung around, startled to see me there. "Oh, Sister, am I ever glad to see you!" Sister Clothilde said. I noted that she was also very embarrassed upon seeing me. "Could you possibly finish supervising the cleaning of this dormitory? I'm already late for my appointment to see Mother Superior."

I immediately decided that preparing lesson plans and censoring mail was less important than aiding in a rapidly deteriorating scene and answered in the affirmative.

Bette began sobbing as soon as Sister Clothilde was out of the room. When she finally regained control, she cried out in despair. "Oh Mother Teresa, I used to love Mother Clothilde. I would have done anything for her, anything she wanted! Now I'm terrified of her and wish that I had never met her. She seems to hate me. I can't do anything right, no matter how hard I try." Again Bette began crying. A little later she stifled her sobs and continued, "I thought being here at the Home was really going to help me, but now…" Again she was sobbing uncontrollably.

At first, I couldn't think of a thing to say. I certainly didn't want to criticize Sister Clothilde, in spite of feeling that she was not handling this relationship very wisely. Suddenly, I was inspired to ask Bette what it was that Sister Clothilde wanted done in the dormitory.

"Well, you can see I was polishing the floor when she came in and blew up because she didn't like the way I was doing it. She didn't even tell me what I was doing wrong!"

I could see at once what the problem was. I walked over to the big industrial floor polisher, turned it on and showed Bette how to polish in small circles to work the wax in and then to go over it in a straight line, thus obliterating the marks of the polisher on the wax. "I learned how to do this when I was just a novice in St. Paul," I laughed, not mentioning that it had been Sister Clothilde who had taught me. "Now, you try it and see the difference it makes," I said, handing the polisher over to Bette.

"Oh, yah, Mother, that looks a lot better!" Bette agreed. She carefully finished the entire floor in the same manner. In the meantime, I checked over the dusting of the dormitory and by the time Bette was through polishing, I was able to assure her that the dormitory looked good and dismissed her to go finish out the morning in the laundry.

Nonetheless, I was most uncomfortable about the way I had handled the situation, knowing that things would probably not improve between Bette and Sister Clothilde. Because Sister Clothilde had more seniority and experience, I had no idea how to approach her as to the way she was dealing with Bette. I finally decided to go to Mother Superior, who had been a first directress in her younger days and seemed to have a good understanding of what it meant to work with the girls.

After I had told Mother John the Baptist what I had witnessed, she replied, "Oh, Sister I didn't realize that Bette had a crush on Sister Clothilde, but I have been concerned about these outbursts of Sister. I'm afraid Bette hasn't been the only one who has experienced them. Sister Clothilde is concerned, herself, and has spoken with me about them very openly. Actually, that is why I begged Mother Provincial to lend us someone who could take some of the stress off her. I can tell you that Sister Clothilde has been very grateful for all you do in the class and you have taken a lot of the burden off from her.

She and I also noticed this happens a lot just before her period. I'm going to have to insist that she sees a doctor about this and see if she can't get help with some medication. Thank you for coming to me. I agree with you about the difficulty of dealing with a girl who has a crush on you, and I agree that the last thing you should do is reject her outright and certainly not by bringing up her past. I think Sister knows that, too, but she just gets out of control at that time of the month."

I was most relieved to hear this, but still remained somewhat troubled about the help Sister Clothilde was in need of. I had never heard of premenstrual syndrome and was without any of the symptoms myself.

A few days later, when Sister Clothilde drew me aside to explain her actions with Bette in the dormitory, she again referred to Bette as a little slut, who *did it* with any man she could get hold of before she was sent to the Home. "I even had her describe what it was like," she informed me. "How she could lower herself so for a few minutes pleasure, I don't know!"

I was surprised that Sister would have the girl describe her love-making in detail and, even so, I knew there was more to it than a few minutes pleasure. Also, it seemed that Sister was using information given her in confidence as a weapon to use when the girl displeased her. Again, I couldn't think of a thing to say in reply; yet I was extremely uncomfortable not saying anything.

Early in May, my monthly one day retreat happened to fall on my birthday. Birthdays are disregarded in the convent, being replaced by little celebrations on the feast day of the saint for whom the sister is named in the convent. Thus on October 15, the feast of St. Teresa of Avila, a little box would be put in front of my place in the refectory and the sisters would put in holy cards, scapulars, rosaries etc. In turn, I could use these as rewards for some of the girls who had done favors for me, as well as to put them in the boxes for the other sisters' feast days throughout the year.

However, despite the lack of celebration on one's natal birthday, I confided to Mother John that I was twenty-nine that day and asked her if I might pack a lunch and take a long hike up the mountain. I explained that I had been raised in Denver, and mountains had been an important part of my life. Mother John thought this was a great idea and readily gave me permission.

I went straight to the Sisters' kitchen, packed myself a lunch and started up the mountain about an hour later. As the aroma of crushed pine needles from under my feet reached my nostrils, I was filled with nostalgia. Memories of the many happy days I had spent in the mountains as a child and of my days at the Flying 'G' Girl Scout Camp with Lynn flooded my entire being.

"I never thought I would ever be doing this again," I sighed. "I really believed my mountain climbing days were over when I entered the order."

I continued up the mountain until I found a level place to sit and meditate. My heart was filled with gratitude for such a birthday present from my Lord. I looked down on the roofs of the convent buildings and peering farther out in the valley, I saw the buildings of the town of Helena. The beauty of the scene drew me into a mystical state of feeling united with the whole world. . . with the entire universe!

Hunger pangs brought me back to the mountain side and after enjoying my lunch, I began the trip down the mountain. My heart was light and full at the same time, even though I felt certain that this would undoubtedly be the last time I would climb a mountain.

When I arrived back at the convent, there was a letter awaiting me from Mother Luke, assuring me that I would be returning to St. Paul in June, as soon as the high school in Helena closed for the summer. I had feelings of excitement, but some dread, too. The Mother House made everyone so much more formal, I realized, because of the good example everyone wanted to set for the young women in the novitiate. Still, I looked forward to working with the novices and postulants again and wondered if I would also be returning as second directress in the Junior Class.

On the day that I told Jeanette that I would be returning to St. Paul the following week, the girl confessed, "Oh, Mother, I really did think I was seeing the Blessed Mother in the attic, but maybe I was imagining it. I've always wanted a loving mother so much. You mothers here at the Home have all been so good to me. Thank you so very, very much."

I gave her a big hug, promised that I would pray for her and wished her well. After I had been back in St. Paul for a time, I received an announcement of Jeanette's baptism. I was delighted and wrote her a letter telling her this and enclosing some little holy cards. A little later I was inspired to write the following poem.

God let me see a soul once.
It was already His,
Although not His child
Not yet born into His family
Nor sharing His life
Yet, it was, if I may compare,
Like a fetus, growing and developing
In the womb of its mother,
Protected by His love and already chosen,
Quickly approaching its birth into the Divine Life

CHAPTER SEVEN

WHEN I WAS a child of two or three, Christian Science Churches were very simply furnished. They were built like Greek temples, complete with colonnades across the front. Inside, at the front, was a lectern, large enough for two people. The American flag and a large basket of cut flowers were on one side of the lectern and the flag of the church and another basket of flowers were on the other side. At the back against the wall were chairs for the two readers and the vocal soloist. Above the chairs, simply painted in gold, was the message GOD IS LOVE. That was all. I knew what these words meant long before I went to school and learned to read.

In Sunday school, I learned at a very young age that God was also omniscient, omnipotent and omnipresent. Along with the message of love, it was the last of these attributes that captured my imagination and filled my spirit. I would lay, stomach down across the board of the swing in our yard, swinging and singing,

> God is Love,
> God is everywhere.
> No matter how high I swing,
> He's already there!

Then I would kick harder and go higher, just to feel His loving presence rush through me. Next I would let "the cat die down" slowly, slowly, my feet dragging, helping in the process, until I was motionless, but still euphoric and lost in the presence of His Love.

Years later, when I discovered that I was no longer a Christian Scientist, I did not repudiate that pervasive presence of light and love, but rather, rediscovered it in a delightful manner in the Sacrament of Holy Communion.

There were to be mystical moments of feeling not only my own essence immersed in Love, but of feeling closely united to each individual kneeling beside me, and then feeling this mutual love expanding to include everyone in the world, the entire universe.

It was to this presence that I joyously consecrated myself, my energies, my life, as I renewed my vows each morning. Once a week I also had to face the watchful judge of the confessional, but I did not let this distract me from the more joyful, and, for me, the more real message of the resurrection, of the new life to come, germinated in me at Baptism and growing and developing at each Communion, through meditation, the Office, my entire life.

A person seeking the spiritual path in the Catholic Church is warned *ad nauseum* about thinking of herself as holy because of the euphoria she might feel at meditation or after receiving Holy Communion. She is put down as being like a child, needing a reward like a piece of candy, to encourage her on the narrow way. I had received this warning even as a postulant, as if they were afraid I might enjoy a bit of ecstasy I didn't deserve. No one, I was taught, could be a mystic or a saint without a lot of suffering first.

Over the years, I developed my own opinion about these euphoric experiences. First of all, in the inmost depths of my heart, I knew they were very similar to the euphoric moments I had experienced after my love-making with Lynn. Secondly, I knew these experiences, from childhood on, had opened my spirit to a greater capacity of loving and being loved than I would have had otherwise. Finally, if euphoria were not holiness, for me it was an effective way to feel close to Jesus, and to receive the energy needed to labor long hours for Him. Besides, euphoria did not eliminate suffering from my life, if suffering was, indeed, the secret to sanctity.

Thus, emulating St. Teresa's practical turn of mind, I began to meditate in such a way as to feel euphoric joy. One way I did this was by singing to Jesus – inwardly, of course. I especially liked a hymn written by the twelfth century Benedictine Abyss, Hildegarde Von Bingham.

> Jesus, the very thought of Thee
> With sweetness fills my breast.
> But sweeter far Thy face to see
> And in Thy presence rest.
>
> Nor voice can sing, nor heart can frame
> Nor can the memory find
> A sweeter sound than Thy blessed name
> O Savior of mankind.

O hope of every contrite heart
O joy of all the meek
To those who fall, how kind Thou art
How good to those who seek.

But what of those who find, ah this
No tongue nor pen can show
The love of Jesus what it is
None but His loved ones know.

Jesus, our only joy be Thou
As Thou our prize will be,
Jesus, be Thou our glory now
And through eternity.

It seemed to me that if joy was such an important part of my life, it probably was for most people. I wanted to do what I could to bring this element, not only into the lives of the girls with whom I worked, but also into those of the young sisters I was teaching.

When I returned to St. Paul from Helena, I was put in charge of the sisters' choir, began a postulants' choir and taught music fundamentals, which gave me even more opportunities to spread the joys of spirituality.

The Sisters of the Good Shepherd chanted the Little Office of the Blessed Virgin every day and sang it on Sundays. Besides this, they usually had a High (sung) Mass and Benediction on Sundays. They also sang the Divine Office, a High Mass and Benediction on feast days special to their Order, as well as on the major feasts of the Church. Thus, the sisters sang from two to five hours a day. I discovered that many of the postulants thought they couldn't sing or at least that they hadn't sung much before entering the Order. I believed that spending so much time singing could become onerous if one did not receive some pleasure in it. I put out a great deal of energy to make the chanting of the Office an aesthetic experience as well as a duty, following the guidelines of the Solesmes monks.

To assist me in this, I requested permission to give each postulant a weekly fifteen minute individual voice lesson to help the sister develop her own voice to maximum capacity. The directress of novices listened to my reasoning and agreed to this arrangement. It was so successful that we extended this to the first year novices, as well. When I felt they were ready, the new sister joined the Sisters' Choir. The difference in the quality of sound was apparent almost immediately. I also began to direct Vespers and Compline daily to aid the other sisters in achieving this end.

It was during this year that I was asked to put together a series of lectures on the history of our congregation from the writings of the founder, the foundress and the journals of various sisters. I supplemented these by including other historical events taking place at the time. I thoroughly enjoyed both the preparation and the delivering of these lectures. I was careful to intersperse them with enough humorous events to keep everyone interested.

My courses in Gregorian Chant at St. John's Benedictine Abbey had sufficed to give me the credits in music I needed to obtain my B.A. I still needed a class in Englsih literature and one in Spanish to complete my requirements. I was able to attend an English literature class with the postulants and second year novices. Since I had had so many courses in Spanish, they arranged for me to take Latin American literature by myself. A professor from St. Thomas came and assigned readings in three different books, one of poems in Spanish, When I had finished reading them, he would come and examine me on them.

I especially enjoyed the challenge of translating the poetry and when I surmised the professor was impressed with my efforts, I hoped to do more of this.

In the afternoons, I taught sophomore English, Spanish and chorus in the girls' high school. There were thirty five students in my English class, which meant reading many, many papers, since I believed that they learned best by doing. One evening, as I was going through a stack of compositions, I picked up one that was very difficult to read. It had atrocious spelling, no punctuation and no use of capital letters. I threw it aside. After completing one or two others, I reluctantly picked it back up to see if I could get any meaning from it. I struggled with it long enough to realize that Wanda was a fantastic story teller. Besides this, the girl's sentence structure, vocabulary and style were excellent. Nevertheless, in order to be able to read it to the class the next day, I had to literally rewrite it.

Wanda was amazed as she listened to me read her story to the class the next day, and was most pleased with the enthusiastic response of the other girls. After class, I asked Wanda if she could come to the study hall I would be supervising that evening. Then I quickly showed Wanda what I had had to do in order to read her story.

"Oh, golly Mother," the girl admitted laughing, "I've never been able to spell."

"'Well, it would help a lot if you put periods at the ends of your sentences and began them with a capital letter," I suggested.

"Gosh, Mother, I don't even know when I'm at the end of a sentence! You know you don't have to worry about those things when you're just telling a story," Wanda insisted.

"Wanda," I broke in impatiently. "You saw how everyone liked your story today. You've truly got some talent. I'd like to help you make them more readable."

"Wow, Mother, do you really think they're any good?" the girl asked.

"I truly do, Wanda. Later on, maybe you could sell them," I assured her.

"Why, Mother, thank you! Yes, I'll come down tonight. Maybe you could help me. I…I . . .guess I never took any of that seriously before. But I will now. Thanks ever so much, Mother!"

While we were working together to improve the legibility of Wanda's stories, I had Wanda read some of her own stories in class, when I hadn't had time to correct/re-write them. I discovered that Wanda couldn't read them either, but she was able to improvise, and thus get by.

Wanda worked hard all year and while she never became a really good speller, by the end of the year, both she and I were able to read her stories with much less struggle.

When I had been in high school, one of my favorite classes had been drama. Now, as Sister Teresa, I decided that it would be fun as well as therapeutic to include some drama in my own English class. I started my students out with a radio play and then went on to more complex stage productions. For the radio play, *The Hitchhiker,* I had the girls use the big institutional floor polisher for the drone of the automobile. I used this suspense-filled play in several different classes and for a long time afterwards, every time I heard a polisher, I would experience that scary feeling in my stomach, wondering if it were Death pursuing the hero of the story, in the form of an ubiquitous hitchhiker.

The school budget didn't have money to pay royalties and I discovered that plays without royalties were usually very outdated. I came up with the idea of having the girls make adaptations of short stories into plays. They did this with several of O. Henry's stories and quite successfully with Edgar Allan Poe's *The Masque of the Red Death* . The revelers, Prince Prospero's guests trying to avoid the deadly plague that was ravishing Europe, wore modern clothing and bore the names of current music and television stars. Elvis Presley took the place of Prince Prospero. The guests went through the different colored rooms by the use of stage lights, until they ended up in the black room at midnight, where they had the unforeseen rendezvous with the Red Death.

As Christmas approached, I wanted to have the girls do something a little different than the usual Christmas play. I wrote a modern musical version of the old French medieval play *The Little Juggler of Our Lady.* Briefly, this is the story of a juggler, who, in spite of being the King's favorite, would be reduced to literal starvation when juggling was out of season. In order to assure himself of regular meals and, in my version, to help change other evils in the world as well, he decides to enter a monastery and become a monk.

After he is accepted, he fails at one thing after another. He can't learn Latin and sing in the choir. He can't write poetry for hymns nor sculpt statues for the Church. He can't even help in the kitchen without burning the food, so he ends up sweeping the cloisters.

On the approach of Advent, the other monks become busy preparing their gifts for the Blessed Mother and her Divine Child. One writes a poem for which another composes a melody. Another carves a new and very beautiful statue of St. Joseph. The cook bakes an immense and delicious fruit cake. On Christmas Eve, the juggler, kneeling in the back of the chapel, is despondent because he has no gift for Mary, nor for the infant Jesus. After the others leave, he is suddenly inspired as to the gift he could give the Blessed Mother and her son.

Rushing out of the chapel, the juggler soon returns with his juggling balls. He goes right up to the statue of the Madonna and begins to juggle. He continues to juggle and juggle and juggle, until towards dawn, several of the monks look in and, full of self-righteous dismay, hurry out to tell the abbot of the blasphemy taking place. When they finally return, they find the juggler prostrate on the floor in front of the Madonna, but not without a sign of her pleasure with his gift. There was a beautiful red rose lying across his heart, now stilled by death.

I used Debussy's *Golliwog Cakewalk* from *The Children's Corner* as the theme for the juggler, both before he becomes a monk and for his swan song at the end. Not being a pianist myself, I was fortunate to find Betty, a junior in the high school, who was quite proficient. She was also very proficient at lying and told me a long tale about her name really being Maureen. She claimed that she was really Irish and that her step parents didn't like the Irish and called her Betty instead. Then, with real tears in her eyes, she begged, "Oh, M...M...Mother Teresa, will you please call me Maureen?"

"Why, I don't see why not," the gullible mother replied. "In fact, I would be most happy to. I like that name for you better than Betty, anyway."

Later I went to Sister Divine Heart, saying, "Sister, don't you think we could call Betty Jamison by her real name, Maureen, since she really prefers it to Betty? Don't you think it's a shame that her adoptive parents made her change it to Betty just because they don't like the Irish?"

Sister Divine Heart began to laugh and laugh until tears were running down her cheeks.

"Well, Sister, at least I know where that story came from," she sputtered between laughs. "Sometimes I don't even think that girl knows when she is straying from the truth! Do you have a few minutes? I want to get her in here, while I face her...and you with the *facts*."

I was both embarrassed and mystified, but was eager to hear the *facts*. When Betty/Maureen arrived, she got a silly grin on her face as soon as she saw me there.

Seeing the grin, Sister Divine Heart said with quite a bit of irony, "Now Betty, am I going to have to get out your folder to prove to you, as well as to Mother Teresa, that you were baptized Elizabeth, that the people you're now living with, when you aren't here, are your *real* parents and that all of you are of English descent?"

By then, both Betty and I were blushing, but laughing rather heartily. "Why did you ever tell me such a story, Betty?" I wanted to know.

"Well," the girl replied, "I *do* wish I were Irish and that my name *was* Maureen! Besides, Mother, I didn't really expect you to believe me!" she exclaimed.

"Well, poor Mother Teresa hasn't had previous experience with you." Sister Divine Heart defended. "You can really tell a good tale and be convincing too, Betty, but that still doesn't make it right. Some day you're going to get yourself into a lot of trouble – as I keep telling you." By then, both Betty and I were no longer laughing. Sister Divine Heart's exasperation was clear. "BUT!" she continued, "since there are so many Bettys in the class right now, why don't we call you Maureen? It would save us all a lot of confusion. Okay?" she asked.

"Why…why…why thanks a whole bunch, Mother!" the girl gasped. "Sometimes you really surprise me!"

"Now don't stretch your luck," I interrupted. "C'mon, Maureen, we've got some practicing to do!" and the two of us left together.

The girl playing the part of the juggler had taken dancing lessons, but didn't know how to juggle, so I had her pantomime the juggling and had her dance at the same time. I also wrote some verses to the beginning melody in the cakewalk that introduced the character.

> Here comes the juggler
> The King's favorite juggler
> Good morning, dear Cantalbert!
> Twisting and twirling
> Dancing and whirling
> He's never dropped a ball as yet!
>
> He's always smiling
> He's always cheerful
> All men know Cantalbert!
> When you're in trouble
> He'll come on the double He's never lost a friend, as yet!

The girls really enjoyed putting on this somewhat different Christmas play. Possibly some of them were astute enough to be aware of my identification with this simple character, who had known both success and failure, and for whom love was the primary motivating force.

On the Feast of the Epiphany (the Three Kings), I had my Spanish class get together a big party for the entire school. They put together four huge and ungainly *pinatas** from chicken wire, crepe paper and paste with sequins added on.

Sister Michael had stored away small gifts for the girls, such as sachets, costume jewelry, address books and small diaries. We put these inside the

---

**pinatas,* a Mexican custom, where baskets are commercially made in the shape of animals or clowns and which are then filled with little gifts and candy . A child is blindfolded and armed with a stick, with which she beats on the *pinata*, until the treasures inside come spilling out, when the children run and grab what they can.

pinatas along with many pieces of candy. The Spanish students gathered the rest of the school together by singing carols in Spanish outside the class-rooms, each class then joining us in the procession, which ended up in the Assembly Hall, where the *pinatas* were hanging.

At first everyone was willing to stand back, while four girls with scarves over their eyes, went to work on the *pinatas* with sawed off broom sticks. When the candy and gifts began to pour out, there was a sudden rush, ev-eryone wanting to get one. The scarves were quickly removed so that those girls, too, would get a chance at the goodies. The hostesses took seriously their responsibility to see that each girl got some candy and a gift.

I felt well loved by both the other sisters and the girls, but not unani-mously. Although I, myself admired Sister Divine Heart very much, I often felt uncomfortable in her presence, sensing that she did not like me. Even worse, I felt she did not even trust me.

During my last year in the Juniorate, nearly all the Junior sisters were assigned an hour or so a day to stay with Sister Patricia, who was in her sev-enties, was losing her memory and had also become bedridden with broken hips that refused to mend.

I enjoyed my times with Sister Patricia because of the candid way she spoke to Jesus. Once, when Sister Patricia was on the bed pan struggling to have a bowel movement, she said, "Lord, I just can't seem to go. It feels like it's right there, but it just won't come. Please, won't you help me, dear Jesus? Did He hear her? Did He help? She was finally able to move her bowels.

After I had cleaned out the bed pan, I handed her a Catholic Digest to read. She chose a story and asked me if I would like to hear it. We both enjoyed it, chuckling together over the humor. Then Sister Patricia began rifling through the magazine looking for something else to read. I picked up a stack of compositions to read and correct.

"Oh, Sister," Sister Patricia exclaimed, not more than a minute later. "Here's a story I think we'll like." Then she began to read again the story she had just completed.

I waited to see if she would laugh again in the same places or if she would come to realize she had just read it. She laughed again in the same places but never came to the realization she had just read it. I felt like laugh-ing and crying at the same time. I quickly found another magazine, giving it to Sister Patricia and suggesting she look it over for a story. I simply could not have endured a third reading of the same story.

One evening, when I went in to take a turn staying with Sister Patricia, as I walked in, I was surprised to see Sister Divine Heart there. Sister Divine Heart was equally surprised to see me.

"Do you help with Sister Patricia, too?" Sister Divine Heart exclaimed.

"Why, yes, I do," I stammered. "I guess Mother didn't know you were already here."

"Well, I am here, so you can leave," she replied rather brusquely.

Hot tears came to my eyes as I walked off. Again, I felt Sister Divine Heart's dislike for me. I tried to think of what I had done to displease her. When I arrived at the the sisters' recreation room, I put it aside.

The next time I went to see Mother Francis, I related the incident to her.

"I don't know why, but Sister Divine Heart seems to dislike me. This isn't the first time I've felt this," I assured Mother Francis.

"Well, all I know is that one time Sister Divine Heart told me that she thought you were on the girls' side," Mother Francis explained.

My jaw dropped. "What do you mean, Mother? Of course I'm on the girls' side. Whose side is she on?"

"Well, I'm just telling you what she said," Mother Francis replied, somewhat amused at the difference in perception of us two women.

Then it occurred to me that not all of the sisters who worked with the girls had the same philosophy as Sister Immaculata, who felt that if you gave trust to the girls, they, in turn, would strive not to let you down. I related my experience in Helena with Sister Immaculata to Mother Francis.

"I truly believe she has the right attitude, Mother, and it is her example I try to follow," I continued, "It is hard to believe that Mother Divine Heart would set herself up and the rest of us, for that matter, into competition with the girls."

"I don't believe that's quite how she sees it," Mother Francis cautioned. "I guess we each have to work out our own ways of working with the girls."

"Yes, I suppose so," I admitted, grateful that I didn't have to work directly under Sister Divine Heart.

On April 24, 1956, five of my companions and I made our final vows. During one part of the ritual, the six of us lay prostrate on the floor, while assistants covered us with a large black pall to symbolize our final *dying to the world*. We remained there during the singing of the entire *Dies Irae* taken directly from the liturgy for the dead.

I had never felt more alive in my entire life. I enjoyed the variety in my work and was well-liked by most of the sisters and the girls. I hadn't experienced any sexual temptations since that last freak brushing of lips with Mother Francis in the fall of 1954. If I thought of sex at all, it was simply with relief and with the belief, perhaps, naively, that I had finally outgrown that type of thing.

CHAPTER EIGHT

In the fall of 1957, it was announced over the news that there was going to be a severe epidemic of Asian 'flu that winter. Since not enough serum would be available in time to immunize everyone, the Sisters of the Good Shepherd were put on the list of those eligible to receive them, because we ran a correctional facility.

When the time came, not one Sister got the 'flu, but about seventy or eighty percent of the girls came down with it in varying degrees. It was a particularly virulent form, causing fevers of 103 to 104 degrees, lasting from four to five days.

During this time many of the sisters worked in the laundry in order to keep up the work of the accounts with the railroads. I was excused from all of my classes, both in the novitiate and the high school. I spent the entire day taking pulses and temperatures, giving out aspirin and keeping records, as well as dispensing the light meals provided for the twenty or so patients.

Quickly, one dormitory was set aside for those girls suffering from the malady. They chose St. Michael's dormitory, because it was on the top floor and thus more effectively isolated the sick from the healthy. For me this wasn't the best solution, since I had to pull up the food and dishes on a manual dumbwaiter.

I would be up in the dormitory by eight in the morning to take the patients' vital signs and dispense aspirin. Next, I would pull up the dishes and finally, the cereal and fruit juice. The distance was three storeys including the high ceilings of an old building. Afterwards, I would go around with warm water, soap and towels to enable the girls to wash their hands and faces. Finally, I would be free to go to the chapel to make up my prayers and eat dinner. By then, it was time for me to return to the dormitory, take the girls' vitals and serve lunch.

The same was true for supper. By the end of the day I was exhausted, but I didn't get the 'flu.

One afternoon, as I was clearing away the lunch dishes, the girls began begging me to open some of the windows to clear out the air. I readily agreed that the dorm could use some clearing out, but I also felt it was dangerous for people with high fevers to be in drafts, especially since it was below zero outside. Besides, the windows were close to five feet tall.

Finally, I got all the girls to promise to stay tightly under their covers until I had finished airing out the room and had closed all the windows. I decided it would be good to open two windows on each side of the room and thus get a cross current to speed up the process. All went well until I went to open up the fourth window. It blew clear out of its casing and into my arms. Fortunately, I somehow managed to set it down without breaking it.

As soon as it seemed that the air was quite clear, I closed the three windows and then approached the last one, being somewhat doubtful as to whether I could get it back into its casing in a permanent way. Some of the girls offered to get up and help, but I held them firmly to their promise to stay in bed under their covers.

It was probably sheer fear that enabled me to finally force the window back into its casing. It fit tight and didn't threaten to blow out again. As the girls came out from under their covers, they were profuse in their gratitude for clearing out the dormitory. I had to leave quickly in order to release the nervous laughter welling up inside.

At first, as soon as a girl's fever was gone, she was given one day to get her strength back and then was sent back to school and to work. We quickly realized that the patients were susceptible to having a relapse, often becoming more ill than before. We opened up a second dormitory for those recovering, but who were able to go to the refectory for meals. I continued with the fever-ridden. It was to be two weeks before I sent the last girls, free from fever, back to their dormitories. In my exhaustion, I couldn't help questioning the *privilege* of having had the 'flu shot.

It was shortly after that memorable experience with the Asian 'flu, that I began giving violin lessons to a girl whose father was a prominent physician in Minneapolis. Mickey had been taking violin lessons for some time at home before she became so incorrigible, that, in desperation, her parents finally sent her to the Home. Somehow she discovered that I played the violin. She decided she wanted to resume taking lessons, because she had heard some gypsy violin music and wanted to play some herself. I was aware of the anger sometimes expressed in gypsy music, and had felt it would be a good release for some of Mickey's own anger. Soon I had her working on some variations on the theme of *Dark Eyes*.

After a few lessons, Mickey brought some pencil drawings she had done of some very tough looking *hoods*. Somehow they were connected to the music for her, but these drawings seemed sinister to me, and I found it impossible to have empathy with them. I did admire Mickey's drawing skills and said so, but Mickey sensed my antipathy and never brought more of them. I didn't even think to alert Sister Divine Heart to these drawings.

A short time later, I went over to class one morning to find a wired window cracked, more windows broken and blood all up and down one of the school halls. Mickey had gone berserk the night before, cutting her hands badly enough to need hospitalization. She never returned. I was greatly saddened by this, feeling that somehow we nuns, myself in particular, had let this girl down.

In the meantime, Sister Divine Heart was retired to a small mission. Sister Louise took her position as the first directress of the girls, who seemed to love her very much, so that the transition went quite smoothly. I was somewhat shocked, therefore, when one evening at the sisters' recreation, I was sent for to help with a crisis in the class. Sister Emily, the new second directress in the class, quickly informed me that there was a girl at large with a kitchen knife threatening to kill Sister Louise.

"Sister Louise is up in the clothes room with some girls and wants you to relieve her there, so she can help find Karen," she said.

"Thanks, Sister," I replied and hurried up to the clothes room on the second floor. There, I found Sister Louise with about twenty girls crammed in the small room with the commercial sewing machines and cutting tables.

"You're here! Great!" Sister Louise exclaimed. "Sister please stay here with these girls and I'll get back as soon as possible." With that, Sister Louise practically ran out of the room, giving no explanation as to why these girls were being detained in the sewing room.

I stood with my back to the Dutch door, which was the only exit from the room. The girls were standing or sitting on the floor. I looked around for some one I knew from one of my high school classes. I recognized no one. I quickly sensed that the girls were not too happy at being enclosed in such tight quarters, for which I could hardly blame them.

"Why are we being kept here?" one of them shouted out.

Since I had no idea, I hardly knew how to reply. When I didn't answer at once, some ugly snickers rippled around the room.

"Well, I don't think it will be for very long," I finally answered, knowing that they realized I was being evasive. However, I fervently hoped this would turn out to be true.

"Why don't we sing for awhile, to pass the time," I suggested, and began to sing one of the songs I had learned at Girl Scout camp, hoping they would be familiar with it. A few of them joined in half heartedly, the others becoming more hostile by the minute. After singing for an interminably long twenty minutes or so, the singing died out entirely and in the silence of the aftermath, I could almost hear the perspiration I felt trickling down my back.

"What will I do if they decide to make a break for it?" I asked myself. No answer was forthcoming. I stood as straight as possible, hoping to give the appearance of strength, in spite of my growing fear. On the far side of the room, some of the girls began to jostle each other, as if daring one another to do something.

I studiously avoided looking at them, but I was becoming increasingly frightened and wondered how much longer I had to remain there. I had been there for forty-five minutes when Sister Louise finally returned.

Out in the hall, Sister Louise informed me, "We finally got Karen, the girl with the knife, and she's on her way to the detention center. Thanks so much, Sister. I don't know what I would have done without you." Then she entered the sewing room to release the girls to their respective dormitories. I never learned their connection with Karen.

As I walked back over to the convent, much relieved that the incident was over, I couldn't help wondering when a similar one would break out. It became increasingly clear to me that so few sisters could not meet the needs of so many disturbed teen-aged girls.

Small family group systems were already being used in France and other places in Europe. These consisted of twelve to fifteen girls, each group having their own kitchen, dining and recreation area. The dormitories were set up with sectional walls, giving each girl some privacy. There was a group mother and an assistant for each group.

The Mother General of the entire Order in Angers, France, had been continually trying to get the superiors in the United States to initiate this system, but they claimed they couldn't afford the structural changes required and that they didn't have enough sisters to support it. Nevertheless, it was becoming increasingly clear that it was a necessary change that should not be delayed any longer.

In the meantime, I had missed receiving Mother Francis' direction and support since leaving the juniorate. By comparison, the Mother Prioress, who was now my immediate superior, wasn't as friendly and was prone to using *cliches* for spiritual direction. It didn't take long, however, for me and the other former juniorate sisters to discover that a simple request would usually bring about an appointment to see Mother Francis.

Spurred on by the evening spent with a group of angry girls in the sewing room, I came up with a plan. I obtained an appointment with Mother Francis in order to present it to her. I intuited that Mother Francis would be favorable to it, having had fairly recent experience with the girls herself.

"Couldn't we at least split up the girls into three smaller groups for recreation in the evenings?" I suggested. "For each group there could be a group mother and an assistant, who would be under Sister Louise's supervision. The girls would still eat in the common dining room and sleep in the dormitories, but at least for a few hours in the evenings, they would have the more personal and emotional support of their own group mother."

"That doesn't sound like a bad idea, Sister," Mother Francis concurred.

Encouraged, I continued with my plan. "We could name the groups after the names the dorms have, Sacred Heart, Our Lady's and St. Michael's. What we'd need to do is designate three separate places for evening recreation," I continued. "The rumpus room and the Assembly Hall quickly came to my mind, but I can't think of a third place. I don't think the dining room would be good and the sewing room is too small."

"I can see that you've really been thinking a lot about this, Sister." Mother Francis let her admiration show. She had heard about the incident with the girl with the knife and of my part in it. "I'll talk with Mother Prioress about it and see what we can come up with. Since they would be supervised by Sister Louise, I don't see why some of the junior sisters couldn't be designated group mothers. I guess I'll have to speak with Mother Provincial, as well, as she is directly responsible for the junior sisters. However, I believe it's a good, workable idea. I'll let you know what they think about it."

I was overjoyed. I firmly believed that Mother Francis would be able to accomplish it. Sister Louise agreed heartily with the plan and was just as happy as I when Mother Francis got it approved.

Since there were only two sisters in the juniorate who they felt were mature enough to be group mothers, I was named as the third group mother. This put me on a schedule that required sixteen to eighteen hour days, but seeing the needs of the girls being better met gave me the necessary energy.

These three groups still numbered about thirty-five girls, but the improvement was noticeable almost at once. However, the third site for a recreation area wasn't at all ideal. It was the long school hallway, where Mickey, my former violin student had gone berserk a few months before. It had been redecorated in the meantime and a small classroom was set up for girls who wished to watch television. Comfortable chairs and couches were purchased from second hand stores for all three groups, making the girls more comfortable. The groups rotated daily, so that the same one wouldn't always be stuck with the hallway. It was far from ideal, but it was a transitional phase that the superiors could agree to.

The primary challenge for me was the conflict of roles in my positions of teacher and group mother. Many of the girls were pleased to discover my maternal side in the groups at night, but then found it difficult to accept my more disciplined role as a teacher in the afternoons. I tried hard to narrow the gap, but there always remained some strain, both for me and for the girls, whom I supervised in both situations. At night, in the groups, I had to watch myself from becoming too involved in giving special tutoring and therefore, more attention to girls who were in my classes.

Cheryl had been in my English class for more than a semester when I became her group mother early in the spring of 1958. I had already learned that in spite of Cheryl's slowness in getting an assignment done, it would be almost perfect upon its completion. Cheryl's penmanship was neat and easy to read and her punctuation and sentence structure was nearly always correct. I also decided that after Cheryl completed an assignment, it was better to have her begin on the current assignment rather than to have her go back to the ones she had missed in between.

Although I required my English students to write four book reports in a semester, I only required Cheryl to do one. Her reports always showed a deep perception and, therefore, I gave her full credit. Besides that, she often made appropriate and often witty remarks during class discussions. The others seemed to understand this allowance.

When I first took over Our Lady's group, I noticed that Cheryl would hang around in the recreation area until she had a chance to have a little conversation with me and then she would ask permission to go up to the dormitory. Sister Louise monitored the dormitories in the evening, so that the girls who wished, could go to bed early.

When I took the rest of the girls up to the dormitory around nine-thirty, Cheryl would be sitting on her bed busy doing some school assignment. I soon discovered that she was slow at doing everything, including making her bed, dressing, cleaning her space, eating, etc. But everything she did was done with care and a certain grace. I also found that while Cheryl didn't seem to have any close friends, there were always those willing to finish cleaning her space and help her in other ways so she wouldn't be late to work or class.

Still, I couldn't help wondering what would happen to Cheryl when she left the Home. Not many would recognize the keen intelligence under the slowness with which she moved.

After Cheryl left the Home, she would telephone me in the evenings and occasionally come out to visit me. For a time she tried to go to school, but after a few months she quit and continued her education on her own, spending much time at the library in her neighborhood. She also tried her luck at several jobs, but was unable to function fast enough to please her bosses. She was thought of as being lazy.

Cheryl's mother didn't seem to mind supporting her. I was certain that Cheryl probably always had a good meal prepared when her mother returned home from work. I could also imagine that their small apartment was kept clean and comfortable.

One evening Cheryl called me and could hardly speak because she was giggling so hard. Sensing my growing impatience, she finally blurted out, "Mother, I bet you could never guess...but...but I've got a...a boyfriend!" again, she burst into gales of laughter.

"Well, Cheryl," I said, "you certainly seem happy about it all, but why is it so funny?"

"But Mother, can you imagine it? Me, with a boyfriend?" She continued to laugh.

It was hard to imagine, I thought. Out loud I said, "Well, I am very happy for you. When are you going to bring him out to see me? I have to approve of him, you know," I added jokingly.

"Do you really want to meet him, Mother?" Cheryl asked. "I know he wants to meet you. I've been telling him all about you!"

"<u>All</u> about me?" I laughed.

"Well, mostly the good things," Cheryl assured me, chuckling. "How about this Sunday afternoon?" she suggested, explaining, "He works on week days."

"That would be fine," I replied and that pretty much ended the conversation.

When I met Tim that Sunday, I discovered he had cerebral palsy and worked at a sheltered work shop during the days, leaving the evenings free to be with Cheryl. Since he loved to read, also, they had met at the library one evening. During their visits with me, the three of us had some pretty lively discussions about some book we had all read. After several months, Tim and Cheryl got married, got an apartment of their own and seemed very happy.

During that same spring of 1958, a girl in my Spanish class prided herself in making sarcastically humorous remarks. I began responding in kind. Each of us seemed to enjoy outdoing the other. Even though I restricted such behavior to the one student, I was pretty chagrined, one night, when one of the girls in my group told me that many of the girls were getting to be afraid to say anything to me, because they feared I might respond in the same sarcastic way to them. I thanked the girl and at once withdrew from the "contest". Soon after, I was able to restore the other girls' confidence in me, but even more remarkable was the fact that Darlene gave up such behavior, as well, and began to make friends for the first time in her life.

One afternoon during my English class, while I was explaining something with the use of the chalk board, I suddenly experienced what I was later to describe as an existential flash. It was hard to describe, but it was as if someone spoke to me saying, "You're giving all of your energies to help others, to helping the young to prepare for adulthood, but in the meantime, what is happening to your own life? I had to squelch such a thought immediately in order to continue my teaching, but that night, during my examination of conscience, the memory of it returned.

"Of course I am giving myself to others," I reasoned to myself. "Isn't that what the religious life is all about? Am I not happy? The rewards of helping others is all the reward I need," I convinced myself. It was a warning that, unfortunately, went unheeded.

It was about this time that I encountered a girl who was a victim of incest by her father. Rosalie had ultimately gone to the police, asking to be taken to the Good Shepherd Home, rather than be returned to her own home, since her mother couldn't seem to do anything about the situation.

"You know, Mother, my dad is on the city council, so I guess his reputation has to be protected at all costs," she said bitterly. "They're telling people that I'm at the Mayo Clinic in Rochester with a rare illness! Doesn't that just grab you?" She began crying.

I was so horrified, I hardly knew what to say. I suddenly felt very naive about things going on in the "world".

"It does seem hard to realize that your own mother wouldn't help you," I finally said. "You were really courageous to take yourself to the police and ask them to bring you here. Do you miss your brothers and sisters?" I asked.

"Well, sure, Mother, but…but not enough to go through *that!*" she quickly replied.

"Of course not!" I hastily agreed. "Nothing would make up for *that!*"

I was somewhat surprised when Rosalie asked me to meet her mother the following visiting Sunday. I found myself feeling anger towards this woman I had never even met, for refusing to help her own daughter. When I saw how beaten down the woman was from bearing five children (she was still nursing the fifth), I also observed how submissive she was by nature and my anger abated somewhat. I realized that Rosalie wanted me to meet her mother so that I would better understand the situation at home.

When Rosalie returned home after a couple years she was treated so badly by her siblings, as well as her uncles, aunts and cousins, that she again took the situation in her own hands. She obtained a live-in babysitting job at a home in Minneapolis which enabled her to finish high school. After that, she won a scholarship to the University of Minnesota and I lost track of her, but felt confident she was doing well. Somehow Rosalie had been able to maintain her innocence in her own eyes and continue on her own. I was to discover that this was often not the case with the rising number of incest survivors. They often felt guilty and unworthy, seeing the experience as some kind of punishment they deserved.

Not only were the new group mothers to counsel the girls in their respective groups, but soon they were asked to censor their outgoing and incoming mail and to write up reports of unusual incidents or other observations in their case histories. I could readily see how this would help their social workers in determining the girl's future, but this put an impossible burden on my already full schedule. Sister Louise finally took over the task of censoring the girls' mail, as it became obvious that, between the two of us, she had more time. This still left me with the task of writing reports in the girls' case histories, which no one else could do.

Then an incident occurred that solved the problem, but lost me a job that I dearly loved. When I received word that I was wanted by the Mother Provincial, I had no idea that this visit would change the entire course of my life. "Sister, how are you?" Mother Luke asked. "I am hearing nothing but good reports about what you are doing with the novitiate sisters and also with the girls under your care." Because the Mother Provincial wasn't prone to giving out compliments, I was momentarily stunned.

"Why, thank you, Mother," I finally stammered.

"When we find sisters talented in working with the girls, that usually receives top priority with us. She is either assigned to work with them in some important capacity or she is sent for training that will help her in that task." Here, Mother Luke paused, as if giving me time to take it all in.

"Wow!" I thought. "Am I being sent to St. Louis to obtain a Masters in Social Work?" A few of the sisters had already done this.

"But in your case, Sister, top priority must go to the novices and postulants, who will be the future of our province." Again the Mother Provincial paused.

"I see, Mother," I replied, but of course I had no idea what was coming next. My heart rate had gone up considerably, however.

"We have decided to send you to the University of Notre Dame to work for a Masters Degree in Theology during the next five summers." This time, when the Provincial paused it was obviously for me to acknowledge I had received an obedience.

I did this in the customary way by kissing the floor. I was glad for the opportunity to think of what to say. I hadn't considered myself as an academic person, but if I was to obtain an advanced degree, this certainly would be the one I would choose.

Before I could actually say anything, Mother Luke continued, "Someone will be given the charge of your group, soon. You will be with her for about a week to help her get oriented. You will be able to finish out the school year with your high school classes. That's about two more weeks, isn't it?" The question must have been rhetorical, because she went right on. "You can continue in the novitiate until you leave, which will be in about three weeks. Then we'll just have to manage somehow without you to conduct the choir for the summer."

By then, I was speechless. Mother Luke chuckled and asked, "Well, Sister, do you have any questions?"

Tears momentarily blinded me. "I can't think of any right now," I stammered. Then I suddenly cried out, "Oh, Mother, thank you so much for such a wonderful opportunity!"

Later, as I knelt in the chapel trying to take it all in, I realized I actually had mixed feelings about it. I loved working with the girls and it suddenly came to me that I probably wouldn't be doing that much more, if at all. Nonetheless, the work I did in the novitiate certainly did not take up all my time. Perhaps I would be able to work some with the girls. However, since I also enjoyed working with the young sisters, I readily accepted my new fate.

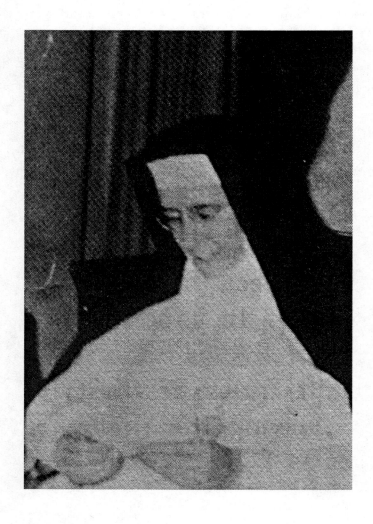

CHAPTER NINE

I WAS PLEASED to discover I would be going to Notre Dame with Sister Michael, who was already in her third summer of the program. I hoped to get to know her better and, in this way, improve our working relationship.

When I had returned to St. Paul, I was assigned to teach three classes in the high school. Sister Michael, who was the principal, let me know that she doubted if I could handle the sophomore English class with thirty-five girls in it. I was not only able, I thoroughly enjoyed it. This helped restore my self confidence, as a teacher, after the failure I had endured two years before I entered the Order. I discovered that I could relate to girls, even unruly ones.

When I began producing plays and musicals, Sister Michael agreed to my having them, but she warned me from the first, that she would not help in any way. She clearly felt over-worked. Although I had not expected any help, this made me fearful to even ask for things like the keys to the costume room.

The Notre Dame campus, with its two lakes, well-kept lawns and bird-filled trees, was in itself, an inspiration for the study of theology. Here, I could develop my love for birds to my heart's content, learning to imitate their calls, in order to entice them to come within my view.

One of the first things Sister Michael and I did, after arriving at Notre Dame, was to attend a concert put on by the college orchestra. It was the first time I could remember having listened to music by Vivaldi. I loved what I heard and decided to find out who made up the summer orchestra. I discovered that anyone, who played an instrument, was welcome. Since I had not brought my own violin, they loaned me a school instrument, and the conductor told me to sit in with the second violins. As the oboe played the A and the others began tuning their various instruments. I suddenly felt the very pores of my skin opening up, as if my whole being had been parched from not having heard instrumental music for so long. It literally felt like moisture was seeping back into my skin. I quickly brushed my eyes and tuned the instrument. The loaner didn't measure up to my violin and I promised myself I would bring my own the following summer. At the end of the period, Mr. Biondo, the conductor came back and told me to sit in the first violins at the next rehearsal.

Now that there was a possibility of my violin becoming a part of my life again, I was filled with gratitude that I had been permitted by my superiors to have it available "for my use" on a pretty continual basis. Up to then, the only time I had used it was when I was a postulant and I played it at the program we put on for the former novice directress and, more recently, when I gave the few lessons to Mickey.

The library at Notre Dame claimed to be the second largest college library in the country. I found an abundance of material on Gerard Manley Hopkins. I not only loved his poetry, but enjoyed the collected letters and other prose writings. The fact that he had been a Jesuit priest, as well as a poet, assuaged my conscience on spending so much time reading his works. I found his concepts on *instress* and *inscape* especially interesting. It proved to be a kind of introduction to existentialism to which I would be much drawn. I wrote the following haiku-like poems, very *a la* Hopkins, with an abundance of alliteration and assonance.

> The rain resting on leaves
> tree's leaves sequin fringed, foliage
> fit for fairy queens.

> Squirrel tracks on the snow
> form shaded pocks in the glow
> from the street lamp's light's flow.

One evening Sister Michael and I were joined by another Good Shepherd Sister at dinner. She was also Sister Mary of St. Teresa of Avila from the St. Louis province. Since we were both tall, we enjoyed the coincidence. When Sister Teresa of St. Louis heard that I was a convert, she wanted to hear the story of my conversion and my subsequent vocation to the religious life. I gave a somewhat abbreviated version of my meeting Lynn at college, which led to my conversion. In explaining my choice of St. Teresa for my name in religion, I related how I had wanted to be a Carmelite, but had been advised by my pastor to visit the Good Shepherd Convent in Denver, since they were a semi-contemplative Order.

Sister Michael became very hostile and exclaimed, "I'm so tired of people entering our order because it's semi-contemplative and not because they want to help the girls."

"But Sister," I exclaimed, "the girls" was the main reason I chose the Good Shepherd over the Carmelites! That visit to the Denver convent was what really convinced me," I continued defensively. Sister Michael remained unconvinced and I refrained from further comment. To myself, however, I wondered how Sister Michael could think I wasn't concerned with the girls. In the past year, I had obviously spent more time and energy with them than she had.

As the summer went by, I gradually came to realize the reason for Sister's antipathy towards me. Sister Michael had been in charge of the Sisters' choir when I first entered. Even then, she was also the principal of the high school and was often late for the rehearsals and sometimes was not even present for the performance in the chapel. The directress of novices felt this was a bad example to give the novices and was hoping for a replacement. When I not only showed a good deal of musical talent, but also a singular love for Gregorian Chant, the novice directress gradually edged me in to replace Sister Michael, beginning when I was only a second year novice. When I was formally made the director of the choir, I had thought Sister Michael had been relieved to have her duties lightened. However, Sister Michael had a beautiful solo voice and considered me an impostor. I refused to feel guilty about this, but felt bad that this would seem to be in the way of a friendly relationship with Sister Michael, as there were many things I liked about her.

On another occasion, in the presence of the same sister from St. Louis, I had been praising the priest who taught my metaphysics course. "In fact, it's my favorite course of the summer," I added. "It's just too bad that he spends so much time bad mouthing Father Hesburgh★, though. That can really get boring!"

"Sister Teresa, how ungrateful can you get!" Sister Michael exclaimed. I was amazed that she took it that I was ungrateful. "Here, Mother Provincial is spending money sending you to Notre Dame and all you can do is to criticize the teachers! Father Hennesy happens to be my favorite priest on the whole campus!"

I immediately became defensive. "Didn't I just say his class was my fa-

★ President of Notre Dame at the time

vorite? I just don't like the way he keeps criticizing Father Hesburgh!" I was soon to learn that it wasn't wise to criticize any priest in front of Sister Michael. In her eyes, no priest could do any wrong. But it cut me to the quick to think she believed me to be ungrateful for being sent to Notre Dame.

By the end of the summer, I had decided on the subject of the first of three research papers. I would entitle it *The Good Shepherd Sister and the Problem of Evil.* The primary evil, with which I had become acquainted, was the abuse many of the girls at the Home had received as children. I drew up a tentative outline and got it approved by one of my professors. I began researching it right away so I could work on writing it during the winter and complete it the following summer. This meant no more Gerard Manly Hopkins. I reasoned that if I did a paper during each of the following summers, I would be free to study for my comprehensives the final summer.

When I returned to St. Paul early in August, I was distressed to learn that Sister Louise had been missioned to Denver and that the family group system had been totally abandoned. Sister Genevieve, who had been put in charge of the class, did not wish to share her authority. I could not believe that Mother Francis would allow this to happen, but it was clearly out of her hands.

Even though the new directress was still in the juniorate, she was a late vocation and everyone seemed to have complete faith in her abilities. Besides, I realized that many of the sisters were more comfortable with doing things the way they had been before.

I tried to enjoy my free evenings recreating with the other sisters, preparing lessons, correcting papers and getting more sleep. However, since I was again teaching the same three classes in the high school, I became aware of the growing discontent among the girls. Sister Genevieve seemed totally unaware of it.

For Halloween, Sister Genevieve staged a very ambitious progressive dinner for the girls. Each of the three dormitories was decked out as a different country, the courses served in each, representing the country. The sisters had been invited to come over and see the transformation of the dormitories and the costumed girls serving in each place. I was most impressed with the amount of work that had gone into it. I could sincerely praise Sister Genevieve and the girls who had worked so hard to bring it about.

When we sisters were ready to return to the convent, without any warning, nor any instructions as to what was expected of me, I was told to remain in the first dormitory and supervise the first course. Fortunately, Sister Genevieve remained, too, so that all I was expected to do was see that the girls remained in the designated part of the dorm and to be sure that the left over food ended up in the pails provided for the garbage.

My job was easy enough, but it was distressing for me to overhear what the girls were saying about Sister Genevieve. They spoke bitterly of her favorites or trustees and the abuse of the power given to the trustees over the others. It seemed strange to me that Sister Genevieve was willing to share so much authority with the girls and none with the other sisters. It was clear that, having so many trustees, she could hardly supervise their use of the power she had given them. I was careful to do only what had been requested of me, pretending I didn't hear the complaints.

When the girls finished the first course, I offered to stay and supervise the rest of the clean up. Most of the girls on the clean-up were not trustees and I was exposed to more complaints. This time I did have to intervene, as there was no way I couldn't have heard them. I pointed out to the girls that Mother Genevieve had been in charge of the class for only a little over three months and they should give her a chance. The complaining stopped, at least until they had finished cleaning up.

As I walked over to the chapel, I was very distressed at what I had heard. It seemed to me that the whole class was sitting on a keg of dynamite that was about to explode.

I made an appointment with Mother Francis to share my observations. "Why, that's strange, Sister," Mother Francis replied. "Sister Genevieve feels in full control and is very satisfied with the way things are going. I know you must be very disappointed because the groups were stopped, but it seems Sister Genevieve knows what she is doing. There are always going to be complainers, no matter who is in charge, as I'm sure you must realize."

"Well, that's right, Mother," I replied, but I realized that Mother Francis sensed that I didn't share her faith in Sister Genevieve.

"Oh, Sister, let us pray that things are not the way you perceive them to be." she said.

"I can surely do that, Mother," I replied as the interview ended.

Sometime in the middle of November, I was eating supper with the other sisters, listening attentively to an interesting article being read out of the diocesan newspaper. Suddenly I heard a noise like thunder of galloping horses, but soon realized that what I was hearing was the stampede of many feet running in the cloister above our refectory, which led to the front entrance of the convent. Without delay, every sister who had anything to do with the girls, ran out of the refectory and on up to halt the mass escape. Fortunately the front doors had been locked and the twenty or so girls, who had planned to run, were huddled in the entry way, not knowing what to do next, because of this unforeseen circumstance.

Mother Francis was able to silence them and then, began to listen to their complaints. They were pretty much the same as those I had described to her, largely that most of the girls were being ignored by Sister Genevieve and they felt they were being unfairly treated by the trustees.

Mother Francis promised to have a talk with Sister Genevieve about certain changes and convinced them to return to class. This was just the first of many riots that were to ensue. Sister Genevieve was unable to see what she was doing wrong and continued on as before. The general disorder which followed, certainly exacerbated the girls' personal problems. Many of them began to disfigure themselves with crude tattoos, using pins or needles and ink. Often by the time they were discovered they had become badly infected. Wrist slashing also became frequent, definitely cries for help. No matter how hard we tried to keep sharp implements away from the girls, they succeeded in getting hold of them.

One evening, I was with one girl for two hours, holding her head on my lap to keep her from banging it on the floor or against the wall. Her eyes were rolled back and she was totally unresponsive to anything I said. Finally, someone sent for an ambulance to take her to a hospital.

A few days later, having had a night off to catch up on some sleep, when I returned the following morning, I discovered an entire dormitory in shambles. Its occupants had been up most of the night breaking whatever they could get their hands on. By the time I joined the young sister, who had been sent to restore order, most of the girls were asleep from exhaustion, but Sister Anne and I knew that when the girls awoke they would start in again. We were at a loss as to what to do. We cleaned up a little before the girls began to awaken. Upon awakening, they began to laugh and swear at us. There was nothing left for them to attack, but us!

"Sister," I said to Sister Anne, "one of us needs to get help. Do you want to, or do you want to stay while I go?"

"You probably have more influence than I do, Sister, so you go ahead, but for God's sake don't leave me here with them for very long!"

This dormitory was close to the Social Service department and I quickly let myself out of the dormitory door which led to a flight of stairs, at the bottom of which was the office. I shocked myself when I heard myself yelling, "If we don't get some help in this dormitory soon, I'm going to let them out!"

The lay social service secretary came rushing out. "Is it that bad?" she cried. She took one look at me and promised help, at once.

I turned and went back into the dormitory and started to tell Sister Anne, who laughed nervously, saying, "It's okay, Sister. You don't have to tell me. We heard you clear in here."

The girls began to get nervous, wondering what would happen to them. In ten minutes a squad of police were there to take the twenty or so girls to the detention center. I really hated for this to happen, but it definitely seemed necessary. A few of the girls repented and begged to stay. Conditions in the state reformatory were worse and they knew it. Sister Anne and I quickly determined which of the girls were truly repentant and those few were permitted to remain. They were very chagrined, and helped Sister Anne and I clean up the dormitory without even being asked.

It was shortly after this incident that Sister Matthew, an older sister with much experience with the girls, was sent for to fully organize the place into the family group system. Sister Genevieve was sent to one of the missions. After all the riots, the numbers of the girls had dwindled to where they could be divided into four groups of about fifteen to twenty girls apiece. I was amazed that somehow the money was forthcoming. Not only were the dormitories remodeled into kitchens, living rooms and smaller dormitories with dividers for each bed, the stoves, refrigerators, tables and chairs and lounge furniture for the living rooms were all new. In a way the girls had won the day, but not without losses among them that were painful to me and the others.

The group mothers and their assistants were mostly young sisters in temporary vows, but they were inspired by Sister Matthew's enthusiasm along with being well instructed by her.

As things settled down somewhat, I got permission to conduct a leather tooling class one evening a week. I went to a Tandy Leather Co. to get supplies, and met a man there, who, when he heard what I was doing, volunteered to come out and help. I was delighted, since I had only done a little leather work before entering the convent.

It turned out that Pete was not only proficient with the leather, he was an excellent teacher as well, having much patience and a sense of humor to go with it. When a girl would make a mistake on her project, he would say,

"We all make mistakes, but there are few mistakes that cannot be rectified in some way." This turned out to be very true.

One evening when the class was going very well, I asked Pete if he would mind if I left for about a half hour, so I could sing Compline.

"Just be sure you do come back, Sister," Pete grinned. "You have to let me out, you know."

In the chapel half way through Compline, Mother Prioress sent for me to come back to the head stall, where the Provincial and Prioress were.

"Sister! Do you hear that hammering noise in the class? It sounds like some of the girls are trying to escape." I hadn't noticed the hammering, because, in fact, it was the girls tapping on their embossing tools in the leather class. The Prioress was clearly relieved when I told her.

As Christmas approached and many of the girls were making gifts for their family members, I met with them more frequently, without Pete, to give them the opportunity to finish their gifts in time. On Christmas eve, I was over there helping and managed to cut one of my fingers rather deeply. They wrapped it in a huge bandage to catch the bleeding, which looked somewhat ludicrous, as I conducted the Sisters' choir as well as the girls' chrous during midnight Mass. After Mass and the procession down a flight of stairs to the foyer where we sang carols for a time, Mother Provincial insisted on looking at the wound and decided, at once, that I be taken to an Emergency Room to have it stitched up. The nurses and doctors found this both amusing and a respite from other casualties such as auto accidents caused by drunken drivers.

Also, in preparation for Christmas, I taught my small chorus of girls the second soprano and alto parts to the more well known of the Christmas carols. Sister Matthew arranged to have us sing at several places where people were shut in and away from their families. The first place was a small hospice for people with terminal cancer. I noted there were tears in some of the girls' eyes as they walked down the aisles singing and also noticed tears of joy in the eyes of many of the patients. Then we were taken to a smaller ward, where the patients were all children from around six to sixteen years of age. They were even more appreciative and, those who were able, joined in the singing. Afterwards, the girls couldn't believe that the children were also terminally ill. One of the nurses explained that they had not been told they were going to die.

We also visited several mental wards in the city hospital. The patients were gathered in a small room fixed up like an auditorium. Again, these patients were most grateful for the singing and also joined in. Then the recreational director asked me if we would go up on the closed ward to sing for those patients. I readily agreed. These patients were restrained in separate cubicles on each side of the aisle, which the girls walked down, as we sang. Since each cubicle had bars in front, it felt like we were in a prison.

We were all shocked, when one of the patients ran to the bars, shaking them and screaming at us. Nothing he screamed made sense, and I kept singing, as did the girls, relieved to continue on and away from him. Even when we had finished and were taken back down stairs, we could hear him screaming. Later, several of the girls told me that it helped them to appreciate their own situation, seeing how much worse off others were.

In the spring, I decided it would help school spirit, if we put out a year book. Sister Matthew was most cooperative and we sent for a kit from a company which helped small schools put out their own year books at a much lesser cost than if a regular printing company did it. Besides instructions, suggestions and clip art were included to aid in putting the dummy together. Again, my evenings were spent over in the class to supervise this. We also hired a photographer, so that each girl's photograph would be included. However, by the time we received the kit, we only had two weeks to meet the deadline required by the company, if the year books were to be available by the end of the school year.

In order to meet the deadline, some of the student staff members and I were up until the early hours of the morning. However, we did meet it and toward the end of May, each girl received her annual. Later, on a return visit, one of the annual staff members said to me, "You know Mother Teresa, you taught me that working hard can be fun."

Besides the year book, I produced one of the best of my stage productions that spring. I had my English class write the script for *A Musical History of America*. This involved some research, which a librarian from the main branch in St. Paul got interested in and gave invaluable help. My chorus, and any other girls who wished, also helped to put it on. I supervised the making of costumes, stage set and make-up as well as directing the actors, dancers and the chorus, but I received a great deal of help from my enthusiastic staff of students.

The musical began with a minuet from colonial times, advancing to a fife and drum piece for the revolution, plantation slave songs, work songs, early jazz and blues, the swing era and on into the rhythm and blues and early bop currently in vogue.

The sister, who did the bookkeeping for the convent, told me, "That was one of the best productions put on by the girls, I've ever seen." I was pleased to pass this compliment on to the girls.

Mother Francis, on the other hand, wryly said, "I really enjoyed your singing of *The Anniversary Waltz*, Sister, letting me know that my voice had been quite recognizable as I used it to lead the chorus behind the scenes. I hoped Mother Francis was the only one to recognize my voice, since I knew not everyone would approve of a nun singing this very romantic song.

"*Pues, asi es la vida,*" I said to myself and thought no more about it.

It would be another fifteen years, during the 1970's, before I would learn what had happened to me that year during the riots, and even, somewhat, during the preceding year. I had put out so much energy to convince my superiors that the girls' needs were not being met. I was satisfied that it was the girls, themselves, who finally made them hear, but it had been a costly way to learn. I would never again be as trusting of administrative authority. I had been *radicalized* before Martin Luther King, the second wave of the feminist movement, or the advent of hippies and their protests of the Vietnam War. What a strange time to be appointed as one of those in authority.

CHAPTER TEN

I WAS APPREHENSIVE, as usual, when I had been told that Mother Provcincial wanted to see me. I absolutely had no idea why I had been summoned. Mother Luke had a very austere *persona*, which had kept me in awe of her. When I arrived at her office, Mother began explaining that the directress of novices was requesting a change of duty and was being sent to Omaha to be the superior there.

Kneeling before her, I wondered, "Why is she telling *me* this?"

The Provincial continued, "I am appointing Mother Francis as the new directress of novices."

"Well," I thought, "she couldn't have made a better choice, but why am I receiving these confidences?"

"I am naming you as the new directress of the juniorate," Mother Luke finally said.

My jaw dropped, and I quickly bent down and kissed the floor, in order to hide my reaction. This act also expressed my acceptance of the new obedience, I realized. To be promptly obedient was thought of more highly than to stop and judge one's capabilities to do the job. That task was certainly the Provincial's, not mine, I gratefully realized, but tears filled my eyes. I wasn't sure why.

"We will announce these changes at the chapter tomorrow morning," Mother Luke continued, "and you will assume your new duties immediately after." Then she went on to tell me the expectations she would have of me. I hoped that I absorbed all of it, in spite of the numbness I was feeling.

The next afternoon, following the chapter, I was walking over to the high school to teach my English class, when from around the corner, I heard, "Did you hear, Sister? Sister Teresa is going to be our new directress!"

"I know, I know! Wow!" the other exclaimed. This was followed by gales of laughter from the two of them. "And just remember, Sister, from now on she's *Mother* Teresa!" The laughing began again.

The words and the laughter were totally understandable to me. These were sisters in their last year in the juniorate, who had not only studied music and the history of the congregation under me, but had undergone the throes of the riots with me. One of them had been a group mother when I was. I slowed down my pace, when I first heard them, but something told me not to slink away, although that is what I felt like doing. I resolutely rounded the corner and they realized, at once, that I had overheard them. I smiled and greeted them.

"Oh, hi…Sis…Mother!" one responded.

"It's good to hear that you're our new mother," the other tried to assure me.

I grinned and said, "I guess we'll all just have to do our best to get used to it."

Teaching replacements for my high school classes were soon found. I was to continue my classes in the novitiate and I wondered if I would be returning to Notre Dame. Within a week, Mother Luke assured me that I would. The Provincial, herself, would conduct the weekly chapter for the junior sisters and would be available to them for counseling. I realized how busy Mother Luke was and tears of gratitude filled my eyes as I thanked her.

Before I left for Notre Dame, I became well acquainted with one of my new charges. The first time Sister Mark came to see me, she expressed doubts about being able to continue with her job as assistant sacristan.

"You know, Mother, I prepare the cruets of wine and water for Mass each morning." Here tears filled the sister's eyes. "You probably don't know that I used to be pretty wild and I drank a lot!" she explained. "I know that some morning I'm going to give in and drink some of that wine. In fact, I already have once," she admitted. "Just a little taste." she quickly added.

I had never personally known an alcoholic, but I felt that this shouldn't interfere with Sister Mark's vocation. There were many other jobs than sacristan in the convent. I said this to Sister Mark and asked, "Did Mother Francis know you had this problem?"

"Yah, I told her all about it," she answered, again getting tearful and blushing.. "She thought that with practice, I would get over it, I guess."

"I'll go speak with Mother Provincial, Sister. She is the one who gives out the charges. We'll see what we can find for you," I assured her.

I decided to check out the story with Mother Francis, first. I discovered that Sister Mark had been correct in assessing Mother Francis' philosophy about handling addictions. In fact, she felt very strongly about it. "If Sister can't overcome this addiction, she should probably leave." she stated categorically.

When I went to see Mother Provincial, before I could bring up the subject of Sister Mark, Mother Luke asked me if I knew about her dilemma. Sister Mark had felt so desperate, that she had gone to see Mother Provincial, herself.

"I can't understand why Sister Francis recommended her for the position, if she knew about her addiction," Mother Luke mused.

"I just asked Mother Francis, Mother," I answered. "It seems that she feels that it is something Sister Mark has to overcome. I really doubt that it is something that she can overcome, but I don't see why, with all the different jobs in our order, she shouldn't be given another one."

"Well, since Sister Mark has been so forthright in telling us about it, I think she should be given that chance," the Provincial agreed. "I think they could use some supervisory help in the laundry. Tell Sister Mark to come to my office at four forty-five and I'll give her a new assignment."

The other junior sisters seemed to be contented with their jobs, so I felt relatively free when I set out on the train, with my violin tucked under my arm, for my second summer at Notre Dame. Soon, I was absorbed in researching my paper and enjoying the weekly rehearsals with the summer orchestra.

Having just acquired a new family, in a sense, I would spend a few hours every Saturday writing a community letter to my new *daughters* in the juniorate. I was surprised at how much I missed them already, but I had taught all of them in the novitiate and thoroughly enjoyed taking this time to address them and to leisurely read the letters they were writing me.

Sister Teresa of the St. Louis Province was the juniorate directress there, and my new appointment added to the things we had in common. However, she was majoring in the liturgy rather than theology.

I was most impressed with what she had to say about Father Joseph Goldbrunner, who was teaching courses in religious education. Since he was also a Jungian therapist, he was applying some of Jung's principles to his teaching methods.

Sister Teresa of St. Louis was adept at taking shorthand and took down Father Goldbrunner's lectures practically *verbatim*. Since Father Goldbrunner was German and English was a second language for him, he was most grateful when she offered him typed copies of her notes. She aso loaned them to me, because I was becoming fascinated with Jungian psychology, although I restrained myself from using time and energy for further study of him, beyond Sister Teresa's notes.

This was Sister Michael's fourth summer at Notre Dame and she still had two of her research papers to write. I was amazed to discover how difficult it was for Sister Michael to express herself in writing. She could verbally tell you something in a logical manner, but when she wrote things down, she would leave out important facts and get off the subject. Since I was almost finished with my first paper, I offered to help her. We got together a few times for this purpose, but Sister Michael found it difficult to receive help from someone younger than she. I tried hard to be as tactful as possible, but it just did not work. I was a little hurt, but relieved at the same time, when Sister Michael found Sister Jean, an older sister from another order, who would help her.

Sister Michael and Sister Jean were also going through a period of temptations of finding men attractive. Sister Jean was openly having a flirtatious affair with a young priest. Sister Michael became very protective of her friend, if any criticisms were made. I knew enough to remain silent on the subject. Gradually I learned that Sister Michael was very concerned that both Sister Jean and the priest would lose their vocations. Sister Michael refrained from getting too friendly with any men, but apparently spent sleepless nights from temptations, as she began to appear with red, puffy eyes in the morning from crying and lack of sleep. I was very sympathetic seeing her like this, and often brought breakfast to her, so she wouldn't have to appear in public before her swollen eyes had a chance to clear.

One evening as Sister Michael and I were walking to supper, she suddenly exclaimed, "Oh, look at that cute brother! I think men with beards are so handsome!"

The remark was entirely innocent, but I froze with antipathy. What I had noticed most about the priests and brothers was how much more money they had to spend and more time in which to enjoy themselves. Many of them spent much of their time going swimming, playing tennis or golf at the luxurious club across the road from the entrance to Notre Dame. They also frequently dined at the very expensive restaurant there. They often had their own automobiles and paid people to type their papers for them, giving them more time for recreation. This double standard of the practice of the vow of poverty did not sit well with me. When I remarked on it, Sister Michael became very protective of them.

"Listen, Sister Teresa, those men deserve all they can get after all the hard work they do during the winter!"

I doubted that any of them worked half as hard as either Sister Michael or myself. This time I knew better than to say anything further and I was most relieved when the end of the summer arrived without any scandals.

Towards the end of that summer session, Sister Teresa of St. Louis and I went to a concert produced by a professor in the liturgy department. The course he taught was called *Eurythmics.* This was a dance form he had developed to aid others in acquiring an appreciation of the subtle rhythms of Gregorian chant. He especially liked to work with children, but was grateful for the enthusiasm of the priests and nuns in the program, who also attended his lectures. I was fascinated with the dancing and, at once, began to plan ways to incorporate it into my teaching of the chant at home in St. Paul.

I was reminded of a novice a few years back, whose parents had been professional ballet dancers. Since the novice danced quite well herself, I prepared a little program for the two of us, in which I played Debussy's *Beau Soir* on my violin, while the novice danced to the music. I had been intrigued with how well the habit adapted itself to and enhanced the grace of the young woman's movements. I wrote the following poem describing the experience.

Oh little white virgin,
For what are you waiting?
You are so quiet and still.
But I can feel you waiting,
    expecting,
        ready.
Is it the sound of a voice
    which makes you rise slowly,
        gracefully
    turning and swaying,
        each movement
    beautifully ordered.
You become light,
    buoyant,
        almost freed from earth

in a joyous ecstasy!

No, you return.

It is not time

for your place to be filled

in heaven.

When I returned to St. Paul that August of 1959, besides my duties as directress of the juniorate, I found Mother Francis full of plans for me in the novitiate. I would not only teach music and the history of the congregation, but two classes on the vows and two more on the religious life. Mother Francis had discovered two books with new approaches to the practice of the vows, which I liked very much. What I was supposed to teach in the classes on the religious life remained somewhat of a mystery, but I soon enjoyed the freedom this gave me in preparing for them. I was so happy that I was to be working directly with Mother Francis again, that I didn't consider, right away, that this would preclude my working with the girls.

I was really eager to put the ideas, inspired by the eurythmic concert at Notre Dame that summer, into my own classes, especially the class in chironomy for the second year novices. The novice who had danced to *Beau Soir* had left, but there was another novice who had studied modern dance and was enthusiastic about teaching some basic movements to the others.

Together we decided to work out a choreography for a tableau. Our theme took in an individual's death, resurrection and entry into heaven. It began with the joyful Easter *Kyrie*, moved on into the bold and ecstatic *In Paradisum,* the recessional sung at burials, and ended with the long and meditative *Alleluia* for the Feast of the Assumption of the Blessed Virgin Mary.

At that time, there was a novice, as tall as I, who was very rigid both physically and emotionally. Sister Daniel had chosen to take the Chironomy and Choral Conducting class offered to the second year novices. Sometimes I would help one of the students get the feeling of the flow of the movement, by placing my hand over the wrist and hand of the student and thus, guide her through. When I did this with Sister Daniel, one day, the young sister stiffened up totally and I had to let go and let her flounder on by herself. Sister Daniel had turned scarlet, but I didn't comprehend the enormity of what had occurred. In fact, I thought that Sister Daniel was angry with me for having *forced her hand*, as it were.

I was delighted that while the novices were practicing the tableau, Sister Daniel was able to forget herself and her body would gradually relax and flow as her face lit up with the pleasure of it. The night that the novices performed the tableau for all of the superiors of the Province, Sister Daniel's face took on a radiant color and her lips and eyes had the look of a mystic lost in contemplation. This helped me to overlook the fact that some of the superiors had been shocked at seeing novices dance to the sacred chant!

A few weeks later, Mother Francis asked me to stop by her office after I finished one of my classes. As I entered the office, Mother Francis said, "Sister, I'm sorry to tell you that Sister Daniel left today. I thought you should know that she told me that she loved you more than she loved Jesus!"

As I began to blush, Mother Francis assured me, "This isn't a reprimand, Sister. That girl had a lot of emotional problems. In fact, you probably helped her more than anyone else had in her entire life. Still, it was good that she decided to leave. I feel she just had too many hurdles to conquer in herself to be able to work with the girls very soon."

I felt abashed that I hadn't realized what Sister Daniel was going through. I wondered if I couldn't have helped her learn to sublimate her earthly love for the love of God. This concept of sublimation was one I frequently used myself.

For Christmas that year, Mama sent me a subscription to a new magazine, *Jubilee, a Magazine for the Church and Her People.* It was put out by a group of lay volunteers in New York City and was a refreshing change from the usual Catholic magazines put out by various religious orders. In one issue, Robert Lax, the editor, published a poem of his own, which he entitled *Tree.* I loved it and began using it at my meditations. After a time, it seemed as if a melody began to form itself around the words. It fell naturally into the first Gregorian mode. I never felt secure about sharing it with any of the sisters, but used it frequently in my meditations. This was to be the first of many such songs I would compose, using the modes I loved so much.

A few days before the feast of the Epiphany (the three kings) on January 6, Mother Provincial received a letter from three Trappist priests asking for over night lodging for the night of the fifth. They also requested to sing a Solemn High Mass on the sixth since they were Asian (Chinese) and this feast had a special meaning for them.

I was able to call an extra rehearsal so the sisters could learn the parts of the Mass special to this feast.

As soon as the three men entered the sanctuary, I sensed that something extraordinary was going to occur. After directing the *Asperges Me*, I turned

around and was immediately struck by the grace and deep intent of the cel-
ebrant. I became so absorbed in watching him that I almost forgot to turn
back to direct the singing of the Introit. I had observed many devoted priests
celebrate Mass, but never anything with quite the depth of this man.

This increased the fervor of my own participation as well as that of the
sisters in the choir. After Mass I was sent to the priest's dining room where
one of the younger priests praised the singing of the sisters. Apparently the
man who had celebrated the Mass with such exquisite beauty did not speak
English, but I could tell by his expression that he too, had appreciated the
singing. I felt an instant rapport with him.

I was amazed to learn that they were on their way to Communist China
to open a Trappist Monastery there. They seemed oblivious of the danger in
which this would place them. I promised to keep them in my prayers. This
experience, which greatly increased my love for the liturgy, would remain
with me for years.

The year of the riots had taught me that those in authority could become somewhat unrealistic in their decisions concerning the girls, because
of their lack of contact with them. Since one of my tasks, as the directress of
the juniorate, was to help the young sisters in their work with the girls, I volunteered and obtained permission to teach a religion class to a small group
of Catholic girls. In this way, I hoped to keep in direct contact with the grass
roots of the specified vocation of our order. I also wanted to try out some of
Father Goldbrunner's methods I had learned the previous summer.

There were several girls in this class who had some training in modern
dance. I told them about Eurythmics and persuaded them to try it out. Together, we worked out several short tableaus, performing them for the rest
of the girls and their parents one Sunday afternoon. In this way, these girls
learned to appreciate the free rhythms of the chant that gave them, in turn,
a new freedom in their dancing.

I was not to have the same success with Sister Mark. A few months later,
she came into my office one afternoon, for her weekly visit, giggling and
blushing. She obviously needed to tell me something that was difficult. As
was my custom, I waited patiently, occasionally saying something to encourage her to speak out. The young sister began telling me in detail about the
escapades she had experienced with the wild gang she had run around with
in high school.

"After we'd get good and soused," she began, "we'd drive out to the

Indian reservation, about twenty-five miles from town, and harass the teen-agers there. Most of them were pretty drunk, too, Mother," she chuckled. "Wow! We'd really end up with some doosies of gang fights. Since we had our own cars, we could leave when it got too rough."

"So how do you feel about that, now, Sister?" I wanted to know.

"Well, I realize we said some pretty bad things to them to get them riled up, Mother. I wouldn't do that any more," she assured me.

The conversation definitely left me feeling very uncomfortable. I wondered if Sister Mark still didn't derive some pleasure from these memories.

The following week, Sister Mark began again, relating how the members of her gang would tattoo themselves with symbols identifying them as members. They used the same crude methods the girls had during the riots. Sister Mark had plenty of scars on her hands and arms to verify this.

"Gosh, Mother, one of the things we liked to dare each other to do to ourselves was to push pins straight into our arms. That was really dumb, huh?" she ended, but her face was flushed, her eyes were half closed and there was definitely a smile on her lips, as if she were in a kind of trance.

I quickly agreed that it was pretty dumb and asked her about her work in the laundry. "You realize, Sister, that many of the girls have had experiences similar to yours and that it would not be good for you to share these stories with them. You could easily lose their respect for you."

"Oh, sure, I know that, Mother," she agreed. I hoped that her limited and closely supervised work with the girls in the laundry helped her keep this resolution.

The following week, when Sister Mark, again, began to regale me with stories of the gang's activities, I asked her if she would like to see a psychiatrist.

"Oh, God, no! No, Mother! No! Not me! I'm okay, now! I don't need any help! Really!" Sister Mark was perspiring profusely and next to tears at the thought.

I said nothing more. That was the last time Sister Mark volunteered stories about her past with the gang, but I wasn't at all sure that these memories were not still causing her problems.

Then Sister Mark requested if she could work with the girls in their groups as well as in the laundry. "You can't get to know them very well, just working with them in the laundry," she argued. I had to agree and promised to speak to Mother Provincial about it. The sister in charge of the laundry reported that Sister Mark was doing a good job with the girls there, so I suggested to Mother Luke that Sister Mark be sent over in the evenings as extra help with the girls. I thought that at least at first, it would be better for Sister Mark to go to a different group each night. Mother Luke agreed and Sister Mark was thrilled to be able to do this.

One evening, towards the end of the sisters' recreation, Sister James, one of the assistant group mothers, rushed up to me. "Mother," she said, "Sister Mark and three of the girls from our group have been missing for about a half hour. We can't find them anywhere! Sister Philip is really beginning to worry. Two of the girls are quite new, although they haven't caused any trouble. But they don't seem to be anywhere in the class!"

"Go back to the group, Sister. I've got to take these papers up to my office and then I'll be right over," I instructed. "Did you tell Sister Matthew?"

"Oh, sure, Mother," Sister James replied. "She thought you ought to know, too, since Sister is in the juniorate."

"Yes, yes! I certainly do want to know what is happening," I responded.

My office was off an unused room above the chapel. When I got off the elevator and stepped into the dark room, I was astonished to see Sister Mark and the three girls. I gasped, "What in heavens name are you and these girls doing up here? Sister Philip is frantic, not knowing where these girls are. She sent Sister James over to get me and Sister Matthew is trying to find them, too. What are you doing over here on the sisters' side, with them?" I asked.

"We just came over to…to get a few supplies," Sister Mark answered defensively. There were a few supplies in a small cabinet in the room, but they were for a small lavatory up there for the sisters' use.

"Sister, these are not for the girls," I spoke tersely.

"Well, they're all out over there, so I thought we'd better come over here and get some," Sister explained. The girls were holding a few rolls of toilet paper to corroborate her story. Not wanting to put Sister Mark in a worse position in the eyes of the girls, I told her to hurry right back over to the group, adding that I would meet them there later.

The following day, when Sister Mark came to see me, I brought up the incident. "Sister, you certainly showed poor judgment, last night, bringing those girls over with you on the sisters' side. First of all, if there were absolutely no rolls of toilet paper over there, you could have come over by yourself to get some. Secondly, you should never take any girls off with you, outside the group, without telling the group mother. Finally, you caused Sister Philip and Sister Matthew a great deal of worry. If you haven't, already, you certainly owe them an apology."

"I did tell them I was sorry as soon as we got back," Sister Mark grumbled. "Even before you got there."

"Why did it take you a half hour to do that one little errand?" I asked.

"I dunno, Mother," she mumbled, "but we didn't do nuthin' wrong!"

"I didn't say that you did, Sister, but you were taking a chance bringing them over to our side. They could easily have run away on you!" I was aware that I was repeating myself, but I didn't feel that Sister Mark was realizing the risk she had taken.

"But they didn't run away, Mother!" she cried out. "Mother, why don't you like me?" Sister Mark suddenly asked.

"Sister, I am appointed to help you to learn our work. It has nothing to do with my liking you or not! I *do* like you! You could be a great help with the girls! I hope you can learn from your mistakes." I said, remaining firm in my declaration.

"Oh, yes, Mother, I can! I…I will! I'm sorry, Mother! It won't happen again, I promise. I want to be a Good Shepherd Sister more than anything." There were tears running down Sister Mark's cheeks.

I dismissed her, after assuring her I would do all I could to help her.

When it was time for me to return to Notre Dame for my third summer, I still had reservations about Sister Mark that I felt obliged to share with Mother Luke. I was reluctant to do this, because I wondered what would happen to the young woman, should she return to her home.

During my previous summer at Notre Dame, I met another juniorate directress of an order dedicated exclusively to the Immaculate Heart of Mary. This woman was in the liturgy program and Sister Teresa of St. Louis had introduced us. Sister Patricia was full of devotion to Our Lady, which inspired me to write my second paper, *The Blessed Virgin and the Good Shepherd Sister.* In it, I put forth Mary as a model of mercy and compassion for both the sisters and the girls. At that time, it was mostly French theologians who were writing about Mary. Sister Patricia, who read French fluently, was willing and even eager to translate some French articles that I wanted to use in my paper, in exchange for some lessons in chironomy. In the process we became friends.

Sister Michael still had two papers to complete, two courses to take, as well as to prepare for her comprehensives at the end of this, her last summer. The romantic problems of the previous summer seemed to have subsided, so that she was able to complete the papers and pass the courses, but failed the comprehensives, not having had enough time to prepare for them. This meant that she would be returning with me the following year, when she would be able to concentrate wholly on the comprehensives. The feelings between the two of us were much improved.

It was during this third summer that I was exposed to the new theology, which was to be the precursor to many of the changes that would be brought about later by Vatican II and, after that, in liberation theology. The profesor of the course on the Mystical Body drew from many diverse disciplines, such as anthropology, physics, psychology, sociology and historical research, in order to get new understandings of Christian principles. These, in turn, would point the way to changes in the liturgical and political structures of the Church. Perhaps the most important break-through would be the Catholic Church's entry into the Ecumenical Movement.

I could hardly wait until I returned home to share these exciting concepts with the young sisters in my classes. I had no idea of the controversy I would thus inspire.

CHAPTER ELEVEN

As a SECOND year novice and young professed sister, I had thoroughly en-joyed the courses I took in logic, ethics and metaphysics, taught by a philoso-phy professor from the College of St. Thomas in St. Paul. In these courses I had been introduced to the classical philosophies of Plato, Aristotle, St. Augustine and St. Thomas Aquinas.

However, these were not the first courses in philosophy I had ever taken. During my final semester at the Colorado State College of Education, three years before entering the convent, I had taken a course in the Philosophy of Education. The professor informed us right away that the official book for the course was John Dewey's *American Education*. He also told us that it could be obtained at the college bookstore, but we wouldn't be held responsible for any of the material in it on an exam. It was evident that he would not be teaching John Dewey. Never having met up with such anarchy in a professor before, I had been a little uncomfortable, but by the end of the class, he had won me over entirely. His philosophical way of approaching life seemed to be just what I had been looking for. Having enjoyed that class so much, I was prepared to enjoy the philosophy classes in the convent.

At Notre Dame I was to study St. Thomas Aquinas in more depth in the class on the Trinity, during my first summer and the class on the Incarnation the second summer. I was grateful for having been given the use of the two very thick volumes of Thomas' *Summa Theologica* to puruse at my leisure during the year.

It was during the third summer at Notre Dame in the class on the Mys-tical Body that I discovered existentialism, with references to the writings of Heidegger, Husserl, Sartre and Camus. The goal of achieving full awareness at each moment and, in this way, assuming full responsibility for one's life, appealed to me.

I was also introduced to the Jungian concept of individuation, where one strove to bring the subconscious and unconscious into one's consciousness and thus become a whole person. To me this goal seemed to be compatible with that of existentialism.

Finally, I was introduced to the writings of Pierre Teilhard de Chardin S.J., the mystic and paleontologist, whose writings were soon to be proscribed by the Church for containing possible heretical material. His combining the mystical with the scientific seemed exactly right to me, but many theologians and scientists were put off by his efforts.

Towards the end of the summer, I came up with the subject for my third and final paper. I entitled it *The Significance of the Meaning of Soma in the Pauline Epistles. Soma,* I learned, is the Greek word for body. Although Paul wrote in Greek, he came from a background in Jewish theology. Previous exegetes (Scripture scholars) had understood his use of the term in the light of Greek philosophy, but current exegetess argued that he was undoubtedly speaking from his own academic Hebraic training. Basically, in the Greek the word would mean the physical body, only, almost as if one were speaking of a corpse. In the Hebraic meaning of the word, it would best be interpreted as it occurs in the word some*body*, i.e. the living person. This certainly threw a clearer light on Paul's teachings about the Sacramental Body of Christ, as well as about the Mystical Body. My deep devotion to the Sacramental Body of Christ inspired me to want to learn all I could from an early source.

I could hardly wait to return home and share all these new ideas with the young sisters, who would be taking my class on the Religious Life. I dreamed of the stimulating discussions I was sure would follow my lectures. Naively, I happily prepared my lectures, certain that the sisters would receive these concepts with the same enthusiasm I had.

Enough did appreciate them, so that the stimulating discussions did occur. It was even more exhilarating for me when one of them would discover a gap in my thinking or would bring up a question I had not thought of and could not answer. I would gladly peruse my lecture notes, or some book in the bibliography from my class on the Mystical Body, until I came up with an answer or clarification. When this would generate even more questions, I was delighted.

Unfortunately, because of the intensity of the discussions, I did not notice that close to half of my students were sitting there with glazed-over eyes from sheer boredom. They were simply not understanding what was taking place. Others were looking at me with shock-filled eyes at what seemed to them absolute heresy.

When I presented a unit on escatology, using the post-resurrection accounts in the *Acts of the Apostles* to discern what life in a resurrected body could promise, one of the novices cried out, "You can't expect us to believe that this old material body will be able to do all of those things! Why, anyone can see their own body deteriorating before their own eyes! When we die, that's the end of our bodies. It's just our souls that go on living. Everybody knows that!"

I was amazed by the outburst. This time I knew I wasn't being heretical. "Sister, it isn't this material body, as we experience it now, that I am describing. The resurrected body is *transformed* into the body we are discussing. Yet, the main characteristics of this body carry over into the resurrected body. That's why Jesus had Thomas put his fingers in the wounds, still present in his hands and feet from having been nailed to the cross. Why, the resurrection of the body is the core of our religion! What do you think Easter is all about?" The novice could not answer, but I knew that she remained unconvinced.

In the meantime, Mother Francis informed me they were having some pretty exciting discussions during the novitiate recreations, stemming from my class. I wished with all my heart that I could be there, too. I could tell that Mother Francis was keenly interested, as well. Mother Francis also laughingly told me that when some novice had brought up one of the ideas in a class taught by one of the priests from the College of St. Thomas, he had quickly replied, "Sounds like anarchy to me."

The only anarchists I had heard of, somewhat vaguely, were murderers of heads of state. My heart leaped a little at the thought of being identified with them.

However, Mother Francis had to tell me that many of the concepts were beyond the understanding of some of the novices and that some of them felt they were actually losing their vocations, because of my teachings.

I took these warnings to heart, since I was very conscientious about how my teachings would affect the lives of my students. I began to encourage the silent ones to speak up, to ask questions and challenge me when they didn't understand. I tried hard to simplify my explanations or to make them more concrete. Since I knew that none of the women in the class were intellectually slow, I gradually came to realize that not everyone thought in a philosophical way. Some of them simply could not deduce facts from principles, as I had first learned in studying geometry in high school and then, again, from a different standpoint, in the course in logic, I had taken in the convent.

I was especially grateful to Mother Francis for standing by me, while, at the same time, providing support for those sisters feeling threatened by the teachings. I knew that she was aware of and appreciated my attempts to make the concepts more generally accessible.

Sometimes, when I would go by Mother Francis' office, as I was leaving the novitiate after teaching a class, Mother Francis would call me in to talk about one novice or other, seeking my opinion as to whether I felt that the sister in question would make a good religious. I felt complimented that Mother Francis seemed to value my observations in this regard. I also came to admire Mother Francis' understanding of human weaknesses in others and her patience in helping the young women to work on them.

After a time, I realized I looked forward to these talks and felt distinctly disappointed when I wasn't called in. Only vaguely did I admit to myself how much closer I was feeling towards Mother Francis.

It was during this year that the Mother House in Angers sent a missive to the Provinces that some of the restrictions, held because we were a semi-contemplative order, were being released. The first of these was the proscription on driving. Up to then, whenever one of us had to go to a doctor or dentist, they had to call on a lay volunteer to take us. In the class, if a trip was planned for the girls, a driver with a chauffeur's license had to be procured.

With the release of this rule, most of the sisters began practicing driving and studying for the written examination. I was no exception. I achieved a perfect score on the written test, but did not do so well on the driving test given by one of the officers. I had worked hardest at parallel parking and passed that part of the test perfectly, but the lay volunteer, who had taken me out for lessons, had not noticed that I was not giving my hand signals clearly, to alert cars in back of me that I was going to turn or stop. Therefore, every time I was told to turn I lost ten points on the test.

When we returned to the yard, the officer prefaced the bad news by saying, "Well, Sister, I hope you don't think I am trying to get back at you, because of some of the bad grades I received when I was in a Catholic school as a boy." Here he chuckled, but went on to explain that I hadn't put my arm out far enough to give a clear signal, and therefore, had earned only 50% on my score. The lowest score acceptable was 70%.

Of course I was chagrined, but did wonder why he hadn't said something after I had made my first turn, although I said nothing. Then he asked for my learner's permit, to transfer its number onto the test. "Well, well," he chortled, "we were born in the same year! How do you like that?"

This fact did not exactly help my feelings about having failed the test, but when he took off his hat, I was in for another jolt. His hair was definitely turning gray and, in fact, he was beginning to lose a fair amount in the front.

"My gosh!" I exclaimed to myself, "Am I that old?" Since personal birthdays were not celebrated in the convent, I even had to figure out how old I was. "Let's see. I was born in 1926 and this is 1962. I'm thirty six! Well," I promised myself, "I'll just have to check it out for myself tonight." That night, squinting into the small hand mirror permitted for shaving my head, I saw a few gray hairs, although not as many as my tester. Also, my hair line seemed intact. By then, I was able to laugh about the whole experience.

When I told Mother Luke how I had failed the practical part of the test, signal lights were installed on the convent car right away. When I went back in two weeks for a repeat test, I also passed that part of the test with a perfect score.

When I returned to Notre Dame for my fourth summer, I was able to take a class from Father Goldbrunner. I admired his application of Jungian psychology to religious education and the spirit of the liturgy, but one day, for an entire lecture, he taunted those women religious, who considered themselves the brides of Christ, just by having taken vows. He didn't' seem to realize that that was what the Church taught (falsely promised us?). According to him, being Christ's bride was a highly mystical state, granted only to a few and of either sex.

I took being Christ's bride seriously and was astonished. Certainly I could share my being Christ's bride with anyone, male or female, who dedicated their lives to Christ, with or without benefit of the vows. However, I definitely felt I had been called (the word *vocation* coming from the Latin *vocare* (to call) by Christ to be His spouse and the relationship I had with Christ had certainly been developed in these terms. The things Father Goldbrunner said made me question the reality of the relationship I was experiencing with Jesus. Actually, by then, I certainly felt more like a seasoned spouse than a bride, but I also knew that the priest's tirade applied to the idea of spouse as well.

"If Jesus is not the love and inspiration of my life, who is?" I asked myself. I knew that I needed to believe in His love and inspiration in order to continue to give myself, wholeheartedly, to the religious life. Did I realize that seeds had been planted in me that would contribute to the loss of my vocation?

I didn't have too much time to dwell on it that summer. Writings about the Dead Sea Scrolls were just then pouring in, giving depth to the understanding of the New Testament. There was so much reading to do that I didn't get much written that summer, but my outline for the paper on the meaning of *soma* was approved. By the time we returned to St. Paul, I knew I had plenty of material to actually write the paper at home during the winter. I felt that this was necessary, in order for me to have time to study for and pass the comprehensives the following summer, when I would also be taking my last two courses.

While I was still at Notre Dame, I received word that Mother Luke had retired and that Mother Francis was named as the new Provincial. At once, I realized that I wouldn't be working as closely with Mother Francis in her new position, but I knew that my colleague would make a fine Provincial. Fortunately, I hadn't an inkling as to what would happen to our relationship.

I had barely been home a week, when I began to notice that Mother Francis would cut me off in conversations that included both of us. At the sisters' recreations, I was careful to try not to walk or sit by her all of the time, but even when I naturally ended up by her, Mother Francis would immediately let me know I was not wanted. She seemed to hate to be spoken to by me or to have to say anything to me. I was aghast at this change in behavior. I could think of nothing that I had done to have caused it. In self defense, I began to be careful not to come within speaking range of the Provincial, and thus expose myself to the cutting remarks that would inevitably come my way.

As the directress of the juniorate, I was directly responsible to the Provincial and I was supposed to report to her, at least once a month on the progress of the young sisters under my care. Mother Francis found it difficult to find the time to do this and when we did make an appointment for this purpose, I would often arrive, only to find that someone else was in with her. Often this person would stay the entire time that had been allotted to me. I would wait as long as I dared, but my own pressing duties would force me to leave without getting to speak to Mother Francis. When I finally would get in, I would be reprimanded for not having been in sooner and then be rushed out. I felt that, somehow, I had become some kind of a pariah in the Provincial's eyes.

However, Mother Francis had highly recommended me to the new novice mistress, as someone who would be helpful in discerning the reliability of the vocations of the postulants and novices. Sister George would regale me with long descriptions of the suspicious actions of this or that novice or postulant and want to know if I had observed the same thing. Her main obsession was with *particular friendships.* At recreations she made the postulants and novices walk in groups of three or four in order to assure herself that none were occurring. When she would approach me about her suspicions of various ones of the young sisters, I never knew how to answer, but I was fearful that the repugnance I felt was probably obvious and would convey my dislike of her gossipy manner and paranoid attitude. It didn't help that it was quite often Sister George, who was in talking with Mother Francis during my allotted time.

After several months, I spoke with Mother Gerard, the Prioress, who was under the Provincial, about what seemed to be happening to me. Mother Gerard scoffed at the idea that the Mother Francis' attitude towards me had changed. She let me know that I couldn't expect the Provincial to have as much time for me as before and closed the subject.

My stimulating classes in the novitiate, working with the young sisters in the juniorate and the writing of my final and favorite paper for Notre Dame kept me going, but at times, I felt crazy when I would receive a rebuke, for no reason, from Mother Francis at recreation. When I experienced a burning in my chest that would last for days, I soon figured out the burning was caused by unshed tears. When I would try to speak with Jesus in the Blessed Sacrament during meditation or my examination of conscience, I would be flooded with doubts about the reality of this relationship from the lecture I had suffered through the previous summer.

Finally, Mother Gerard admitted that she had begun to observe that Mother Francis' behavior towards me during recreations did, at the least, seem rude. She suggested that I speak out about how this was making me feel. After almost nine months of intense suffering, I did as the Prioress suggested.

"Mother Francis, this past year has been hell for me," I began. "At recreation you cut me off any time I speak to you and sometimes when I'm speaking to someone else. I even try to avoid being near enough to you for this to happen. Time after time, when I come for my monthly report, you are engaged with someone else for the whole time and I have to leave without seeing you. When I finally get in, it feels like you are hardly listening to what

I have to say and that you rush me out as soon as possible." By this time, tears were running down my cheeks.

"Sister, I know that I have had to spend a great deal of time with Sister George, this year. Being the directress of novices has been difficult for her, although I believe it is getting easier for her now, probably with thanks to you, too. She has nothing but praise for you, in your work with the novices and postulants. Of course, I know how valuable your work with them is and I appreciate it, believe me," the Provincial replied, deftly avoiding the first issue, which I had mentioned.

"Well, thanks, Mother," I replied, not knowing what else to say, but feeling most dissatisfied with the results of my confrontation. However, I left the interview hoping that at recreation, Mother Francis would become her old friendly self. The first time I spoke to her during the recreation, even though it was only a comment added to the general conversation, I received a look from the Provincial that told me to back off.

A few days later, when I was, again, alone with Mother Francis in the Provincial's office, I brought up that specific event.

"Sister, I don't remember that at all," Mother Francis denied. "you must have misinterpreted my look," she laughed.

"Well, Mother, some one else has noticed your…your…" I hesitated to use the Mother Prioress' term *rudeness*, "your brusqueness with me at recreations." Perspiration was pouring down my back. I would not expose Mother Gerard as being critical of the Provincial.

There was a long pause before Mother Francis spoke again. "Well, Sister, perhaps I have been…brusque, as you say, without intending to."

I was relieved that Mother Francis hadn't asked who had noticed her actions towards me at recreation. "Mother," I finally continued, "you and I have worked closely together for almost eight years. I…I guess…I guess I have come to love you during that time. The way you've been treating me this past year has been very painful!" Here, I really broke down crying.

Although this declaration of love had no sexual connotation in it, it was still frightening to the Provincial. Religious sisters simply did not speak of their love for one another. There was another long pause, while Mother Francis gave me time to control myself.

Finally, speaking slowly, she shared an event, which had occurred at a recreation the previous summer, while I was at Notre Dame.

"One noon, at recreation," she began, "shortly after I became Provincial, one of the older sisters made the remark that Sister Teresa had me wrapped around her little finger and that now, since I was Provincial, you would be getting your way about everything."

"But. . . but Mother, that's not true! If anything it's the other way around! It's *you* who have *me* wrapped around *your* little finger. Why, I've never refused you anything!" I exclaimed, tears again welling up in my eyes.

"Yes, Sister dear," the Provincial agreed, "you are absolutely right! But now we must let bygones be bygones. That is the past. Please, don't be so emotional about it. Can't you see the spot that put me in? I am truly sorry if I have caused you suffering. Now, please, pull yourself together."

I kissed the ground, as if acknowledging a fault (being emotional) and left the office. I was not in control inside, but I had no more to say and would be better able to pull myself together out of this woman's presence.

"Why didn't she tell me about this a long time ago?" I wondered to myself. I went to the chapel to kneel before the tabernacle, close to the Presence of my . . of my . . .? I had no strength to face this other dilemma, which had been festering inside of me. I finally left, without feeling comforted. In fact, I felt abandoned and a little crazy.

Sometime in May, Mother Francis again sent for me. I knew it wasn't about the juniorate sisters, but I didn't have the slightest idea what was coming.

"Well, Sister Teresa," Mother Francis began, "I've been giving a lot of thought to our last conversation. I've decided that after you finish at Notre Dame this summer, I'm going to send you to the mission in Omaha. There, at a smaller mission, you'll be able to get hold of yourself. . .of your emotions . . .better than here at the mother house. I've already spoken to Mother Mechtilde, your former novice directress, about it and she is delighted that you will be coming there. She wants you to be the principal of the high school. The lay woman, who has been doing this, has felt inadequate and has not wanted to do it. She would rather go back to simply being the science teacher."

There was a pause before I realized that I had been dismissed from one obedience and given another in the same sentence. When I did figure it out, I quickly kissed the floor, denoting my submission to the will of the Provincial, and left the office, too shocked to say anything. It was beyond my comprehension how I could be treated like this after years of devoted giving. I knew I had to block it out and continue on the best I could.

I looked forward to my return to Notre Dame, as a surcease from all that had happened this past year, but I wondered why I was even being allowed to finish, since the whole purpose of getting my degree in Theology was so that I could teach the postulants, novices and young professed on a college level. Well, I was returning. I had completed my paper on the Pauline Epistles and was more determined than ever to pass the two courses and my comprehensives. I would prove…I would prove to Mother Francis . . .that I wasn't as emotionally unstable as she thought. I would not let this woman break me.

Two days before I was to leave for Notre Dame, Mother Francis announced to the group at the end of the noon recreation, that Sister Barbara would be returning to the Mother House the next day, around ten in the morning. This was done so that those who were free would come to the foyer and greet her. Then she pulled me aside and told me that Sister Barbara was to be the one to replace me as juniorate directress.

I determined right away that I would be there to greet Sister Barbara the next morning, to congratulate her on her appointment. Later that day, Mother Francis met me in a hall and thanked me for giving Sister Barbara her new obedience. I stared at her uncomprehendingly.

"You didn't know that we usually don't give out such important obediences by mail? When you congratulated her this morning, that was the first she heard of it." Mother Francis laughed and hurried on, leaving me stunned as I stood there in shock.

That night I began having cramps and diarrhea on the hour. When the crecelle* clapped the following morning, I felt a little better and dressed for meditation and Mass. However, by the time Mass began I had to leave the chapel. The cramping would come on sooner and sooner, until I was running down the hall to the lavatory every fifteen minutes. By then, there wasn't anything inside of me to come out, but the cramping was severe and I couldn't be certain that I should stay away from the lavatory. When Sister Assistant came to see how I was faring, I told her what was occurring. "I've taken nearly an entire bottle of Pepto Bismal, but it isn't helping at all."

Soon Sister Assistant came back with some Kaopectate, instructing me to take the largest dose suggested. It worked quite quickly and I fell into bed and slept soundly until the crecelle went off the following morning, the morning I was to leave for Notre Dame.

----

*crecelle Two pieces of wood hinged together, with a handle. It clapped when shook thus giving the signal to rise.

After Mass, Mother Francis hurried up to me and asked if I would be able to leave. "I'm sure we can get your plane ticket changed until tomorrow," she assured me.

But I did not want to be present when Mother Francis would tell the others that Sister Barbara would be replacing me. "Oh, no, Mother, I'm sure I can leave today. That Kaopectate really did the trick." I smiled wanly and after breakfast, finished my packing in plenty of time to make my flight.

One of the ways I kept my sanity that summer, was to study for my comprehensives by *lecturing* on the subjects I would be tested on. I would get up on the top, unused bunk in my room and give forth with a German or French accent, imitating the accent of one or another of my professors. One afternoon, as I was giving an especially dramatic discourse on the Trinity, I was interrupted by a knock at the door.

"My gosh!" I thought, "Did I get too carried away? Was I speaking that loud?" Finally I said, "Come in," as I quickly slid down from the bunk.

The door opened a little and a nun I had never seen before peeked in. "What are you doing?" she asked, when she saw that I was alone.

I had to laugh. "Well, believe it or not, I'm studying for my comprehensives." I was also blushing furiously.

"What...what is your field?" the nun wanted to know.

"Theology," I answered. "It seems to help me remember by pretending I am lecturing on the subject. Just now it was on the Trinity. I guess the accent adds a touch of humor. At least it does for me," I added.

"How wonderful that you got to major in theology!" the nun continued. "I wish I were studying something like that. Sometimes I don't think I know anymore about my religion than the third graders I teach during the winter. Uh...would it bother you if I stayed and listened for awhile?"

Again, I laughed. "It would probably help," I admitted. "It'll make it more realistic. In fact, if you have any questions, go ahead and interrupt me." Then I felt a twinge in my throat, as I realized that the next year I wouldn't be teaching in the novitiate. "Well," I thought to myself, "I may as well take advantage of this willing student." I continued the lecture with a French accent.

Because I felt close with Sister Patricia, who had helped me by translating the French articles for my second paper, I related to her some of the painful events of the past year. Sister Patricia was most sympathetic. Then, one day, when I was walking across the campus with the other Sister Teresa, we came upon Sister Patricia.

"When you two get together," exclaimed Sister Teresa of St. Louis, "it's as if an electric charge sets off. Your faces light up and all of this energy comes pouring out."

I laughed it off, saying, "Well that's because we're both such high energy people." Then I noticed that Sister Patricia looked as if she had been slapped. She quickly excused herself and walked off.

"Hey, I hope I didn't say something wrong!" Sister Teresa of St. Louis said.

"Well, if you did," I tried to assure her, "I sure don't know what it was."

Sister Patricia avoided me for the rest of the summer. For me it was another very painful rejection. I poured over my studies even harder.

The day of my comprehensives finally arrived. It was a written examination, in which we would write on five of the six subjects we had been instructed to prepare. We began at nine in the morning until noon, during which time we would write an hour each on three of the subjects. After an hour off for lunch, we would return for two more hours to complete the ordeal.

By the time I had completed the fourth topic, my writing arm was aching so much, I wasn't sure I could even lift my pen. My mind was also so fatigued, I could hardly think. Somehow I grasped my pen and began writing, hardly aware of what I was expressing. I didn't even care. I could only think of getting out of there and falling on my bed.

Nevertheless, I was most relieved to learn that I had passed and wrote home to tell them the good news. Shortly after, I received a telegram from Mother Francis saying that Mother Gerard would be attending my graduation. No one had done that for Sister Michael, the year before, but I was not too elated by the honor. I suspected that Mother Francis had arranged for it to make me feel better. It did not make me feel better at all.

Two days before the commencement exercises and one day before Mother Gerard would be arriving, I offered to go to the electric train station in South Bend with Sister Teresa of St. Louis, in order to help her with her luggage. She had one more summer at Notre Dame and there was no reason for her to remain for the commencement.

After I saw my friend off, I crossed the street to wait for the bus that would take me back to Notre Dame. It was still quite early and there were no others around. Then a sleek Lincoln Continental drove past me and stopped in front of a motion picture theater marquee. Two well dressed black men got out and rushed into the theater, while the driver remained in the car with the motor running. I wondered what could be taking place this early in the morning.

Then my attention was diverted, when I heard footsteps approaching from the opposite direction. I looked around and saw a large black man, shabbily dressed, approaching me. He didn't seem to see me, but kept coming right for me. Just in time, I stepped forward and out of his path.

When I turned around to return to where I had been standing, I was horrified to see that I had been standing right in front of a huge billboard with a larger than life depiction of a man about to stab a woman, whose one breast was exposed from having had her blouse torn down. I immediately walked away as far as I could and still be in place to get my bus when it came.

In the meantime a pickup truck, with sides attached, drove up and parked across the street from me. Two black men leaned on the side facing me and stared intently at me.

I remembered hearing news reports of black uprisings during the summer and while I was entirely sympathetic with their cause, I didn't particularly want to become a martyr that morning.

Thankfully, more people began appearing on the street, some white, and I was able to relax a little. In fact, I was treated to a little comic relief, when a small man with a parakeet on one of his shoulders, walked past. I could hear him speaking lovingly to the bird, apparently oblivious of anyone else around. Finally the bus arrived and I returned to Notre Dame.

Since I hadn't been told when Mother Gerard would be arriving, I was relieved when someone came to my room and told me to meet the Prioress in the dining hall for supper. When I saw her standing in the cafeteria line, it did feel good to see someone from home. However, Mother Gerard was very formal with me, having very little news from home to share with me. I decided she was afraid of receiving confidences from me, as to why I was not returning to St. Paul.

When it was time for the commencement exercises, the following day, instead of standing in line with the other graduates, I was in the pit with the orchestra, in order to play the processional and recessional. At the rehearsal in the morning, I had met the person who would be receiving her degree right before me, so I felt certain I could get in line in time. Actually, we were taken over to see the improvised stage on which the faculty would be seated and we would receive our degrees. Then we were handed copies of the program and that was the extent of the rehearsal.

According to the program, there were about a dozen Ph.D.s before those of us receiving our Masters. I was shocked when only one of the Ph.D.s showed up. Since I was the second in line to receive my Masters, I hastily put down my violin and ran clear across the front of the platform and in front of the audience in a most undignified manner. I wondered what Mother Gerard was thinking.

By the time I got up to the platform, they had called my name and since I wasn't right there, the provost put my diploma on a small table.

"I'm Sister Teresa!" I gasped, quite short of breath. The priest gave me a big grin, retrieved my diploma, handed it to me and shook my hand. That night at supper, Mother Gerard seemed not to have noticed a thing. I suspected she had not even been present.

The following day, I was relieved that Mother Gerard's plane left for St. Paul before mine left for Omaha. I truly looked forward to working with the girls, once more, but I realized that the past year had left a deep scar inside and that I would never be quite the same again.

"Well, maybe it's all for the better," I hoped.

CHAPTER TWELVE

WHILE AT NOTRE Dame, I had been introduced to the writings of Pierre Teilhard de Chardin S.J. Because of his teaching on evolution, his writings were later banned by the Church. I was unaware of this and asked Mama to get me a copy of *The Phenomenon of Man*. It was with this book I discovered that I could read something out of my field and in some ways, beyond my understanding, yet grasp enough of it to keep up my interest and widen my vision. The mystical section at the end gave me the desire to read others of his works.

The anathema on his works were finally withdrawn and I obtained a copy of *The Divine Milieu*, a selection of essays on mysticism. The one on detachment was especially helpful to me at this time. In it, Father de Chardin taught that detachment did not mean that one did not become deeply involved with one's assignments, but that one always had the readiness to leave them, when asked, and then become just as deeply involved in the new assignment. For me, this was both a way and a challenge.

I threw myself into my new involvements with all my energy. Along with being the principal of the high school, I assigned myself to teach three classes, which I knew I would enjoy. Two of them, I felt, would benefit the entire school, one being dramatics and the other journalism. The third was a religion class, in which I used the methods of Father Goldbrunner.

The journalism class was putting out a weekly news sheet by the end of the month. As the students advanced in their knowledge of journalistic writing, this was increased to two sheets and by the end of the first six weeks, they decided to continue with a weekly news sheet and began to put out a monthly newspaper.

That Christmas, I had the girls put on the Little Juggler, which for them, would be the first time. The beautiful Afro-American, who played the lead, did the best job of all the jugglers to this point. I told Ginny this and because she also received much praise from her peers and the other sisters, her self esteem was raised immeasurably, a thing which she badly needed. When I met her mother after the presentation, I learned that Ginny, too, had been a victim of incest. Her mother was still carrying feelings of guilt about this, although she had left her husband, when it was discovered. The mother was very pleased with her daughter's performance and was grateful to me for having given Ginny so much encouragement.

Florence was the girl assigned to help me in the school. She was responsible for cleaning the three classrooms, the library and my office. Florence came from an impoverished family, made more so by an abundance of children. Her father was a laborer and handyman but could not financially provide for his ever increasing family. Finally, welfare workers stepped in, placing the children in a temporary orphanage until they could find homes for them. Florence became incorrigible while she was in the orphanage, from having been seperated so abruptly from her mother, so they placed her with us. She had been here almost two years when I arrived.

Florence and I would work very hard on Saturday mornings to get our work done so we could read Antoine d' Xuperey's *The Little Prince*. Florence became the little fox in the story, whom I both tamed and became responsible for. In this way, I was able to open Florence to enjoy the beauty of poetry and classical music. I would play my violin for her, on occasion, and Florence would make little book marks for me, with favorite selections from *The Little Prince*, or poems she wanted to share. This was most healing for me as well as beneficial to Florence.

I was also asked to direct the choir of the contemplative Sisters Magdalen. I looked forward to this, since I had never before had the opportunity to work with the contemplatives. For some reason, it had been believed that they were not capable of singing Gregorian chant. Not realizing this, I got hold of some *Libers* for them and easily taught them to love and appreciate it. They sang it beautifully. The rehearsals were interspersed with much laughter and high moments of ecstasy. I felt that I was among spirits very kindred to my own.

After rehearsals, the portress would take me to the door leading from their cloister to the Good Shepherd Sisters' side of the convent. It became difficult for me, when the nun would grasp one of my hands, holding it tightly to her bosom. I would assure her that it was wonderful for me, as well, and then would have to let her know that I needed to leave, having duties elsewhere. I became uncomfortable with these displays of affection, because I was no longer certain of the clarity of my own feelings.

Before leaving home, when I had told Mama I was going to enter the convent, Mama had cried very hard at the prospect of the loss of our relationship. However, as soon as Mama had returned to her home in Denver, she wrote right back that I should do whatever would make me happy. Actually, Mama admitted later that we had become closer, perhaps, than if I had been married and had my own family.

Shortly after I had become fully professed, Mama had developed a bleeding ulcer. She awoke one morning hemorrhaging from her mouth. She didn't even make it to the telephone, before she fainted from weakness. They would never know how much later she regained consciousness and was able to complete the call for help. At that time, the rules of our order did not permit me to go to be with her.

Later, while I was in Omaha, Mama was again in the hospital with the ulcer. This time I was sent to Denver to be with her, while she was hospitalized. We had been sitting silently for a time, when Mama said, "You aren't happy anymore, are you?"

"Oh, yes," I lied in a squeaky little voice. "I am still happy, but this past year has been a little hard," I finally admitted. My feelings of loyalty did not permit me to share what had happened between Mother Francis and me. I realized that I hadn't convinced Mama and had probably made her feel worse that I couldn't be entirely honest with her. But it was still difficult for me to admit even to myself that I was still deeply affected by that experience.

One day, when I was speaking with Mother Mechtilde in her office, she asked me if I would like to think of getting a Masters degree in Secondary Administration, so that I could be a certified principal of the high school.

"Another Master's degree?" I asked myself. To my superior I said, "If you think that would be best, Mother." I kissed the floor accepting this new obedience.

"You could take one or two courses at Creighton University and gradually get it. During the summers, you could probably take more."

In January I signed up for two courses. I was able to complete them, but by spring I was definitely feeling the strain of so many duties. I had discovered that Lynn's order offered this degree and that I could get it in five summers as I had at Notre Dame. This college was also near Omaha. I asked Mother Mechtilde if this would be possible. She had already asked Mrs. Winston if she would mind being principal for a summer. Thus, it was arranged for me to transfer my credits there and the summer of 1963 found me matriculating to enter their graduate program.

I was secretly hoping that Lynn would happen to be there for the summer, but I was surprised when I actually met up with her. Now she was Sister Caritas, and was also doing graduate work there. After eleven years, both of us had gone through many changes. Vatican Council II was in process at the time, and I realized that Sister Caritas was very conservative about the changes being proposed, whereas I was very much for them.

I also noticed that the tip of Sister Caritas' nose still turned up giving her a mischievous look, even when surrounded by a veil. In other words, I knew that I still loved her, conservative or not. I wrote a few poems to her, in which I said this between the lines, but Sister Caritas never let on that she got the message. She simply acknowledged that she was happy that I was still writing poetry.

Later on, when the two of us were taking a walk around the small lake on the campus, I said, "I haven't told you about the misunderstanding I had with my provincial last year. It was really painful to be sent away, although I am enjoying my work in Omaha."

Sister Caritas quickly responded, "You know, Sister, our confessor is very understanding and is especially good with spiritual direction. He hears our confessions on Thursday afternoons, beginning at four o'clock. I know that he would be very helpful to you and I also know that since you are a religious it would be all right for you to go to him."

I immediately understood that Sister Caritas did not wish to hear more and, thus, become more involved. "Thanks, Sister," I replied. "I'll give him a try." I hoped Sister Caritas didn't notice the tears at the edges of my eyes.

Nevertheless, I enjoyed the summer there very much. I spent much time listening for bird calls and praying and writing. Besides the poems for Lynn, I wrote one which I sent to Mother Francis.

> I had a little chat with a bob-white, today
> I hope no one overheard, because
> We spoke quite frankly of love.
> I told him how precious he was to me
> Because of you,
> Who taught me to listen for birds
> And to thrill at their song.
> He understood.

Do you?

It, too, received no reply, but the following poem, which I sent to Florence along with the feather it described, was much appreciated.

> "First impressions," so they tell us,
> "Often deceive."
> And we must admit
> This is true.
> See this feather
> On one side no hue to delight us
> But blown over, shows bright blue.
> See these hard eyes, not even a clue
> To lead us
> To a heart whose beauty is new.
>
> See these hard eyes change at a cue
> Because we love her, too.

I found the women professors were more personal and less egotistical than many of the male professors I had had at Notre Dame. I was challenged by them without being pushed into competitiveness.

Much to my surprise, I enjoyed the class in Statistics because the professor let us know how even something based on mathematics could be used to favor the goals of the statistician. I also learned how to extract square root from some other students, who taught this to their eighth graders during the winter. They had worked out a very clear set of eight steps to accomplish this.

My favorite class was one in the Philosophy of Education. While it differed very much from the one I had taken many years before, this teacher had us write experiences from our own teaching, applying some of the principles we were learning in the class. Despite these things which I enjoyed, intuitively I knew that I would not be returning there the following summer.

One night, during my sophomore year in high school, as I lay in bed reading the historical novel, *Anthony Adverse*, I read a particularly graphic account of Anthony copulating with his slave-mistress. I started masturbating for the first time in my life. I had never heard of anyone doing this, nor had I been taught of its rightness or wrongness. As I approached climax, I became so frightened at my increasing lack of control, that I stopped short of orgasm. A year or so later, I had a similar experience and had somewhat of a climax with its attending euphoria, but still remained fearful of the lack of control and had little desire to repeat it.

Most of my girl friends were not dating and we rarely talked about sex. I sometimes day-dreamed about passionate embraces and kisses, but my fantasies of love-making never seemed to go beyond that.

Later, as I listened to the girls speak of their early sexual experiences, I wondered at my own sexual immaturity. While sex was not freely spoken of in my family, it was not prohibited either. I couldn't remember hearing of any warnings or punishments for touching or playing with my genitals, but I couldn't even remember wanting to play with them. I did like to sleep with one hand in my crouch, but no one ever reprimanded me for this (did they even know?) nor did I feel guilty about it. It simply gave me a secure and comforting feeling. During high school, once, when spending the night with a girl friend, Jeannie pulled the covers off me, and seeing my hand in my crouch, jeered at me and told me I was dirty. After that, I was careful not to indulge myrself in that way when sleeping with a friend, but I still didn't believe that I had done anything wrong.

Perhaps the joy and euphoria I sometimes experienced in a mystical way through music, poetry and natural beauties, delayed my desire to discover the joys of sex. It wasn't until my relationship with Lynn in college, that I arrived at any sexual sophistication.

We nuns in Omaha were beginning our annual eight day retreat, when during the night of November 3, 1963, I awoke myself masturbating furiously, my imagination filled with very sexual imagery. I abhorred and found pleasure in it at the same time. I froze to a halt with the masturbation, but the imaginings were harder to control. I lay there aghast at myself. I felt my entire being sink into a kind of despair. Towards rising time, I tried to sing to Jesus, but I felt that somehow I had betrayed Him irrevocably.

Following the directions given me in the novitiate, as to what to do under such circumstances, I candidly spoke to the retreat master in the confessional. He surprised me with his reply.

"Well, Sister, what you ought to do when this happens, is to get it over with as soon as possible and go back to sleep. You aren't guilty of anything, when you are caught by surprise like that."

At first, I was unable to do this, feeling too much like a traitor to Jesus. Even when I tried out of desperation, not having heard of the clitoris, I was often unable to achieve orgasm or any kind of relief, in order to go back to sleep.

Also, according to the directives I had received as a novice, I spoke to Mother Mechtilde about it. Mother was sympathetic about my dilemma, but it was obvious to me that she was also very uncomfortable when the subject was brought up. By then, I was being haunted by sexual imagery even during the day and, as I told Mother Mechtilde, it made me feel like a wolf in Good Shepherd's clothing. I drove myself more and more so that I would be exhausted by the time I went to bed. I also obtained permission to shoot baskets in the girls' gymnasium at night to help in achieving this purpose, and, thus, being able to sleep.

Sister Pauline, the only Afro-American nun in the Province, who had also been under me in the juniorate, was attending the Sacred Heart Academy full time in order to get her Bachelor's degree. She began to join me in shooting baskets at night, as a release from sitting in classes all day.

I had gotten the idea of relaxing by shooting baskets from having worked with Marie, a girl of thirteen, who had been sexually molested by her father from the age of eight and then physically abused by her step-father. Marie was always getting into trouble for picking fights with the other girls or for yelling at the nuns for no apparent reason. I discovered that if I let her yell, she would finally stop and begin to cry. Ultimately she would speak of her old hurts and the anger behind her behavior in school. I obtained permission for her to go to the gym, whenever possible, to shoot baskets and in this way, release some of her anger. What Marie and I could have both used to greater advantage was a punching bag. Although I experienced some relief from this physical activity, I no longer had self-confidence in my dealings with the girls. I finally requested to see the woman psychiatrist, who came once a week to work with the girls. She had also seen other sisters in the past. Dr. Sands and I bonded quickly, even though the doctor was a mother of six and was carrying her seventh child. She was near my age and about my height and had gone through the oppression of being *too tall* for a woman. Dr. Sands empathized with my experience with Mother Francis and pointed out that it was probably my declaration of love that got me missioned. At the time that I told Mother Francis that I loved her, I was not feeling sexual, in the least. Now, because of the temptations I was experiencing, I wasn't certain what my feelings for Mother Francis had been.

Dr. Sands shared her own experience of having been rejected, but by her own family because of her size and clumsiness. This had given the doctor the impetus to prove herself by entering a man's field and overcoming the sexism in medical school and psychiatry.

"You know, Sister," she said, "I believe that all good psychiatrists and counselors have been rejected at some time or other. It makes us sensitive to the pain of others. That's probably why the girls like to come to you for counseling." This was naturally gratifying for me to hear.

Dr. Sands and I also had similar reading tastes and we would enjoy discussing ideas we had read about and suggested books to each other. Two or three hours would go by rapidly in animated conversation, when Dr. Sands would suddenly exclaim, "Oh, Sister, I've got to go! It's already past the time when I told the baby sitter I would be home.

I thoroughly enjoyed talking with someone who shared my interests, but I began to realize that we rarely got down to speaking of my problems.

CHAPTER THIRTEEN

ONE MORNING DURING March of 1964, when the clapping of the *crecelle* awoke me, I discovered that I had been and was still crying. I couldn't determine the specific cause of the tears, so I arose and dressed, weeping all of the time. I felt certain that when I would arrive at the chapel, I would stop. I didn't. All through meditation, the office and Mass, tears flowed without sound, but endlessly, causing my nose to run. Towards the end of Mass I went back to Mother Mechtilde's stall and told her what was happening.

"Go up to your room, Sister, and I'll get up there as soon as I can," she promised. When she came up shortly, with breakfast on a tray, this only increased the tears, so Mother Mechtilde decided she had better cancel the appointment the two of us had with an architect, to discuss plans for a new high school building. Then she called Dr. Sands, who felt that I should be withdrawn from my stressful situation and spend some time on a psychiatric ward. This meant getting me admitted to the local Catholic hospital that had such a ward. It also meant getting another psychiatrist, since because of her large family, Dr. Sands was not affiliated with any hospital. By then, I was feeling desperate enough to comply with any plan.

As soon as I arrived at the ward the tears stopped. It felt to me like a matter of self preservation. I had to be admitted to the medical ward, as there were no openings on the psychiatric unit. At first, this was not bad. I was exhausted from all the crying and slept for close to twenty-four hours. Then I began to receive a battery of psychological tests, many of which I had studied in college and in my work with the girls. I was amused to learn that I was considered a *sophisticated* case, because of this background. Sophistication had never before been one of my attributes.

When the psychologist began to administer the Rorschach ink blot test, after two or three cards, I slowly began to realize that when I saw anything remotely sexual, he was really bothered. I could well imagine that this was because I was wearing a religious habit. I found myself taking perverse pleasure in his discomfort and didn't attempt, in the least, to squelch the sexual imagery, which was right at the edge of my consciousness, anyway. I found myself furtively watching for his responses — beads of perspiration breaking out on his forehead and a general flushing from his shirt collar up. He started clearing his throat and, once, even pushed his chair back as if to make his escape. Then he resolutely began writing again as I droned relentlessly on and on.

It was hell for the rest of the time on the medical ward. I simply didn't fit in with their routine. I certainly didn't need to stay in bed all day. Mother Mechtilde came to see me frequently, bringing cross word puzzles, which I worked on by the hour. Never before had I enjoyed that pastime, nor would I ever touch one afterwards. After almost a week of this, the charge nurse suggested that I get permission from my doctor to take walks on the grounds. This made a vast improvement, but the next day, I was finally able to go over to the psychiatric unit.

I arrived at supper time, where we patients all ate together at tables of four. I was the only nun there and it took me half the meal to even raise my eyes, much less to speak to anyone. When I finally forced myself to look up, the others were also sitting with their eyes modestly cast down. I smiled inwardly, thinking what good nuns they would make, including the man among them. By the end of the meal, we were talking hesitantly to one another. I wondered if each of them was wondering how crazy the others of us were, as I was.

The next day I saw patients returning to the ward after they had received electroshock treatments. Other patients would immediately go and sit with them, during that frightenly disorienting period of loss of memory. I was grateful that my therapist did not believe in that technique.

I actually enjoyed the Occupational and Recreational Therapies, referred to as O.T. and R.T. The Occupational Therapy class was doing leather work. Following Pete's example with Good Shepherd girls, I enjoyed helping my companions, when they made a mistake, by showing them how they could change the pattern a little and still come out with a worthy piece of work.

Unfortunately, the therapist was condescending towards us, speaking to us as if we were naughty children or mentally retarded. One afternoon, one of the men patients began to *act crazy* . He was so good at it that I, myself, was a little taken aback. Slowly, the others and I became aware of his charade and joined in, all done in a non-violent way. Even when we saw that the therapist was becoming frightened, we didn't let up. The next day, we were relieved to see that she had gotten the message. She treated us as if we were normal adults, although, of course, in many ways, we were not.

Volleyball was the main attraction at Recreational Therapy, although table games were provided for those not so athletically inclined. I had enjoyed playing volleyball in my youth and gladly joined in the games, again discovering that the physical exercise released a lot of my tension. I also used my height to good advantage up by the net, clipping the ball over the net, in a way that it was impossible for the other side to return it.

I said my prayers in the special chapel provided for the psychiatric patients.

I felt no devotion. All I felt was an indefinable pain. I found these unscheduled hours the most difficult.

The elderly priest, who said Mass each morning, was himself a patient. He said Mass slowly and with much care. I wondered if such scrupulosity with every action was not the cause, or at least a symptom of his basic problem. Having an altar boy (a young man) with a facial tic, which caused him to keep his head turned to one side, did not help. The young man kept fumbling with the cruets of water and wine and dropping the small towel the priest used to dry his fingers. I could feel the priest's irritation.

One day, a group of us were taken to a nearby bowling alley, which had been reserved for our use for a few hours. I was surprised to see the priest among us.

The first floor of the psychiatric unit, where I stayed, was completely open. We had access to exits and could have left any time, although, incongruously, there were detention screens on the windows and we had to get the nurse to unlock the bathrooms, when we wished to bathe. The second floor was a locked ward and the patients on the third floor were even locked in their rooms. The poor people on the fourth floor were in restraints. I had heard that the priest was on the third floor.

At the bowling alley, the priest chose not to bowl and sat somewhat apart from the rest of us. I went over and sat by him. "You celebrate Mass beautifully, Father," I told him.

He turned towards me and replied, "Thank you, Sister." When I saw the pain interlaced with anger in his blood-shot eyes, I felt pierced and looked away quickly. Since he seemed to have nothing else to say, I gradually withdrew and involved myself in a game.

When we returned to the hospital, as we were all gathered near the elevators, I was surprised to see the priest dart off down one of the halls.

An attendant quickly followed and soon returned leading him back to the elevator to return to his room.

He was totally submissive, but his face was beet red and his head was hanging down on his chest. Suddenly I felt connected to the anger I had seen in his eyes. I knew that if I were locked up in a room all of the time, I too, would try to escape.

In the meantime, I was receiving wonderfully amusing and warm letters from Sister Pauline, my buddy in shooting baskets. Actually, they were miniature collages made from cutouts from magazines. with little hand written messages tucked in here and there. I wondered how she had ever found the time to make them, considering she was still going to college full time. I was extremely grateful for the love and respect tucked in between the lines. They were probably the most healing things of my entire stay.

Dr. Forbes' diagnosis for me was depression brought on by repressed anger towards my father. I agreed with the depression, but I felt absolutely no anger and I knew I had dealt with the anger I had felt towards my father long before.

At times, I felt chagrined, feeling that I was less affected by my depression than most of the others on the ward. However, the head nurse quickly punctured any complacency I might have felt.

"Let me tell you something, Sister," the nurse began one day. "I'm probably more afraid of you than anyone else on the ward, in spite of your being such a *good girl*. Yes, you make your bed each morning, go to meals and R.T. and O T. But," she continued, "nice people like you, with all that repressed anger inside, are likely to blow up at any minute and become very violent."

I was most surprised by this assessment, but felt secure in myself that this would not happen. However, it felt very strange to know that the nurse was expecting this momentarily.

After two weeks on the psychiatric ward, I returned home. At first, I felt much better, the temptations diminishing quite a bit. One afternoon I was in the auditorium with my drama class when the school bell sounded about a half hour early. "Stay here!" I ordered the surprised students and stomped down the aisle, through the back stage and into the main classroom, where I told the students and teacher to stay where they were. I hurried towards my office where the bell was. Florence, who was the official bell ringer, was loitering in the hall outside the office, before going to her next class.

"For heaven's sake, Florence, why did you ring the bell a half hour early?" I asked, not very kindly.

"I...I...don't know," the frightened girl answered. "Was it early?"

Momentarily, I thought perhaps my watch was wrong and looked in at the clock in the office. It agreed with my watch. "Did you look at the clock?" I asked.

"Well," Florence stammered, "someone in my class told me it was time. I . . I guess I forgot to look!"

"Well, run downstairs and tell Mrs. Winston the bell was a mistake. We need every minute we have to rehearse our play!"

Florence was glad for the opportunity to leave. She discovered that Mrs. Winston had kept her class, noticing that the bell was early. When she returned to the office, I had already gone back to the auditorium, for which she was probably most grateful.

At the end of the school day, I again asked Florence how it had happened. "I told you, Mother. Someone in English told me it was time!" Florence was on the verge of tears.

"Well, after this, you check the clock yourself, young lady! There is a clock in every classroom and you're the one with the responsibility to see that the bell rings at the right time!"

"I'm sorry Mother," Florence said, breaking out into tears.

"Well, don't let it happen again!" I admonished and walked away without offering any comfort.

That night after Compline, while I was examining my conscience, I realized I had been harsh with Florence. I remembered how loyal the girl was to me and how hard she worked to keep the school clean. It would be years later before an adult Florence would confess that she had never learned to tell time and that she had been depending on other girls to tell her all along. Unfortunately that incident was followed by similar ones and the disturbing images and broken sleep patterns returned. When Mother Mechtilde called Dr. Forbes, he suggested I return to the ward and he would try other medications. I learned how it felt to be a *recidivist*.

At the hospital, the next morning at Mass, I discovered that the same priest was celebrating Mass, with the same man assisting. I was amazed that the priest had been able to tolerate him. Then I discovered that the *altar boy* was now on the open ward. Even though the tic remained, he must have improved.

I would discover myself watching him to see if he ever held his head straight. One evening while he was watching television, his head did straighten out. However, the following morning he was not at Mass. A nun rushed into the chapel and asked me to give the responses, which I was happy to do. The priest did fine with his own ablutions and I could feel his relief with the situation.

At breakfast, I found out that the *altar boy* had run away early that morning. I wondered if his tic had gone away. When he returned three days later, the tic was back.

No one on the ward spent much time with him. I realized that because he looked so crazy, he was too threatening to the rest of us. *We* could pass for being sane. I felt enough guilt about it that I tried to hold a friendly conversation with him. I found it quite difficult to converse with someone whose face was constantly turned away.

I dreaded going to Mass the morning after the altar boy returned. I wondered how the priest would accept having his former, unwanted assistant back. For some reason I never learned, the man with the tic never assisted at Mass again.

During this second admission I made friends with a woman who was also depressed. It was easy for me to see why Gloria was depressed. She had four sons and a husband, each one needing a clean white, starched shirt every day, five days a week. This meant twenty-five shirts to wash and iron each week, along with preparing meals, cleaning house, shopping etc. etc. It was the shirts that seemed to be the last straw for her. She definitely resented the nuns, who ran the school her sons attended, and enforced the rule of daily, clean, starched, white shirts.

Nether Gloria nor I spoke of our problems much, but often played pool together. Gloria seemed to never tire of watching me, in full habit, bending over the table, carefully placing my shots. In the evenings, we played table tennis and, while Gloria accompanied us on the piano, we sang and harmonized together.

One evening, as the nurse came with fruit juice and sleeping pills (everyone was required to take a sleeping pill, whether they felt they needed one or not) Gloria and I decided we weren't sleepy yet. No one had ever stated what time we had to be in bed. Everyone obediently took their pills and naturally went to bed shortly after.

"I'm not tired yet, Sister, are you?" Gloria asked with a quirky little smile.

I could guess what was coming next. "No, I'm having too much fun singing."

""What do you say that we fool this little nurse and put our pills under our tongues until she's gone."

"That's an excellent idea, Gloria!" I responded with enthusiasm. "But be sure to act like you're swallowing," I advised.

Gloria laughed uproariously, but stopped quickly as the nurse wheeled the cart into the room.

"Well, girls," the nurse addressed us. 'What'll it be this evening? We've got grape juice, tomato juice and orange juice."

"I'll take grape juice," Gloria requested.

"Make mine tomato juice," I added.

The nurse handed us each a little paper cup with our chosen fruit juice and followed that with a little pill, each in an individual container. We thanked her and went through with the little charade we had planned. The nurse smiled and went on to the next patient. As soon as she was out of the recreation room, we took the pills out of our mouths, put them in a Kleenex and went back to singing, as before.

A half hour later we were still singing, when the nurse returned, incredulous at our sustained energy.

"Aren't you sleepy yet?" she asked.

"I'm not," Gloria responded. "Are you, Sister?"

"Not at all," I answered and Gloria resumed playing the piano.

"Well, you'll have to be quiet now," the nurse remonstrated. "Everyone else had gone to bed." She left and quickly returned to the nursing station, undoubtedly to get advice as to what to do next. Gloria and I realized that our little joke had run its course. We quickly swallowed our pills and retired to our respective rooms. As I lay in bed, waiting for the pill to take effect, I thought, "Why, I'm just like one of the girls. I wonder how many times they've gotten by with something like this."

When Gloria left, I became friends with Marjorie, another woman in deep depression. She lived alone with her husband, all of their children having left to begin their own families. Marjorie loaned me a mechanical device and a book that would help me learn to play contract bridge. This way, when Marjorie's husband would come in the evenings, I could join them in a game. I was more than grateful for the distraction.

After Jim, Marjorie's husband, would arrive, when I got the signal from Marjorie, I would set up a table for us to begin the game. I would usually deal out the cards, but the game soon became filled with trauma. Marjorie had trouble concentrating and Jim would look at her with imploring eyes, asking, "What's wrong, Marjorie? Is it something I've done? Why are you so depressed?"

Marjorie would shake her head and with tear-filled eyes, would answer, "No. It's not anything you've done. I don't know why I'm depressed. I just am!" I observed that Jim seemed to be very tender and caring of her.

The next day Marjorie assured me that Jim was a wonderful husband and that she was a terrible wife. Finally, I blurted out, "How are you so terrible?"

Marjorie couldn't answer me. According to her, it should have been obvious.

When I was preparing to leave, they were considering shock therapy for Marjorie, who was desperate enough to agree to anything. I was glad I wouldn't be there to see Marjorie so frightened and confused. However, I hoped the treatments would help this miserable woman.

Seeing this couple together made me realize how very lonely I was. I thought of all of the nuns I dearly loved, and wished that just one of them could hold me in her arms and let me cry. I felt this would be all I needed, but of course, I knew better than to request it.

I was sad to have to be in the hospital during Holy Week. Easter was late that year and the trees and flowers were blooming in abundance. In spite of myself, my spirits rose. I found I could sing to Jesus, again, and even put to music a poem of Caryll Hauslander, that seemed to me to have been written for Good Shepherd sisters:

I am your reed, dear Shepherd
Glad to be, glad to be.
And now, if you will,
breathe out your joy in me
And make bright song
Or fill me with the soft moan of your love
When your delight has failed to move
or keep your flock from wrong.

Make children's songs
or any songs, to fill your reed with
breath of life.
But at your will, lay down your flute
and take repose

While music infinite is silence in your heart
And laid on it, your reed is mute.★

Holy Week is the very moving and dramatic preparation for the culmination of the liturgical year, when the Church commemorates the passion, death and resurrection of Christ. It was always the high point of my year. It provided a companion for me, a companion with whom to go down into the depths. A companion, who had been deeper than I, deeper than I cared to go. With Him, I sang the lamentations of Jeremiah, the prophet, concerning the Messiah and his death. These were solos sung during Tenebrae, the term used for Matins and Lauds during Holy Week. The word, itself, means darkness and as each lamentation is sung, another candle is extinguished, casting the participants further and further into darkness, as the hour progresses.

I usually sang at least one of these solos and when I had been at the Mother House, I had coached the other sisters, who had been assigned to sing one. The haunting melody they were set to, was more expressive to me than the words. The psalms, too, were sung to a beautiful tone★, used only during Holy Week.

The drama of these days was heightened by the progressive singing of the *Christus Factus Est*. It began on Wednesday of Holy Week, the first of the three days of Tenebrae. We sang it as if it were happening at the moment. *Christus factus est pro nobis, obediens usque ad mortem.* "Christ is delivered for us, obedient unto death."

On Holy Thursday, we would add *Mortem autem crucis,* "even the death of the cross." Finally, on Good Friday, at the darkest hour, we were given a glimpse of the victory to come, as if to see us through. *Propter quod et Deus exaltant illum et dedit illi nomen quod est super omne nomen.* "Because God has exalted Him and has given Him a name, which is above all names."

Holy Thursday, which coincides with the Jewish feast of Passover, was when Christ and His disciples gathered in the upper room for the Last Supper. At the beginning, Jesus had asked His disciples to bring Him a basin of water and a towel. Then He went around to each of them, washing the dust

★ *The Reed of God* by Caryll Houselander

★ A psalm tone is a short melody, lending itself to the form of the psalm. There are eight, one for each of the eight Gregorian modes.

from their feet, expressing both His humility as their leader and His love for them. He knew that one of them would betray Him.

We nuns gathered in our community room to reenact this scene. The twelve oldest sisters, representing the twelve disciples, would be seated in a circle. The superior, representing Christ, and flanked by sisters, one bearing a basin of water and the other a towel, went around to each *disciple*, bathing her feet. During the ceremony the sisters would sing the beautiful *Ubi Caritas.*

> The love of Christ has gathered us together.
> Let us be gay in Him and cheerful
> Let us love and be in awe of the living God,
> And love each other with honest hearts.
>
> Where Charity and Love abide, there is God.
>
> So, now, that we are gathered here, together,
> Let us take care not to be isolated in ourselves.
> Let ill will, quarrels and disagreements stop,
> And Christ, our God, be among us.
> Where Charity and Love abide, there is God.
>
> And, together with the saints,
> May we see your face in glory, Christ, our God,
> That is, straight, unmeasured joy
> For ages on unending ages.

For me, this hymn epitomized what the religious life was all about. But having missed Tenebrae, I returned home on Holy Saturday in time for the Easter Vigil. In the darkened Church, the Paschal candle was lit from a flint, a new fire symbolizing the resurrected life of Christ. Then small, individual candles for the congregation were lit from this one, providing the only light in the Church. While the priest vested for Mass, the statues which had been covered for Lent were unveiled.

Between the Epistle and the Gospel, the Alleluia was heard for the first time since the beginning of the forty days of Lent. To emphasize this joy, it was sung three times, each time a half tone higher. On the day of Easter, and for the following week, the celebratory *Haec Dies* was sung. "This is the day the Lord has made. Let us rejoice and exult in it." It was followed by a longer and more rejoicing Alleluia, which truly exemplified what has been written of these long and trailing alleluias, that they express the depths of our joy, when words fail us.

At Benediction on Easter Sunday, some of the Sisters Magdalen actually wept, when I went over to their chapel to direct them in the motet they had rehearsed for the occasion. Also, on the following day, the girls were delighted that I would be with them, when they put on their version of *The Masque of the Red Death*.

That night, as I prepared for sleep, I thought to myself, "With so much love all around me, how can I be depressed?

CHAPTER FOURTEEN

A WEEK OR SO after my return home from the hospital, I was surprised to receive a letter from Mother Francis. There had been no communication between us since I had sent the poem from college the summer before. I waited until I went to my room that night to open it. That had been a wise decision. I was shocked at what I read.

> My dear Sister Teresa,
>   I have just heard from Mother Mechtilde that you are home, once more, and seem to be doing well. I want you to know that I am planning a visitation to Omaha early in June and, if your physician feels you are able, I would like you to return to St. Paul, when I do. We can really use you here in the novitiate.
>   Sincerely in Christ,
>   Mother Francis

A surge of anger welled up. *If your physician feels you are able...*

"What about how I feel?" I wondered. "How do I feel?" I then asked myself. "Well, first of all, I'm scared," I continued. "I'm not even sure if I am back on my emotional feet, even here in Omaha, much less in St. Paul! The sex visions have gone away almost entirely." I laughed at the juxtaposition of the words sex and visions. "Sex visuals?" I laughed again, but the laughter was without release. "Would they start up again in the presence of Mother Francis? But...but I never did feel sexual towards her!" I exclaimed. "Can't you love someone without being sexual? Did Mother Francis think that's what I meant when I told her I loved her?...Did I feel sexual and just didn't realize it? NO! Then why...what...where did all these gross feelings and imaginings come from?"

I knew that the answer to that was not forthcoming. I had been asking myself that ever since November 3, of the past year. I reached for a sleeping pill, glad that my doctor had given me a supply, for moments like this.

As I went about my duties during the following weeks, I realized that a part of me was looking forward to working with the young sisters once more. But would we have those exciting discussions again? Could I? Was I that enthusiastic about anything these days? Could I feel that way again? Ever again? I would like to, but I had doubts.

The medication I was taking had done away with the imaginings and the painfulness from the depression had let up, but I didn't feel much enthusiasm inside. All I felt was a dullness, like I wasn't fully alive.

I returned to St. Paul with Mother Francis in June. Seeing the Provincial again had not stirred up anything in me but dread. Even after I came to feel more secure that I didn't feel at all sexual towards her, it wasn't much better not feeling anything at all.

Mother Francis wisely kept my duties to a minimum for the summer. I taught music fundamentals to the postulants, directed the postulant choir and the sisters' choir. In spite of these precautions, by September I wasn't able to do even that much. I would sit in an easy chair in an old office they gave me and stare.

"I am being passive aggressive," I told myself, wishing I had never heard of the term. "It would be more fun, if I were just being that and not knowing it!" I exclaimed, trying to dredge up some humor about it.

Finally, Mother Francis sent me to a psychiatrist, one who was more fatherly than the one in Omaha. I didn't even know whether I preferred that or not. He didn't believe in institutionalization. but where was I to go, while the new medication either took effect, or didn't?

Fortunately, at that time, the chaplain's cottage was not in use. Our present chaplain worked in the chancery office and lived there, as well. I stayed in the cottage, various sisters bringing my meals there, when I simply could not make myself get up. I felt guilty about it, but not enough to get myself over to the convent.

After a couple weeks, I was able to transfer back to the convent and begin, again, to take up my duties. I still felt dead inside, but I could plod on. Strangely enough, my singing voice had taken on a new vibrancy, which I couldn't explain, not feeling vibrant at all. I definitely had to control it, or drown out the others entirely. Every now and then I would let it soar, as if to say, "To hell with you," but then I would feel guilty and reign it in again.

Several months later, when I was in talking with Mother Francis about stepping up my duties, she said, "You know, Sister, you have really matured during these past two years. You seem to be much more steadfast and stable. I used to be amused when the young sisters from your classes in chironomy would get up to direct (here Mother Francis rolled her eyes and pretended to be singing with all her heart). How did you feel when they were imitating you like that?"

I was stunned. "I…I…I guess I didn't know they were imitating me," I stammered.

"Well, I for one, certainly prefer the level-headed and mature sister you've become," she assured me, and quickly dismissed me. Did she sense that I was on the verge of tears?

"So this is maturity?" I asked myself as I walked away from the office. "I'm afraid that I hate it! What is going to become of me?" I wondered. "Can I go on like this for the rest of my life? I certainly don't want to, regardless of what she wants!" But the mere wanting – or not wanting – didn't change things much.

Apparently my new demeanor continued to please Mother Francis. Shortly after the New Year, she called me into her office and gave me the obedience of resuming the directorship of the juniorate. The sister, who had taken my place almost three years before, had proven somewhat inadequate, because of her own scrupulosities. She was literally begging to be relieved from the position. I had overheard some complaints from the various young sisters that their directress treated them like children. I knew I could improve on that, but I was fearful because of my own lack of self confidence as to my relationship with Jesus. This still seemed to me to be the basis for finding the strength to observe the rules of the religious life, as well as for the joy I had once felt in this observance. I felt that I had made a little progress in my strivings to reestablish this. Perhaps, again being in charge of the young sisters would secure it, more. I had accepted the obedience long before these thoughts had gone through my mind. I had never refused Jesus, in the person of my superiors, anything yet.

In May of 1965, Mama came for a visit. For the past few months, she had been writing me, telling me of her loneliness, and asking me if I couldn't consider leaving the order and coming to live with her. I knew how desperate she must have felt, to have asked this. Mama had always taken pride in her independence.

As difficult as living in the convent had become for me, the thought of readjusting in the world, after all these years, was terrifying. What I replied, to her, was that I didn't feel like I could go back on the vows I had taken and feel right about it. This was also true.

At the beginning of the visit, I tried to explain my feelings to Mama, that I still loved Jesus and wanted, above all, to remain in His service. I truthfully meant what I was saying, but I was also aware of my cowardice about going back out into the world. Was Mama also aware of this?

In spite of the unhappy beginning, this visit turned out to be the best we had ever had together. When Mama realized that she wouldn't be able to persuade me to come home with her, our conversations became animated like old times. I played my violin for her for an entire afternoon, playing all of her favorites.

At the end of the visit, Mother Francis arranged to have me drive Mama to the station. It was the first time I had been permitted to do this.

I stood and watched as Mama walked down the ramp, leading to her coach. When she turned, waved and smiled, I waved back, but was stunned by the premonition that this would be the last time I would ever see Mama alive. Everything in me wanted to run after her, to shout out, "Mama, don't leave!" My throat became blocked by a huge lump and my feet were as if glued to the pavement. I watched as she boarded the railroad car and was out of sight. Tears blinded me momentarily.

"Don't be so silly!" I exclaimed to myself. "Of course, I'll see her again. Look how healthy she is." I returned to the car and to the convent.

Shortly after this incident, the Good Shepherd Order was released from being a semi-contemplative order altogether, as this was becoming more and more of an obstacle to our apostolate. Among other things, it meant that we were allowed a home visit of three days every five years, which would be staggered, so that others could cover for those who were away. Mother Francis felt that I could greatly benefit by this and saw to it that I was one of the first to go. My sister Margaret was delighted to have me come for a visit, but I was somewhat uncomfortable not having been in a private home for over fifteen years, and was further dismayed to find that her daughter would be sleeping in the living room, so that I could have her room. However, I was grateful for the privacy and Patty seemed to enjoy playing like she was camping. It turned out to be a pleasant enough visit, the three boys and Patty enjoying the novelty of having a nun in their agnostic household.

Shortly after my return to St. Paul, everyone was surprised when Mother Francis was asked to leave the St. Paul Province, to become the provincial of the Cincinnati Province. It was rare that anyone was asked to leave their province and go to another. It didn't seem possible that an entire province didn't have someone capable of leading it. Whatever the cause, Mother Francis was asked to do this, and difficult as it was for her, she accepted. This meant leaving her elderly parents, who lived in St. Paul.

She was replaced by Mother Gerard, who had been the Prioress of the Mother House for some time, and was well qualified. I found that I was relieved to be under someone else.

Late in June, Mama's ulcer was reactivated and she was again hospitalized. This time surgery would be required. Margaret was able to be there with her, so I did not go. The surgery was a success and a day later a little party was held in her hospital room to celebrate her seventy-ninth birthday. I was able to give her greetings over the telephone.

I was totally unprepared, therefore, when Margaret called me on July 10, just six days after the party, to tell me that Mama had suddenly died that morning, while being X-rayed. They had attempted pulmonary resuscitation, but were unable to revive her.

I staggered down to the provincial's office to let her know. All I could think of was the image of Mama waving at me at the train station and the premonition I had had less that two months before.

Mother Gerard took me into her arms as I wept. I suddenly realized that this was the first time I had been held like this since entering the convent. I felt somewhat bitter, that it took such a calamity to be cared for.

Arrangements were made quickly for me to go to Denver for Mama's funeral. I had very mixed feelings about it. Somehow it seemed too late. Mama had carefully made arrangements ahead of time for the cremation of her body and a simple service. She had requested donations for eye transplants, rather than flowers. I was grateful for this simplicity and the lack of a casket. I certainly preferred my memories of her at the railway station to that of a corpse. I wept at the funeral and, except for the first time in the Provincial's office, that would be the only time until twelve years later when my tears were finally relased. I simply could not face the fact that Mama was gone forever.

Margaret had come from her home in Sacramento, California to be with Mama in Denver, during the surgery. Her husband, John, came to join his wife after Mama died. Because he had forbidden Margaret to visit me in the convent, we had not seen each other for fifteen years. Either because he had mellowed with age, or no longer believed the strange ideas he had about the Catholic church, John agreed to come for supper at the convent on the day of the funeral, so we could be together. The two of them even remained for a visit that evening.

It was the kindness of Sister Michael, my companion at Notre Dame, that I would remember most vividly from that trip. She had arranged to serve the supper for me and my family. Remembering how close Mama and I had been, Sister Michael was very sympathetic towards me and spent much time with me during the remainder of the visit. She took me over to the girls' high school, where she was the principal, and showed me the things she had done to make it a pleasant place for the girls. She conveyed much enthusiasm and energy for the school in Denver and I could see that the girls liked her very much. It was such a wonderful change from the woman Sister Michael had been in St. Paul and at Notre Dame. By the end of the visit, I felt as if we were old friends. It gave me hope that I, too, could get over my depression and be enthusiastic about life, once more.

On my return home, I found that there were five sisters in the juniorate, who had doubts about their vocations, a rather high number for a small juniorate of fifteen or so members, nearly one third of the whole group.

One of them was the younger sister of one of the nuns who had entered with me. I remembered Sister Henry asking us to pray for her little sister, that she would have a vocation to our order. I had joined in the prayers and rejoiced when her sister entered a few years later.

Sister Joseph was intelligent and responsible and I had enjoyed having her in my classes. However, when she was still a novice I had noticed a certain lethargy and sadness about her, so much so, that I mentioned it to Mother Francis, who was still the directress of novices at the time. Mother Francis thought it might be an iron deficiency and after Sister Joseph had been taking iron supplements for a time, she did seem better.

By now, Sister Joseph was approaching her final vows. During one of her visits to me she said, "You know, Mother, Sister Henry and even my whole family, put a lot of pressure on me to enter the convent. When I had been out of high school a couple years and hadn't fallen in love, I did begin to think I had a religious vocation. I certainly wasn't interested in going to college and developing a career."

"So what was it that you really did want, Sister?" I interjected.

Tears filled the young woman's eyes, as a deep blush spread over her face. "I know it sounds silly, Mother Teresa, but what I really want is to have children and be a good mother, to my own children, that is."

"That doesn't sound silly to me, Sister. It sounds to me like you have a real vocation, a real calling to it," I assured her with vehemence. "Your vocation is every bit as valid as ours."

Sister Joseph was genuinely surprised at the heartfelt answer. "Do you really think so, Mother?" she asked, knowing full well that I meant what I had said.

"Oh, Sister," I replied, "I guess I'm the last person, who should be talking to you this way. But, yes, I truly believe that you have a strong vocation to motherhood and that you will not be happy until that is what you are doing.

However, I would like to make an appointment for you with Monsignor O'Reilly. You definitely should have a second opinion on such an important matter. Would you agree to this?"

"I would like that, Mother. Thank you so very much," the young Sister replied.

I was not surprised when the Monsignor agreed with my assessment. This was a great disappointment to Sister Henry, who was permitted to come and visit her sister to see for herself how much she wanted this change. Within a year of her leaving, Sister Joseph was married and pregnant with her first child. She seemed very happy and most contented.

Another junior sister told me about having been sexually active with a boy during her sophomore and junior years in high school. They had planned to marry, but during their senior year, the boy had fallen in love with someone else and finally married this second woman. In her shock and grief over the incident, Sister Matthew had decided that she was meant to be a nun and help others. Now, she was having intense sexual temptations at night and was becoming nervous and frightened. She still felt that she wanted to continue being a nun. She genuinely loved working with the girls and seemed to do well with them.

In an oblique way, I let her know that I, too, had had similar temptations, so that she wouldn't feel so alone in this trial. I obtained some sleeping pills for her and also got permission for her to have her set of trap drums at the convent, to give her something to do that she thoroughly enjoyed. Sister Matthew played the drums over in class and soon had several pupils. These things helped, but I wasn't surprised to learn much later, that Sister Matthew had left and was married.

Sister John the Evangelist had difficulty in speaking of her problems, but was becoming very irresponsible about her prayer life and her duties with the girls. She would leave her keys out over in the class, would be late to prayers, would forget little assignments she had been given and, also, was unable to sleep. She told me it had something to do with her childhood, but was unable to be specific. I finally got permission for her to see a psychiatrist, which she was willing to do.

After the doctor saw her, he felt that Sister John should be admitted to the psychiatric ward, with which he was affiliated, for further tests, observation and possible treatment. After she was once admitted, Sister John was not allowed any visitors for a full week. When I was finally able to visit her, I was impressed with the cheerful decor of the ward in comparison to the one I had been in, in Omaha.

Sister John hurried us to her room, where, after closing the door, she threw herself into my arms, sobbing and begging me to take her home. I sensed that the psychiatrist seemed somewhat punitive or at least unsympathetic in his attitude and after a few days I was able to have her released.

Sister John was so happy to be back home that her behavior improved for a time. Then one evening at supper, she did not appear. We were unable to find her anywhere in the class or on the convent side. During recreation, she telephoned me to inform me that she had run away.

"But you don't have to worry, Mother." she assured me. "My older sister is coming to pick me up. I think being with her for awhile will help."

"Sister John, do you realize how much worry you have caused us?" I was quick to respond. "However, I'll tell Mother Provincial where you are and we'll go from there. Give me your sister's telephone number so I can reach you there."

Mother Gerard was furious with Sister John for having broken cloister, but agreed to let her stay at her sister's for the rest of the week. When she returned she had made the decision to leave. After being dispensed from her vows, she entered nurses' training and seemed to make a good adjustment. I couldn't help wondering what had occurred in her childhood to cause so much distress.

In the meantime, a young sister in Omaha had written me, saying, "Could you possibly come and see me, Mother? I simply can't put what I have to tell you in a letter." Since there were several junior sisters in Omaha,

Mother Gerard decided that it would be a good idea for me to go there and see how all of them were doing.

Sister Rachel, who had first requested to see me, was having trouble with the vow of obedience, which I thought might have come from her having been in a family where the father had been domineering and the mother excessively passive. I persuaded Sister to see Dr. Sands, the psychiatrist who had helped me, to aid her in working out her problem. Sister Rachel received much help from Dr. Sands and was able to renew her vows for another year, which gave her time to make a further decision about her vocation to the religious life.

I was dismayed when I found out that another of the young sisters was still very happy being a religious, but was most displeasing to the Superior. Mother Mechtilde was no longer the Prioress in Omaha and I barely knew Mother Charles, who did not feel that Sister Philip was strict enough with the girls and did not believe that she was trying hard enough to become more so. After I talked about it with Sister Philip, I could see that the two of them had very opposing philosophies about working with the girls.

While I was probably more sympathetic to Sister Philip's methods, I could also see that she was quite immature in many ways. She had entered the order right out of high school and, now, at the age of twenty-one, was being asked to be a full time group mother.

When I returned to St. Paul, I requested Mother Gerard to bring Sister Philip back to the Mother House, where she would have supervision and example in working with the girls in a less responsible position. It didn't seem right to send her home without giving her an opportunity to mature. I was dismayed to find Mother Gerard's mind was made up. At the end of the year, Sister Philip was asked to leave. I was upset, but totally powerless in the situation.

★ ★ ★ ★ ★

It was around this time that Sister Euphemia, who had been in the juniorate the first time I had been the directress, came back after a years's leave of absence. She had held some kind of office job and had lived with a sister and brother-in-law. She told me that what she had seen of her sister's married life, helped her decide to try the convent, again. Living singly in the world did not enter into her realm of possibilities.

She asked me if she might speak with me some time. By now, a cloister had been established for the juniorate, so I had to see her in one of the convent parlors, since Sister Euphemia was fully professed. During one of these visits, we found ourselves in a passionate embrace. I had been taken completely off guard, because I had not felt in the least attracted to her. It happened again on three or four more occasions, the conversations before-hand getting shorter and shorter. I found myself furtively locking the door behind us, so that we would not be discovered. My resolutions, beforehand, not to indulge in these embraces, seemed futile. I finally had to refuse to see her. Shortly afterwards, Sister Euphemia was missioned, so the pressure was taken away, but my own apparent neediness was haunting.

As if to exacerbate this realization, Sister Gabrielle suddenly appeared at the Mother House in St. Paul on her way to the main Mother House in Angers, France. Usually, getting to go to Angers was considered a great privilege and a thing of joy, but it was more often young sisters, who were thus honored, to get special training. In fact, Sister Gabrielle had been one of the young sisters, who had been sent long ago to Angers for specialized training. She had come from French speaking parents. By now, however, she was semi-retired and was well into her sixties.

It was obvious to see that Sister Gabrielle was not happy. I had only known her briefly on previous visits to St. Paul, and had liked her very much. She was a small, bird-like woman with a demure sense of humor and was generally beloved by all of the sisters.

I was most unpleasantly surprised to hear that Sister Gabrielle had be-come emotionally involved with one of the lay social workers in Seattle, Washington. They did not say sexually involved, but if she was being sent clear out of the country, it must have been a serious relationship. Sending her to the Mother House in Angers seemed the only solution. She certainly would have found it impossible to adjust in the world, after fifty odd years in the cloister.

I found myself fantasizing sweeping her up in my arms and running away with her. My own fears of *making it* in the world, cut the fantasies short.

"Sister Gabrielle, I'll be praying that things will work out for you in France," I promised her. When I spoke to her with such compassion, the older woman fled from the room in tears.

Having to counsel so many sisters, who were unsure of their vocations, and the incidents with Sister Euphemia and Sister Gabrielle, showed me how vulnerable, I, myself, had become. I thought about seeking counseling, once more, but really had little faith that it would help. Instead, I continued taking sleeping pills at night and several psychotropic drugs that had been prescribed for me, during the day, and was thus able to put off the inevitable. It would take still another series of incidents with another troubled junior sister, that would begin my own long process of leaving the convent.

Sister Elizabeth was demanding much of my time, energy and endurance. She did not want to leave the order, but was overwhelmed with guilt feelings and scrupulosities. She would be in my office for over an hour, weeping and trying to express her feelings. Then, out of gratitude, she would bring flowers from the convent gardens for my office. She began writing poetry, also leaving them on my desk. The poetry showed that she had a gift with words and that she was deeply sensitive.

Some of her problems stemmed from having been brought up in a very restrictive environment. Her mother had raised her and four siblings by herself. Being the oldest of the five children, she was often responsible for the care of the others, while the mother was working. Sister Elizabeth had been deprived both materially and emotionally.

Not having the time or energy Sister Elizabeth seemed to require of me, I persuaded her to see the fatherly psychiatrist I, myself, had seen when I first returned to St. Paul. Sister Elizabeth resisted this suggestion at first, but finally agreed to see him once. He quite won her over, but not in time to keep her from going into a psychotic depression, during which she refused to eat, drink or get out of bed.

When I approached Mother Gerard about this, she forbad me to take meals to Sister Elizabeth's room, or for any other reason, to go in there. She felt Sister Elizabeth was doing these things to get my attention.

After two days, I became concerned that the young woman might become badly dehydrated. I tried to reach the psychiatrist by telephone, only to discover that he was out of town for the weekend.

The following day, which was a special feast day, we sisters were conversing with one another at supper, instead of eating in silence while someone read to us, as was the custom. One of the junior sisters rushed into the refectory and came right to me, forgetting to get permission from the Provincial, according to custom.

"Mother Teresa! Sister Elizabeth is hammering on her door, begging to get out and screaming for you!"

"But her door isn't locked!" I exclaimed.

"Well, that's what she is doing, anyway," the harried sister insisted.

I left at once, also forgetting to get the standard permission to leave the refectory. By the time I had gone up the three storeys, where Sister Elizabeth's room was located, the young woman seemed totally out of control. She clung to me for some time, sobbing and mumbling incoherently. At first, I thought she was running a slight temperature, but when I took it, it was normal. I was finally able to get her to drink a little water and ultimately to go to sleep.

By this time, the sisters' recreation was over and they had sung Compline. I went right to the Provincial's office to report what had happened. Before I was able to say a word, Mother Gerard was berating me for giving bad example in the refectory, by getting up and leaving without permission. I readily apologized and then began to relate what had happened.

Mother Gerard quickly interrupted me, saying, "Sister, I think you are handling this situation most unwisely. I thought I told you to stay away from Sister Elizabeth's room entirely. When she gets hungry or thirsty enough, she will come out on her own. She's probably been drinking, when you aren't there, anyway. I absolutely forbid you to go up there again!"

I was shocked. I kissed the floor and left. In the chapel, after I had said Compline in private, I began my nightly examination of conscience. Mother Gerard's assessment of the situation seemed to me entirely insensitive and even cruel. Suddenly I felt overwhelmed, not only by the situation with Sister Elizabeth, but my own, as well. I felt that I could no longer tolerate such an unfeeling environment. It seemed to me that what we all needed was the opportunity to express and to receive affection and support from each other. I also knew this was not within the boundaries of the rule for religious. I went on to realize that the vow of chastity, not only precluded sex, but even normal expressions of affection for one another. "No wonder Sister Euphemia and I had begun embracing," I thought. I realized that it was similar to what I had felt at Notre Dame after going so long without hearing instrumental music. My very skin was parched from the lack. Now, my whole being was desiccated from lack of affection and no matter who gave it, I couldn't resist. It was like being given a drink after days in a desert without fluid.

Now I understood completely how Sister Gabrielle had succumbed to having an affair with a social worker. I could imagine myself doing the same thing, when I would be too old to adjust to the world. I decided that I would ask to be dispensed from my vows and leave as soon as possible. Having made the decision, I was able to sleep that night without the need of a sleeping pill.

After the first Mass the next morning, I again went to the Provincial's office. Mother Gerard was stunned when I told her that I wanted to be dispensed from my vows. She quickly dismissed me, promising to see me right after the second Mass. I did not attend the second Mass, but began going through my papers and to pack.

Where I would go did not enter my mind.

Later, when I returned to Mother Gerard's office, the Provincial said, "Sister, I hadn't realized how distraught you were. . . are, apparently. You have given of yourself unstintingly for a good many years and we do appreciate it, but I see now, that you need a respite from so many duties. I urgently advise you to let me send you to a mission for a year, to think over more clearly as to whether you want to leave."

Tears of frustration rolled down my cheeks. What I felt I needed was encouragement to take this terrifying step.

"Sister," Mother Gerard continued, "four of our superiors will be making a private retreat at an ocean-side cabin near Tillamook, Oregon. What would you think of going to join them? It seems to me that it would be a good setting for you to get yourself together, before making a decision you might regret later. They will be leaving from the Portland convent tomorrow afternoon. I can probably get a plane reservation for you this afternoon, so that you can be there in time to leave with them." Actually, I was grateful for the reprieve and agreed to at least make the retreat.

A few hours later, Sister Louise, my long time friend from our days in the novitiate, was driving me to the airport. As we were leaving, a group of postulants were walking up the driveway coming back from their afternoon recreation. Sister Louise had to stop the car, in order to get by. As soon as they recognized me, they stopped and began singing the last motet I had just taught them, having no idea they would not be seeing me again. I was afraid I would begin to cry. "Sister Louise, please! Let's leave!"

Sister Louise put her window down and told the postulants they were going to make us miss a plane. They quickly moved on. On the way to the airport, Sister Louise tried to tell me that I was too much of a perfectionist. It only made me angry that my friend could offer this advice without having any idea what had taken place. I simply remained silent, knowing that she meant well.

As we entered the airport parking lot, I started to cry, knowing that I would never again see the Mother House, where I had felt so much at home for so many years, beginning with that very first day sixteen years ago, kneeling in the visitor's chapel.

CHAPTER FIFTEEN

I DID NOT make the retreat with the superiors. They did not have a retreat master, but were using the tape recording of that momentous retreat in Omaha, which I had made in November of 1963. As soon as I recognized the retreat master's voice, I knew I could not go through that one again. I offered to do the cooking and shopping. I spent the rest of my time walking on the beach. Even though it was late October, the weather was fair enough that I was able to do this.

I was intrigued by the curious three-rock formation to the south of our cabin. One of the rocks had a tunnel running through it, formed by years of wind blowing on it just right. Someone knew the formation was called The Three Sisters. It became indelibly imprinted on my mind, as I walked up and down on the sand, trying to rethink my life. In a way, it was the most serious retreat I had ever made.

I carefully thought about my dedication to Christ and to His Church. I disregarded the memories of Father Goldbrunner's diatribe, and asked myself what it meant to be Christ's spouse. Could I still consider myself as such? At times, I still felt His closeness and also the joy the thought of Him would bring. At other times, I was filled only with sexual images and a constant aching in my groin. Mostly I felt quite starved for affection.

While I knew that I had given myself quite literally, heart and soul to Jesus, I was also aware that, in part, this dedication could have come from an unconscious sublimation of my illegitimate love for Lynn. Nonetheless, I had thrown myself entirely into working with and for Him. I began to realize that working and being with women, almost exclusively, was what had made me blossom out so much in the beginning. Also it had been most uplifting to have my gifts recognized and suspected that this could happen. I did not even consider where I would go, if I did leave, which was obviously the important question. Was the utter darkness of my terror the reason for this avoidance?

I finally decided that since I had made such a total investment in the order, I would take Mother Provincial's suggestion and try to regain my dedication on one of the missions. I suspected that I might simply be procrastinating from fear of the unknown. At the same time, however, I decided to let my hair grow.

I was sent temporarily to Helena, with the understanding that my duties would be kept minimal. The superior there had been with me in the novitiate and we were good friends. Mother Thomas spent time with me without expecting me to speak of my problems. However, after a few visits, she began to speak of the problems in the Helena Home. The first directress was somewhat naive, as Sister Joan d'Arc had been in Portland. They had not been able to initiate the family group system and, in fact, the province was considering closing the home within a year.

I offered to help in the laundry in the mornings and to supervise a hallway between two dormitories at night. I was asked to sleep off an empty dormitory, where trouble makers were sometimes sent.

One afternoon, I was walking through the assembly hall between classes, when a girl approached and asked if she could speak with me privately. After we had stepped away from the main flow of traffic, she asked, "Mother, do you know what a lesbian is?"

My heart froze, but I actually was not certain of the meaning of the word. "I'm not quite sure, Myrna. I'll look it up and let you know," I hastily reentered the flow of girls going to classes. When Webster confirmed my suspicions, I realized the question had not been sincere, but a lead-on. I felt like running away. I knew I needn't bother informing Myrna.

The following day I got permission to call Monsignor O'Sullivan. He had been my confessor in St. Paul ever since I had been in the novitiate. I had also had private interviews with him. He had always been most helpful and had been the priest who had helped me when Sister Joseph had told me of her vocation to motherhood, I was certain he would understand my present situation and would give me good advice.

Indeed, he told me, at once, that I did not need to remain in the convent until I had another breakdown. Then he cautioned me not to go live with relatives, should I leave. "You want to remain as independent as possible," he advised. "Afterall, you do have the education and experience that should bring you a good job," he assured me.

A few nights after that, Myrna got herself in trouble and ended up in the dormitory off which I was sleeping. I was hardly surprised, when at about midnight, I heard a knock on my door. When I opened the shutter, Myrna claimed that she was hearing noises on the fire escape.

I put on a robe, carefully adjusted my night veil and went out to investigate. First, I turned on all of the lights and then opened the door to the fire escape and looked up and down.

"Well, if anyone was there, they're gone now," I announced. Leaving all the lights on, I sat on a couch, keeping the lead in an innocuous conversation. After a time, I yawned and declared, "I haven't heard a thing, have you?" The question was rhetorical. I got up to return to my room, saying, "If you want to leave the lights on, Myrna, you may." A few minutes later, I saw the lights go out through the transom above my door. Nothing more happened that night.

A couple of days later, Myrna tried to incite a riot in her dormitory. Only two or three others were really into it, and after a suspenseful morning, they were removed to the county detention hall. Mother Thomas asked me if I would continue to sleep off the problematic dormitory, but I felt I had to refuse. This was the first time I had ever done anything like that. But, in fact, I was distraught enough, that I requested to return to my cell in the convent.

It was shortly after this incident, that I was missioned to the convent in Seattle to be the principal of the school. Even though I had had to be hospitalized, while I had been principal in Omaha, I looked forward to having another chance at it in Seattle. It was clear to me that being principal had not been the cause of my hospitalizaion. With Monsignor O'Sullivan's assurance of my capabilities, I was hopeful for a new and challenging beginning.

Shortly after I arrived in Seattle, I enrolled at the Jesuit run Seattle University to continue my work towards a Master's degree in Secondary School Administration. My faculty advisor was a Catholic layman, Dr. Jamison, who was very interested the the work we nuns were doing in the high school at the Home. He offered to become involved in the program as a consultant. I was pleasantly surprised and immediately accepted the offer.

Both as teacher and as principal, I had felt the futility in trying to determine the grade placement of many of the girls, who came to the Good Shepherd schools. Their abilities and backgrounds often did not correspond with their chronological ages.

While perusing some magazines for a short paper in one of my classes, I ran across an article on non-graded schools and became interested in the concept. I soon found other articles about experiments taking place all over the United States, especially in Florida. This was one educational experiment being tried on all levels, which was a pleasant surprise, as I had found that most creative innovations were taking place only in the primary grades.

When I mentioned the subject to my advisor, he told me that they were trying it in several of the public schools in Seattle and arranged for me to tour and visit them. I was most impressed with what I saw. First, I noticed that in these schools, there seemed to be very little competition. Progress was very individualized. With the aid of reading laboratories, some students had been able to break through reading blocks that had kept them at third and fourth grade levels. On the other hand, gifted students were earning college credits in certain fields.

From speaking with some of the teachers in these schools, I had learned that there were history, literature and science books available with a secondary interest level, but with a reading vocabulary of the third or fourth grade. There were also news events papers like this.

I spoke to Professor Jamison about non-grading our high school. He not only agreed that it would be a beneficial thing to do, but knew of some educational grant monies available in the area and suggested that I apply for some in order to get the special reading materials I wanted and to set up a reading laboratory.

I called this endeavor Project Grow, set up a proposed budget with Dr. Jamison's help, held meetings with my faculty, the students and their parents and thus achieved valuable input and support for the program. By the time we received the grant that summer, everyone involved was solidly behind the project or, at least were willing to give it a try. We sent for the materials and during the summer, hired some student teachers from the University to tutor in reading and mathematics.

The interest I had in this program made life easier for me, in that it aided me in putting off examining my vocation to the religious life, or, even more to the point, to think of where I would go, if I did leave. Nights were still a torment, with sexual images and unrelieving masturbation. I finally asked, once more, for psychiatric help.

An intelligent and sensitive psychiatrist, who worked with the girls one afternoon a week, agreed to see me on that evening. The two of us would have animated conversations about such things as life after death, the new findings in physics and psychedelic drugs. He felt that I simply needed the opportunity to speak about such subjects, in an intellectual way, thus making my life interesting enough to carry on with my more mundane duties. I began to suspect that it was he, who had such a need.

He also took me off one of the three psychotropic drugs I had been taking, explaining that it wasn't compatible with one of the other two. He didn't realize that this undermined my faith in the psychiatric profession, since the doctor in St. Paul had assured me that I could take this combination of drugs for the rest of my life, without any side effects.

Then began a series of incidents, which led to my eventual departure from the order. When I first arrived in Seattle, the girl assigned to the cleaning of the school had actually graduated in January and was still at the Home, unable to return to her family. It was difficult for Elaine to have to remain there, not going to classes and her future being so indefinite. I had her begin to organize the totally unorganized library and to do some typing for me, as well. She was grateful for the distraction from worrying about her future and gaining experience at the same time.

Elaine's social worker finally found a live-in situation for her. Because she had just turned seventeen, finding a job was more difficult. After a few weeks, she came back to the Home for a visit. She already had a boyfriend and seemed happy with her situation, although she still didn't have a job. Then, several weeks later, she returned and asked to see me privately. It turned out that she really wasn't happy with her situation. Her foster mother had been well intentioned, even having introduced her to the boy, but she also expected her to attend their church and become more of a family member than Elaine really wanted. She saw her stay there as a temporary thing, until she could be out on her own. Nonetheless, she continued to date the boy, for whom she felt no attraction, out of a sense of obligation.

Then Elaine met up with a former girl friend, who was looking for a roommate and could even get her a job, if she lied about her age. Her social worker felt she wasn't ready to be completely on her own yet, so Elaine simply left on her own, the situation having become intolerable for her. She felt especially good being financially independent for the first time in her life.

"Well," I commented, after hearing her story, "It sounds like you are much happier in your present situation, but aren't you still under the supervision of your social worker?"

"Well, in a way, I am still on probation, but I was never formally put on probation by a judge," Elaine explained. "She is a social worker, not a probation officer. I really don't think she can do much about it, especially since I'm financially independent. When I'm eighteen, I'll be entirely on my own, so why not now? I've finished high school and I've got a job. I really don't need her anymore. I just hope I don't run into her any place," she added.

"Are you telling me this, so I will get in touch with her and let her know where you are?" I asked.

Elaine's eyes grew wide with horror. "I certainly do not want that, Mother! I. . . I thought you'd understand. Babs, my roommate,...well, she likes to be with women. I think that's why Mrs. Wells didn't want me to move in with her. But, she's really been nice to me, Mother, and helpful, too. Don't you see, Mother?"

Again, I froze. It seemed like I must have a scarlet L up and down the front of my habit.

"Well, I do believe you aren't doing anything illegal," I finally answered. "At least it doesn't seem so. If Mrs. Wells ever asked me where you are, I might feel obligated to tell her, but she probably won't. I've never even had a conversation with her about any of you girls."

We had been walking towards the school exit, where I would let Elaine out. Just as we arrived, Elaine suddenly hugged me, crying out, "I knew you'd understand, Mother Teresa! Thanks so much for all your help!"

When she finally let go, she saw that my eyes were glistening.

I quickly said, "I am so happy for you, Elaine!"

"Goodbye, and God bless you, Mother Teresa," Elaine said. "I'll pray for you. Honest I will."

That was what the nuns usually said to the girls when they left, but in my confusion, I had forgotten. I hastily replied, "Thank you, Elaine and, of course, I'll pray for you, too." I quickly unlocked the door and after Elaine departed, I hastily locked it and walked down the hall. I felt foolish, exposed and frighteningly lonely.

I didn't return to my office, but went straight to my room, for a long, frustrating and unreleasing cry.

When Elaine returned again for a visit, I was very involved with Project Grow and told her I didn't have time for a private visit. I knew I had hurt her, but I couldn't risk further exposure. I didn't feel sexual towards her, but the girl's sympathy could have easily tempted me to confide in her, which I knew would be most inappropriate.

At the beginning of that summer of 1967, one of the sisters, who had been in the juniorate under my direction, was sent to Seattle to help during the summer. Sister Dolores sensed my depression, in spite of Project Grow.

She told me that the young sisters felt that I was at least ten years ahead of the order and that was why I had been sent away. Since this was somewhat true, I didn't correct that impression.

The two of us got permission to swim and play tennis together once or twice a week. I had played a lot of tennis in high school and found it most releasing. At these times we would speak of the reforms in the order, which we hoped would come about. It was encouraging to me that the young sisters had taken my teachings to heart, which might bring about some changes, but sexual images continued to haunt me at night, unless I capitulated and took a sleeping pill.

In the fall, the books and supplies for the reading lab arrived and I felt real excitement over the prospect of the advantages this would bring the girls. I worked for hours into the night, besides seeing that Project Grow functioned during the day.

That same fall of 1967, saw an influx of *flower children* into the Home's population. The Haight, in San Francisco, was not the only place to find them.

There was a large hippie community skirting the edges of the University of Washington. I had read with interest some articles of Timothy Leary describing the mystical experiences he was granted with the use of LSD. I also read of the bad trips others experienced. I soon discovered that some of the girls had been adversely affected by it, but there were also the others, the enlightened ones, the new, peaceful revolutionaries.

For some reason, these latter felt an affinity with me and would hang around my office, wanting to talk. Some of them hoped that I could get them out of the Home. When they discovered that I didn't have the authority nor the will to have them released, they removed themselves from the group. Most of them, however, remained loyal to the little *coterie*. I thought that it was the teachings in my religion class, on the primacy of love, that drew them to me. Even some of the Protestants among them, were asking to take my class.

One day, during my Music Appreciation class, one of the girls gave an excellent report on Bob Dylan, finishing it by playing one of his albums. In the ensuing conversation, they began trying to persuade me to go visit the hippie village by the University. They felt certain that the hippies there would like me and that I would like them. My stomach clenched and my skin became icy cold. Had they somehow divined my thoughts about the possibility of leaving?

"Well, maybe someday I could get permission to go for a visit. I think I might like that," I admitted.

Ramona, who was exceptionally bright, was doing a research paper on Hemingway, under my tutelage. She would come down to the school on weekends to get help with her paper and then regale me with her sexual escapades with men, on the weekends when she went home. Ramona claimed that her mother was more or less aware of what was going on, but she didn't want to report her and thus prolong her stay at the Home. She wanted to have Ramona released so that she could go to a larger high school with more college preparatory courses. Also, Ramona confided, her mother liked having a cheap baby sitter.

"I really like it here, Mother. I want to finish my high school here," she claimed. I suspected that she also wanted to remain at the Home to antagonize her mother.

One day, when Ramona was sick and not in school, at the beginning of the Music Appreciation class, Ramona's best friend told me that she had a message for me from Ramona and proceeded to give it to me in Spanish. Ramona wanted me to hold her in my arms. I quickly responded in Spanish, "Que cosa!" (what an idea!) and began the class.

I felt that Ramona's desire came from her wanting to be the little girl she had never been allowed to be. She was the oldest of four children and had had to assume a lot of the child care, because her mother, who was also quite bright, got herself a job that took her away from the home for hours at a time, making it necessary for Ramona to assume the care of the others, at a very early age. I had sympathy for both of them, but by this time, I felt totally incapable of trusting myself to take anyone in my arms, for whatever reason.

One morning in late September, I awoke with a migraine headache that I knew would keep me in bed for several days. After another day of rest from the pain, I would be able to to be up and at work once more. About two weeks into October, it happened again. This time, when I awoke the third day, free from the headache, but exhausted from the pain and lack of sleep, I suddenly knew I could not go on in this manner any longer. It was more frightening for me to continue my life as a nun and possibly bring ignominy on myself and the order, than to leave and go out into an unknown world, where I knew I would not have nearly the appreciation and esteem I held in the convent.

I got up, went to my superior and told Mother Dorothy of my resolution. The prioress was very sympathetic and felt, that indeed, I had struggled long enough. She called Mother Gerard right away, so the process for the dispensation of my vows could begin. I was told that I did not even have to remain in the convent until this was achieved. I simply had to continue practicing the vows, as well as I could, under the circumstances. On a practical level, this meant that I could not legally marry nor purchase any property, until I had received the dispensation from Rome.

I also learned that the Mother General from Angers was visiting in St. Paul and would be coming to Seattle in a few days. Mother Gerard thought that perhaps I would want to wait until I had an interview with the General. That was the last thing I wanted. I knew that this time I must leave. The possibility of going to the Mother House in France was absolutely terrifying. Mother Dorothy took me shopping for clothes that afternoon, which was Saturday. It was some time during that afternoon that I decided not to go back to using the name Georgette, which I had never liked, but would go by my first name, Anne.

That evening when I went into the refectory for supper, I was abashed to see the traditional flowers and the small box, filled with holy cards and other little gifts at my place. It had entirely slipped my mind that it was October 15, the feast of St. Teresa of Avila. It was almost beyond my capability to seem happy and grateful for the little remembrances. I left recreation early, with the excuse that I had something to attend to in the school. No one, from among the sisters or the girls, was to know I was leaving until after the fact.

I had already spoken with Dr. Jamison about the possibility of my leaving. He felt bad that I wouldn't be seeing Project Grow through, but was very sympathetic with my predicament. He knew of a teaching position in eastern Washington that had just opened and promised to help me attain it.

On Sunday Mother Dorothy tried to find an inexpensive place for me to stay, until I got a job. She telephoned three different women's residences in Seattle, since she felt that I shouldn't be alone for awhile. As soon as they learned how old I was (I was forty-one by then) none of them wanted to take me in. They felt that I would not fit in with the other occupants, who were mostly in their late teens or early twenties.

The next morning Mother Dorothy went over to the school to let the teachers know I would not be over. She ran into Mrs. Green, who taught typing and shorthand in the high school, and decided to confide in her as to why I would not be back in the school. She also spoke of not being able to find a place for me to stay while I was seeking employment. Mrs. Green suggested that I stay with her. Mrs. Green's husband was a building contractor and was up in Alaska on a project for the winter. She was not even Catholic, but she and I had become friends and I was relieved and happy to accept her offer.

Mother Dorothy gave me a purse and billfold with a hundred dollars to tide me through until I got a job. Not having been shopping for seventeen years, I felt that was more than generous.

After Mrs. Green's last class, I went off with her, still in my habit, but carrying a suitcase with my new clothing and the purse. Mother Dorothy had also given me permission to take my violin.

Arriving at Mrs. Green's beautiful suburban home, we continued a somewhat strained conversation, until finally, Mrs. Green said, "Aren't you going to show me your new clothes, Anne?"

I was grateful for the tactful way she was helping me make the transition, but being addressed by my new name was a shock, nonetheless. I excused myself, went to the guest bedroom and took off my habit. I didn't feel anything – relief or grief. I remained numb as I put on the new clothing.

Mrs. Green was obviously relieved and more relaxed with me in my new attire. She congratulated me on my good taste, got an appointment for me with her own hairdresser the next day and advised me as to what make-up was current.

I was truly grateful for Mrs. Green's interest and help, but was emotionally still numb. "Will I ever find joy in being a woman of the world?" I wondered.

CHAPTER SIXTEEN

As SISTER TERESA, I had forgotten all about the problems I had had with my very fine, wispy hair. It did have a good wave, which helped some and Mrs. Green's hair dresser did a fine job making the most of it. Afterwards, Mrs. Green took me to a department store and left me alone to make choices of lip stick and blush, the latter of which I had never worn before. I absolutely could not bring myself to wear eye makeup, even though it was currently in vogue.

While Mrs. Green was teaching during the days, I did dishes, vacuumed the rugs and any other chores I found waiting. I also prepared supper in the evenings. I perused the magazines lying around the house, but Mrs. Green didn't seem to have any books available. I was simply too numb to care.

Mrs. Green did lovely work with crafts and proudly showed me items she had made from pine cones, dried flowers and grasses, bits of bark, shells etc. I was especially taken with the large cones from Ponderosa pine trees.

Through Dr. Jamison, I was contacted by the superintendent of schools in the little town of Colville, Washington, where a position for an English teacher was open. Colville was on the other side of the state, close to the border with Idaho.

Mr. Pierce, the superintendent asked me to make the trip to Spokane, where he would meet me and give me an interview. I bought the necessary round trip ticket on the train that ran between Seattle and Spokane and left the following Saturday. The hundred dollars was diminishing rapidly.

I had the interview that afternoon, but had to stay overnight in a hotel, before I could return to Seattle. However, the interview seemed to have gone well, which was encouraging.

When I returned, Mrs. Green and I went grocery shopping and I insisted on helping with the purchase. I became anxious, however, as I saw the hundred dollars melt away.

In my interview, I had learned that Colville was nestled in the mountains and definitely had snow in the winter. Quickly, I realized I didn't have a winter coat, which I wouldn't have needed in Seattle. Besides that, I would need money for rent and groceries until I would receive my first check, which would not come until the following month.

The next day I called Mother Dorothy and told her of my situation. Remembering my inheritance of four thousand dollars, when Mama died, I asked Mother Dorothy if I couldn't have that. Mother Dorothy promised to call Mother Gerard with the request and sent another hundred dollars to me, via Mrs. Green, to cover expenses until I obtained the inheritance or received my first check.

Dr. Jamison arranged to take me out to lunch on Wednesday, when he told me that Mr. Pierce had been impressed with me. This was a relief, but I still felt somewhat insecure about it. Dr. Jamison also told me I would probably need a car fairly soon, since Colville was large enough that I couldn't walk everywhere, but small enough not to have public transportation. He offered to help me find a good second hand car. I was extremely grateful for this, since I would have had no idea how to go about getting one. I told him I would call him as soon as my inheritance arrived.

When I still hadn't heard from Mr. Pierce by Thursday, Mrs. Green insisted that I call him to find out if I had the job. I suddenly realized that my presence in Mrs. Green's home was becoming a strain for her.

When I made the call, I discovered that I did have the job, but that they wouldn't need me until the seventh of November, when the new grading period began. This was only the twenty-seventh of October, which meant almost another two weeks with Mrs. Green.

When I told Mrs. Green, she insisted that I call back and tell Mr. Pierce that I needed to come that weekend. She told me that it would be good for me to find an apartment and get settled in, before I began teaching. I was embarrassed that I hadn't thought of that, myself, and called Mr. Pierce the next day to tell him I needed to come Saturday, which was the next day. He promised to come and pick me up in Spokane and help me find an apartment. I was grateful and relieved that I wouldn't have to buy a bus ticket from Spokane to Colville. After paying for the one way ticket to Spokane, I was already into the second hundred dollars. Mother Dorothy hadn't known when my inheritance would arrive.

Mr. Pierce picked me up in Spokane late that Saturday morning and took me to an available apartment. It was furnished and seemed nice enough, so I paid my first month's rent, taking over half of what was left of the one hundred dollars. I walked down town to J. C. Penny's, the only department store in town, and tried to apply for a credit card, but although they knew I was going to teach at the high school, they refused to issue me one, because I had no credit rating. Reluctantly, I bought a set of sheets, a pillow and a blanket. I hardly had any money left for food, much less a winter coat. By then, it was getting late, so I rushed over to the grocery store and got food for a few days. As soon as I got home, I quickly put together a sandwich, which I hastily ate, made my bed and fell in it right away, thoroughly exhausted.

Early the following day, I went down town, where I found a pay telephone and called Mother Dorothy to give her my address, so she could mail my inheritance as soon as it came. The call took all but a little change of my money. I still hadn't called my sister, Margaret, to tell her that I had left the convent, but that would just have to wait.

I found the library, got a card and checked out a few books. They were able to direct me to the Cathoic Church. Exhausted by all the walking and my own emotional turmoil, I returned to my apartment, read a little, ate lunch and then felt rested enough to walk over to the Church in hopes of meeting the pastor. As soon as I told Father Smith of my experience with music, he asked me to direct the choir. "We have a fine organist, but she knows little about singing and finds it difficult to play and direct the choir at the same time. She'll be delighted to have your assistance," he assured me.

Right away, he telephoned Mrs. Delaney, the organist, who invited me over to her house for tea that very afternoon. Mrs. Delaney had a very comfortable older frame house on a corner, with a huge and beautiful garden in the back. After she had showed it to me, we went on in for tea and cookies. The friendly atmosphere brought my appetite back and I found myself enjoying the woman's stories about her past. She was a widow, whose two children lived on the coast. It was evident that she was eager for company. She seemed to understand why I wasn't eager to talk about my immediate past, but when she learned that I played the violin, she exclaimed, "Oh, my dear, you'll have to bring it over so we can play together! I love the violin! Surely you have some music?"

I was quick to assure her that I did and was excited about the prospect of playing music with someone who was obviously a serious musician. We planned to meet Wednesday afternoon and Mrs. Delaney invited me to stay for supper. When she discovered I didn't have a car, she insisted on coming to get me and promised a ride home.

"Listen, my dear, when you're ready to go shopping for food, let me know and I'll come and take you to the store. Do you have some food now?" she asked.

"Oh, yes. Yes, I do," I stammered, overcome with the woman's generosity and thoughtfulness. "That would be most kind of you, thank you. I surely will let you know," I promised, wondering when I would have the money to go shopping again.

Late that Tuesday afternoon, Mr. Pierce stopped by my apartment to see how I was faring. When he learned I didn't have a car, he made arrangements for the high school librarian to pick me up and take me to school until I got my own. "I know Mrs. Gleason will be happy to give you a ride," he assured me. "But you may as well come over to the school some day this week so I can show you your room and give you a list of your classes. You'll have three ninth grade English classes and two of remedial reading."

"Oh, dear, I haven't had any training in remedial reading," I blurted out.

"Well, we have two sets of SRA reading laboratories, which I'm sure you'll find quite helpful," he assured me. "It will be good for you to have a chance to look them over, however, to see how they work. Also we have a couple of speed reading machines, which we let students, who are planning to go on to college, use to increase not only their speed, but also raise their comprehension scores. You won't have to help them at all. Why don't I come over to your apartment around one on Thursday afternoon and we'll take you on a tour of the school."

"That would be wonderful, Mr. Pierce," I replied. "I'll be looking forward to it." Inside, I was grateful that I wouldn't have to cancel my appointment with Mrs. Delaney, the next day. I was most thankful to Mrs. Green for having encouraged me to come to Colville a week before I began teaching.

The following day, I enjoyed playing music with Mrs. Delaney as much as I had thought I would. The older woman began planning right away for us to play at various events around town. "I can't forget that you do have a full time job, however." she sighed. "Well, enough of that. I'm starved! How about you?" With that, she led me into her kitchen, asked me to set the table, while she finished putting our supper together. I was comfortable enough to eat heartily. The pot roast with potatoes and carrots was a welcome relief from variations on peanut butter sandwiches.

Before parting, Mrs. Delaney gave me the hymnals they used in Church and told me which ones the choir would be singing the coming Sunday. I gulped as I remembered that I had accepted the job as choral director, and was relieved to have a chance to look at the music ahead of time.

On Thursday, Mr. Pierce came to pick me up and take me to the high school, as promised. My main classroom would be where I would teach the English classes, there being a special room for remedial reading. I was instantly impressed with the SRA labs, as well as relieved, since I was certain they would work for me and my students. When he handed me my schedule, I saw that I would supervise a study hall immediately after lunch and had a free period in the morning in which to prepare for my classes. It all seemed quite possible.

"If you'd like to come in on Saturday morning to work on lesson plans, I could come and get you," Mr. Pierce offered. " I have some work to do then, myself."

"I would like that, thank you, Mr. Pierce."

"Mrs. Gleason often comes in on Saturdays and you could not only meet her, but she'd probably be happy to take you home, if I stay longer than you need. I can get so much more done when there's not a lot of people around."

He drove me home and when I went to go in my apartment, there was a notice on my door that there was a registered letter waiting for me at the post office. I quickly summoned up the energy to go get it, as I realized it must be my inheritance. After picking up the check, I went over to the bank across the street to open a checking account and get some much needed cash. I thought of Mama and was comforted with the feeling that somehow she was still helping me.

On Friday morning, Mrs. Delaney took me grocery shopping, as she had offered, as well as to the telephone company to arrange for a telephone, which they installed that afternoon. First, I called Dr. Jamison to let him know I had the money for a car. He thought he could have one for me by the following weekend and generously offered to drive it over to Colville. "I'll get my son to drive our car, and it will be like a mini-vacation for us," he explained.

Then I called Mother Dorothy to let her know the money had arrived. Next I called Mrs. Green to tell her I was doing well and to give her my address and telephone number. Finally, I called my sister, Margaret.

My memories from my visit at Margaret's, which I had had over a year ago, helped me immensely to be able to imagine my sister in her home, as I broke the news. At first, she wondered why I hadn't come down to be with them in Sacramento. I explained how Dr. Jamison had been helpful in finding me a job right away, which I felt I could hardly let go by.

"What about coming down for a visit during your Christmas vacation, then?" Margaret asked.

"That's a good idea!" I replied. "I can't make definite plans now, but as soon as I get the school's calendar, I'll see about taking a bus down to Sacramento."

Then I went back down town to get the much needed winter coat. I had already experienced how cold it was becoming in the evenings. I found a pea green coat with a quilted lining, which I was sure would keep me warm.

That evening after a good meal, I decided I would use some of the money to buy a record player and some records to play in the evenings to assuage my loneliness, while I ate my evening meal. That seemed to be the time I felt it most. I felt a little guilty about spending money on such a luxury item, but quickly banished the thought as I realized I needed to take care of my emotional needs as well as the physical. Besides, I knew Mama would have approved.

Then I began to think of lesson plans for my English classes. I remembered allowing Ramona to write a paper on Hemingway and how much she had benefited from this. I wondered if it would be possible to let some of my students write research papers. I believed that most students had a good understanding of grammar by the time they reached the eighth grade and most of them wouldn't use what was contained in high school texts, after they graduated. But how would I know which students had a good concept of grammar and usage and which did not. I decided to make up a diagnostic test to give to the entire class and use those to let me know who needed more work on grammar and who did not. I stayed up most of the night working on the test, believing I could put it on a ditto master the next morning and have it ready to administer the following Monday.

I decided that those students, who were proficient in grammar, could be working on their papers, while I was teaching grammar to the others. When I would give them all time to do assignments in class, those who were working on papers could get passes to the library, while the others would do their grammar assignments. The class, as a whole, would do the literature section together. I would also encourage those writing research papers to use the town library. It was the first time I had felt this much enthusiasm for anything, since I had left the convent and now I was free from having to make the decision of leaving or remaining.

The following Monday morning when I met with my first ninth grade English class, I introduced myself and carefully took roll, trying to put names with faces in my memory. Then I laid out my plan to the students. I passed out my diagnostic tests, which took up the rest of the period. My free period was next and I was able to grade most of them in that time. I was pleased to note that over half the class did well on them. I did the same for my second English class and was able to correct most of them during the study hall I supervised after lunch.

As I helped individual students in the remedial reading classes, I was pleasantly surprised to find how interesting the stories, provided by the SRA lab were. Somehow they were able to make them interesting at every level of reading ability. Not only were they interesting to me, but to the students, as well. and not only were they interesting, but I was learning things about science, geography and history as well.

After I finished with my last English class, I completed the day with the second class in remedial reading, leaving me with the last set of diagnostic tests to take home and correct.

That night I discovered that about two thirds of each class would be able to write term papers, which was a pleasant surprise. Of those, two or three from each class decided they would rather not write papers. Most of those writing papers went to the library during the grammar period. I had told them to have a tentative outline for their paper by Friday. When I discovered most of them hadn't made an outline before, I prepared a lesson on making outlines, which I taught the whole class. This delayed getting in the outlines for the term papers until the following week. However, I was delighted at the diversity of subjects on which they had chosen to write.

In the meantime, I received an invitation one evening from Mrs. Haroldson, to come over for Sunday dinner. The Haroldsons had two children in the high school, although neither of them were in any of my classes. However, Jim and Julie had heard about the term papers and had told their mother about them, since they wanted to write one, too. Joy Haroldson was impressed by the idea and said she would have liked to write one herself.

At dinner, I discovered that Mr. Haroldson was a dentist and Joy tried her hand at oil painting. The conversation during the meal was interesting and, afterwards we three adults went to see Dr. Zhivago at the only motion picture theater in town. I was moved by the story, but it would be the scenes in the ice and snow in Siberia that would remain with me.

Later in the month, the Haroldsons took me up to their cabin at the edge of a lake in Canada, in order to close it up for the winter. The lake was surrounded by mountains and, again, I had the pleasure of smelling the needles of many conifers and seeing the beautiful colors of the few deciduous trees. I was more than happy to help with the chores, interspersed with a wonderful picnic lunch. At one and the same time, I was happy in the company of a family setting, but after leaving them, I was assailed by feelings of unreality and of being uncomfortably different. I began to doubt that I would ever fit in enough to have a family of my own.

After riding to and from school with Mrs. Gleason, the librarian, a few times, the older woman invited me to her home to have dinner with her. She, too, was a widow, with several children, none of whom lived in town. She remained alone in their family home, which was most comfortable, but the woman's loneliness was obvious. I bought some dishes so I could return the favor, but we really did not have much in common to speak of, even though we both read a good deal. It was the first of many experiences I would have, where the main topic of conversation was about children, in which I had nothing to contribute. If I spoke of my own childhood to make some comparison with their stories, I could feel that they felt it strange that I found my childhood experiences comparable to those of their children. My experiences as a surrogate mother to many girls over the years didn't seem comparable at all.

It was the librarian, who told me that Joy Haroldson came from a wealthy family, which had established a very successful lumber business in the area, and that it was the woman's money that enabled them to have such a lovely home and the cabin in Canada. She definitely felt that Joy had married beneath her status. I had noted how polite Mr. Haroldson was with his wife, but felt they were truly a happy family. At least I hoped so. It was important for me to believe this.

Mrs. Delaney had me over for a Thanksgiving meal, at which one of her sons and his family were present. The couple had children about the age of the Haroldson's and the main topic of conversation was of their adventures, which, again, made me feel out of it, with very little to add. I was grateful that when Mrs. Delaney and I were alone, the two of us had other things to talk about.

One evening in December, I received a long distance telephone call from Ramona and several other girls from the Home in Seattle.

"How did you ever get hold of my number?" I asked. They admitted they had wheedled it out of Mrs. Green. Their wanting to know how I was doing made me realize just how much I was living on a somewhat superficial level, but I hoped this was a necessary step in making the adjustment to my new life. I told them about my students writing term papers and shared some of the topics with them.

They regaled me with stories from the convent, telling me who the new principal was and that she had abandoned Project Grow. This news brought tears to my eyes, not only because I hated to see that happen, but also I could understand how difficult it must have been for the young sister, who had been under me in the juniorate, to come in to a new program of which she was totally ignorant and unprepared. When Dr. Jamison had delivered my car, he hadn't told me of this.

As Christmas drew near, I decided to go by bus to Sacramento to visit Margaret and her family, but because of time limitations, I would fly back. It had been years since I had ridden on a bus and had never made such a long journey that way before. My height made it very uncomfortable most of the way, since my long legs were jammed against the seat in front of me, unless I had the seat to myself, when I could turn sideways and stretch out a little. This did not happen often. I was on overnight and was able to sleep very little. I was relieved that I had made plans to fly back.

After resting some after the bus trip, I was able to enjoy visiting with Margaret, speaking fondly of Mama and getting to know her four children some, although they didn't seem to be home much. They were all in high school and had a lot of outside interests. Johnny, who had been born prematurely and had cerebral palsy, as well as being blind, was often the only one home in the evenings.

We planned a trip to San Francisco, which was a first for me. Again,

Johnny was the only one of the children to come with us. The day was sunny and bright and with very little wind. For this to happen in December was a real treat.

I was amazed when I learned that Johnny could give the make, model and year of a car passing by, just from hearing it. I also learned he played trumpet and had perfect pitch. He belonged to a band and also sang with it.

We went to Golden Gate Park, the Cannery and Ghirardelli Square and had a delicious seafood dinner at a restaurant on the Wharf. I was intrigued by the artists and musicians selling their wares on the sidewalk. With their bright costumes and long hair, I wondered if they were hippies like the ones my students in Seattle had described. Their friendliness made me certain that I would return there some time.

January first was the twenty-third wedding anniversary of Margaret and John and we went to a very nice restaurant, having cocktails before dinner and wine to drink during the meal. I became very uncomfortable with my fuzzy thinking and some loss of equilibrium and wondered how people could enjoy getting drunk. I determined never to drink that much again.

The next day, which was also the day I was returning to Colville, I awoke with a severe headache from the drinking. I was relieved the plane trip would make the journey home much shorter, although I would have to take a bus from Spokane to Colville. By the time I arrived at my apartment, the headache was gone and I actually looked forward to returning to my classes the following day.

In spite of having made a few friends and feeling I was doing a creditable job at the high school, I was struggling with feelings of alienation and depression. My evenings and weekends became almost unbearable. Finally, I went to a physician in town to get a refill on my prescription for Stelazine. He gladly made out the prescription, but also referred me to a psychiatrist in Spokane, whom he felt certain would help me. It was February, however, before I could get an appointment.

When I had left the Order, I had written to Florence, the girl who helped me in the school in Omaha and Marie, whom I had helped in curbing her temper by shooting baskets. They had both written to me ever since I had left Omaha. I felt it would be unfair not to let them know of my whereabouts, as I realized they depended somewhat on my advice and support. Florence had married and very recently had a daughter, whom she had named Teresa. I sent my namesake a huge teddy bear for Christmas, since teddy bears had been my favorite toy when I was a child.

Marie had moved around some, getting trained as a psych tech at one point. I was amazed and not too happy, when I came home one afternoon and found a letter from Marie, telling me she was on her way to Colville, giving me the time when her bus would arrive. By the time the letter arrived, it would be the following evening when I was to meet her.

Realizing my own vulnerability and feelings of insecurity as I was adjusting to my new life, I felt unable to cope with someone who was probably even more insecure than I. It seemed that it took every bit of my energy to live through each day. Besides that, my apartment had only one bedroom and I did not look forward to sharing my bed with Marie or anyone else. The couch was definitely too small for a bed for Marie, who was almost as tall as I and much heavier. However, there was no way to reach Marie and tell her not to come.

The next evening, I arrived early at the bus depot, which was not even open and watched as Marie and the driver got off. The latter dragged out three huge cartons from the baggage unit under the bus. Since no one else got off the bus, I knew they all belonged to Marie. This told me that Marie had come to stay.

Somehow I was able to hold back the tears of anguish smarting my eyes.

Instead I gave her a welcoming hug and together we squeezed the cartons into the trunk and back seat of my car.

After we arrived at my apartment, I said, "Marie, you should have written me sooner, telling me you wanted to come. This is a one bedroom apartment and I really can't afford something larger."

"Oh, that's all right, Mother .. er I mean Anne. I can sleep on the couch. I've done that lots of times!"

"Just look at that couch, Marie. I don't think you could even spend one night on it, it's so small." Then seeing tears filling Marie's eyes, I quickly added, "Well, we'll just have to do the best we can. At least it's a double bed."

As the weekend approached, I felt desperate enough to tell Marie that I would take her down to Spokane on Saturday and help her find a job and an apartment.

"It is simply too crowded in my apartment and I doubt if you can find a job in a small town like Colville. Spokane is only seventy miles away and I'll come down on weekends and either visit there or bring you back to Colville. I'm not abandoning you." Marie did not cry this time, but stoically accepted my will. "We won't take all your things, just enough for you to get by for a week. In a couple weeks I'm going to be seeing a psychiatrist there and afterwards we can do what ever we want." I was taking it for granted that Marie wouldn't be working on weekends. I forgot entirely that I would have to be back Sunday mornings to direct the choir.

The first thing we did when we arrived in Spokane was to buy a newspaper and look for jobs in the want ads. We didn't see anything for psychiatric institutions, but there were several ads for aides in nursing homes.

We bought a map of Spokane and went in search of the nursing homes. By the time we had found the first one and Marie completed an unsatisfactory interview, (unsatisfactory because they only needed part time help which wouldn't have covered Marie's expenses) it was time for lunch. We found an Arctic Circle and wolfed down hamburgers, French fries and milk shakes, which made us both feel better.

The afternoon became more and more discouraging as we searched out the other nursing homes, only to find that the jobs had been covered or that they only needed part time help. We found a Kentucky Fried Chicken, where we bought supper and finally headed back for Colville. Fortunately, Marie fell asleep in the car and it wasn't necessary to try to make conversation.

Since Marie was Catholic, the following morning she went to Mass with me, but she was unhappy because she had to sit alone, while I directed the choir.

I asked her if she would like to sing with us, but she declined, saying she wasn't a very good singer. However, the offer made Marie feel that she was going to get to stay in Colville. As a matter of fact, I didn't feel like we could go through another Saturday like the one we had just experienced.

Marie began to complain that she didn't have anything to do during the day and wondered if we couldn't get a television. I had never owned one and couldn't see that one would be necessary, so I bought an inexpensive radio. Magazines began to appear around the house, which told me Marie had some money, but she never offered to help with food and I realized she probably didn't have much.

In the meantime, my students who were writing term papers were running out of materials from the town and school libraries. I showed them how to use the *Reader's Guide to Periodical Literature*, and told them to make lists of magazines or books relating to their subject and promised to try and get some of them in Spokane. I took Marie with me, but finding a job was not discussed. It was then that I found out that Marie didn't like to read books, which brought out a huge difference between us.

Marie kept the apartment clean and did the laundry, but felt inadequate to cook supper. I discovered that having to cook for someone else as well as for myself, was a powerful incentive to prepare good meals. Marie was a most appreciative consumer.

When it was time for my first appointment with Dr. Colson, the psychiatrist in Spokane, I had to insist that I go alone this first time and gave Marie money to take in a movie while I was gone. As I drove down, I had an intimation of how dull Marie's life must be, since I was gone most of the five days, but I had no idea of how to help her discover friends her own age. After supper in the evenings, I always had papers to correct. Besides that, I was so caught up in my own problems, I didn't have the energy to take on Marie's.

The visit with the psychiatrist was most unsatisfactory. When he found out that I had been a nun, he spent forty of the fifty minutes I had paid for confiding that he was an exorcist. For me, exorcism was only something I had read about, not with much interest. He laughed that if his colleagues in the building they shared ever found out, he would probably be kicked out. It was hard for me to feel empathy. Finally, he told me I would have to do something about my hair, should get contact lenses and gave me the name of a charm school, where I could get help in selecting clothes and how to act "in the world." This certainly didn't inspire confidence that I was doing anything right, at the present. However, he took me off the Ritalin and Stelazine I had been taking and put me on Elavil and a new prescription for a sleeping pill.

Before I left Spokane, I got an appointment with an ophthomologist, and visited the charm school, where I was told their main purpose was to help young girls, who were interested in becoming models or working in commercials on television. However, they felt they could help me, so I decided to give them a try. I realized it would be good for me to get a new permanent, which I could do in Colville.

Over a period of time, I felt that the Elavil was an improvement over the other medications and was glad I had made a follow up appointment with

Dr. Colson, in spite of his being an exorcist. At least he hadn't suggested that I needed exorcising.

After two sessions, he didn't seem to have the need to speak of his exorcising experiences, or perhaps he sensed my definite disinterest. He was pleased with my attempt to get used to the new contacts and while he wasn't too impressed with the permanent, even suggesting I try wearing a wig, I didn't tell him that after three sessions at the charm school, I knew what they were teaching was not for me. None of the women teachers nor the wives of the male teachers at school acted like the instructors at the charm school wanted me to. I was relieved that I hadn't had to pay for the entire ten session course, but could pay for each session as it occurred.

One night shortly after Marie and I had gone to bed, Marie asked if we couldn't snuggle. I felt ashamed that I hadn't thought of Marie's need of comforting and gladly complied. I was totally unprepared for the consequence that both of our bodies were inflamed with sexual desire and before I knew it we were making love. I was filled with conflicting feelings about it, but couldn't bring it to an end. Shortly after, Marie fell asleep, but I was awake for the rest of the night, aghast at myself but feeling some pleasure from it in spite of myself.

I had discovered through one of my students that the man whose place I had taken at the high school, had been fired because he had been caught making lewd suggestions to one of his male students. I realized that Marie was still a minor and that if we were discovered, I could be in deep trouble. I determined that it would not happen again.

Even though I had been very faithful to the choir rehearsals and attending Sunday Mass, I couldn't bring myself to receive Holy Communion. I would go down from the choir loft and kneel in the back of the church while the others received. This little act of duplicity did not help my self respect. Now, after the experience with Marie, I realized that I should go to confession, but simply could not bring myself to do it.

★ ★ ★ ★ ★

The brightest thing in my life was the success of the term papers of my students. They were most enthused and when they began to finish them, I had them present their papers to the class. Even those who had not written one, enjoyed hearing them. Most of all everyone was learning.

One evening when I came home from work, Marie was not there. I looked around for a note, but there was none. I put my things away and began to prepare supper. Finally, Marie came in all smiles.

"I bet you'll never believe what I did today!"

"Well, give me a try," I replied, glad that I hadn't started to scold her.

"There's a nursing home in town and I've got a job there. I'll be starting tomorrow."

"Well, congratulations!" I immediately responded. "After supper, why don't we go out for a root beer float to celebrate."

When I came home a week later, there was a thirteen inch black and white television installed in the living room. It had taken Marie's entire paycheck to obtain it. I was more embarrassed than angry. I finally realized that if you had been brought up with a television, life would be quite difficult without one. Besides, I didn't really expect Marie to help with our combined expenses, since she was barely making minimum wage. I would just insist that she buy her own clothes and take care of her recreational expenses.

I began joining Marie watching some of the later programs just before the ten o' clock news. I had to laugh out loud when I saw the women in commercials walking, standing and sitting just like I had been taught in the charm school.

In spite of my promise to myself, occasionally Marie and I would make love.

I really wasn't sure how I felt, but I knew it was risky on my part to let it happen. I came to realize that it was my own neediness that kept me from stopping it all together, especially when I knew I wasn't really in love with her. Such lack of will was unprecedented in my life and added to my depression.

As the weather turned for the better with the coming of spring, my mechanic told me how to get to a beautiful secluded picnic spot in the mountains surrounding Colville. It was by a rather large stream, swollen from the winter snows. Both Marie and I loved it. Although Marie had never had the opportunity to spend much time in the wilderness, she sensed my happiness with it and was soon learning the calls of various birds and enjoying climbing over rocks, as well as the smell of crushed pine needles. We got into the habit of packing a picnic lunch and spending our Sunday afternoons there. As a result we became closer.

However, Marie did not help in keeping the few friends I had made. The Haroldsons invited me over for a Sunday dinner and when I told them about Marie, they were glad to include her in the invitation. With the weather being so nice, we were all out in the back yard by the garage, where Marie saw a small motorcycle just inside.

"Oh, boy!" she cried with delight. "Could I take a ride on your motorcycle? I used to ride one all the time!" Mrs. Haroldson finally gave her permission, but I could tell it was with some reluctance. Marie had told me how she and one of her brothers had owned a motorcycle together and how much she had enjoyed riding, but I found myself wishing Mrs. Haroldson hadn't been talked into it.

When Marie got it out and started the motor up, it was evident that she was familiar with the procedure. She took off with a wave and it was two and a half hours before we saw her again. Mrs. Haroldson kept asking where she could have gone and I certainly had no idea. We remained standing by the garage the entire time, looking in the distance and listening for the sound of the motor. When she did return, I asked her where she had been and let her know how worried we had been. It was evident that Marie did not see why we had worried and only made matters worse when she offered to pay for the gasoline. We were never invited to the Haroldsons again.

Mrs. Delaney also invited the two of us over for a meal and while a similar crises didn't occur, it was also the last time I was invited to come over and play music.

The worst fright I received was the night I had been correcting papers until about eleven p.m. I thought that Marie had gone to bed, when she came slouching in, her eyes and lips swollen and handed me the half empty bottle of my sleeping pills.

"I...I took shum of your shleeping pills and now I'm schared. I took too many, I guess." With that she fell on the floor, utterly unconscious. I tried to arouse her, shaking her and splashing cold water on her face. Neither the shaking nor the cold water had any effect. By then it was quite chilly outside, so I put my coat on and put Marie's on her the best I could. My terror enabled me to drag her out the door and down the flight of stairs to the ground floor and, even with more difficulty, push her into the back seat of my car. I drove over to the emergency room of the town hospital, where those on duty got Marie out of the car and onto a gurney. I remained there while they pumped her stomach, and being assured that she would probably be all right, left to at least get some rest before teaching the next day.

I called the hospital the following morning and was told Marie was sleeping normally and would probably be released later in the day. Of course it was next to impossible for me to keep my mind on my classes, at the same time that it enabled me not to think continuously about her predicament. I was ashamed, but I couldn't help wondering what might happen when the story got around town.

Marie telephoned me shortly after lunch to tell me that she was ready to come home. I told her she would have to wait in the hospital lounge until school was out and I was free to get her. I was relieved that no one asked about the call and, in fact, no one in town ever brought up the subject. I was certain Marie was unaware that she had been instrumental in my losing friends, although she did apologize about taking the sleeping pills.

I persuaded Marie to see Dr. Colson, which she finally agreed to under duress. Afterwards, when Marie started sobbing and begged me not to make her go back, I realized the mistake I had made in lining up the two of them together. I didn't insist that she go again.

About this time, Margaret sent me a newspaper article about the scarcity of teachers in California, telling of *teacher scouts* going to neighboring states to find applicants. It even gave the dates when one would be in Spokane and an address to send a letter, if one had an interest in being interviewed. Of course, Margaret wanted me to see if there were any vacancies in Sacramento. By this time, I felt independent enough to do that; I knew Margaret and John would expect me to have my own apartment. Quite soon I sent a letter speaking of my interest in teaching in Sacramento.

The school district replied almost by return mail, giving me a date, time and place to be for the interview. Now I thought I should tell Mr. Pierce, my superintendent, of my plans and tender a resignation. He was very understanding of my wish to be near my sister. Then he asked me a very unforeseen question.

"Haven't you had any problems with Eric, John or Tom in your afternoon remedial reading class? We sent them in to you at the beginning of the new semester, because they were causing problems in their English class."

"Why, no. They haven't been a problem at all," I answered in surprise.

"Well, I kind of guessed that, since you never complained, but I was surprised, and pleased, I must say. I also liked your idea of having your better

English students write term papers. You can expect a good reference from me and Mr. Smith, (the principal) when you make your application for a job in Sacramento."

I didn't say so, but I gave most of the credit to the SRA labs for my success with the *problem* boys. Also, the diagnostic test I had administered to them showed that they were a year or two behind in their reading ability. Perhaps on some level they were glad for the opportunity to get themselves caught up.

By late April, I was offered a job teaching English in a junior high school in Sacramento on the same side of town and fairly close to where my sister lived. I accepted with alacrity.

Early in May, I woke up one morning crying hysterically and beating my pillow. At first, I didn't know why, but I knew I was extremely angry from a feeling of having been betrayed. I found it hard to breathe, and was crying in great gulps to get air into my lungs.

Suddenly I screamed a long and piercing cry. Realizing where I was, I stopped, wondering if I had awakened anyone, or even if someone outside the building had heard. Nonetheless, I began beating my pillow and sobbing again, not caring if anyone had heard, although I didn't scream again..

Then I asked myself what was provoking such great anger. The answer was forthcoming. I felt betrayed by Jesus. This meant I felt betrayed by God, in the Second Person of the Blessed Trinity This brought me up short for a minute. It was pretty terrifying to be angry with God.

But angry I was! "I worked as hard as I could to please You," I said. "I was faithful to the rules and regulations of the Order. I even overcame the temptations of the last few years enough that at least I didn't bring scandal on the Order and on the Church. Or on You." There was no reply. I felt abandoned and, thus betrayed.

After my sobbing subsided, I began to question the existence of God, for the first time in my life. I wondered why He would want his chosen ones to give up affection and expressions of love, including through sexuality, when He had created us with these needs. I had long been uncomfortable with the descriptions of His jealousy and violence in the Old Testament from the time I first read the book of Exodus and even more so, the Prophets. I finally concluded that if there was, indeed a God, He was some One who was far beyond the comprehension of mere human beings. I decided that when I left Colville, I would stop attending Mass. I was definitely no longer a Roman Catholic.

It was only then that I gratefully realized that Marie had been at work that morning.

In early June, when school let out, I rented a U Haul, packed it with our few possessions and Marie and I began our trip down to Sacramento. I had great hopes that life would improve, being near my sister.

CHAPTER SEVENTEEN

MARIE AND I actually had fun on the overnight trip to Sacramento from Colville. We sang *Do You Know the Way to San Jose?* with Dionne Warwick everytime it came on the radio and when we ate supper at a restaurant just after crossing over into California, I ordered my first daiquiri and slipped a few sips to Marie, who was just under twenty-one. Even after a short night in a motel, we were quite exhausted when we finally arrived at Margaret's the following evening and were more than content to sleep on the living room floor for the night.

The next day we were able to rent a furnished one bedroom apartment, fairly close to the school where I would be teaching and also near Margaret's home.

It was much more spacious than the apartment in Colville and with nicer furniture. Spending so much time with Marie on the trip down, I noticed how innocent she was, in spite of her difficult childhood. One way this innocence expressed itself was the absolute trust she had in me. Marie apparently had no idea of the struggles I was going through adjusting to life in the world . Her trust and dependence made me uncomfortable but I had no idea how to deal with it without destroying her confidence in me, which she seemed to need very much.

I drove over to Sacramento State College to see about the three upper division English courses I needed to be fully certified as a high school English teacher in California. I was able to enroll in two summer classes at the campus in the city and a third class to be offered up at South Lake Tahoe later in the summer.

The first class was on eighteenth Century English Literature. The professor looked like Sigmund Freud and his lectures were obtuse; they did not lend themselves to help me like or even understand John Donne or any of the other writers we studied. I had to be satisfied with a C. The class in Twentieth Century Drama was most interesting and I easily earned an A.

When I went to the Sacramento Public School Administration building to give them my transcript, I learned that because of my twelve years of teaching in the convent, plus the one year in Colville, my salary would be over nine hundred dollars a month, almost three times as much as I had earned in Colville. I could hardly believe my good fortune. Marie was jubilant when I shared the good news. The following weekend she approached me about needing a car for herself, if she was to get a job in a large city like Sacramento.

"Marie, I won't be getting paid that salary for another four months," I remonstrated. "There's no way I could help you get a car now."

"Well, can't we at least go look?" Marie asked. "We have time now. After you start teaching, you won't have time."

I knew this would probably be true and decided that it wouldn't hurt to look at a car dealership down the street and around the corner from our apartment. With Marie's encouragement, I ended up buying a new car for myself, even though the Fairlane was quite satisfactory. The first salesman had told me they would give me a six hundred dollar trade-in for the Fairlane, but when I was in the office with the dealer, he quickly said they couldn't give me more than three hundred dollars, which would leave me with a monthly payment of seventy-two dollars. I wondered why the discrepancy with what the first salesman had told me, but was unable to say anything. Besides, I reasoned, earning close to a thousand a month, I should be able to swing the monthly payment. Actually, I just didn't have the nerve to get out of the deal. In a haze, I found myself signing the contract and becoming the owner of a new chartreuse Ford Futura Falcon.

Unfortunately, this would not be the last time I would act on the spur of the moment without sufficient planning.

The class in Lake Tahoe on the American Transcendentalists wasn't of great interest, but at least I understood it enough to get a B. Nevertheless, the two weeks turned out to be a very healing experience, because every afternoon I would go to the lake, wade out until the water was up to my neck and then float on my back, taking in the beauty of the surrounding mountains and the brilliantly blue sky. The current of the lake gently drew me back to the shore, where I would lay in the warm sand, and even sleep a little. After several trips out to the middle of the lake and back, I would be restored enough to return to the motel, eat some supper and do my homework for the next day.

When I returned home, Marie had purchased two plaster black cats, which she had hung on our living room wall behind the couch. I was amazed and grateful at how much this made the apartment our own.

One evening, when I was visiting Margaret and John at their home, John suggested that he and I do some dancing.

"I never was the dancer Margaret is and I haven't danced for years!" I demurred.

"Then it's about time you're getting back into it," John insisted, as he got up and put a Benny Goodman record on their turn table.

The music quickly brought me back to my years in high school and college, which were not years filled with dating and dancing with men. But, as with the salesman who sold me the Falcon, I didn't have the energy or will power to refuse.

Even though John was barely my height, somehow I found myself able to follow him. Wisely, he avoided doing any fancy steps; however, I was acutely uncomfortable with how tight he held me. I was barely aware when Margaret got up suddenly, announcing that she was going to bed. When we finally sat down, he remained very close to me. He tried to kiss me, but I automatically turned my face away. "Margaret won't care," he assured me. It sounded like a "line" to me and I again refused to kiss.

"I…I thought you were going to introduce me to some of your friends at work," I finally stammered, as I moved away from him.

"I will," he said, "but I thought you could use a little practice first."

Somehow I found the strength to get up, saying, "I need to go home and get to bed myself."

At home in bed, I lay there stiff with fear, wondering if I had made him angry enough to break off any more visits with Margaret. I ended up sobbing in great gulps, filled with fear and the feeling that there were no answers to this unforeseen problem.

Finally, it was time to prepare for the classes I had been assigned; one in seventh, another in eighth, as well as two ninth grade English classes and a class in Journalism. I was surprised to receive very detailed outlines of the subjects I was to cover. Especially disheartening was learning I was to teach Shakespeare's *Julius Caesar* to the ninth graders. To counteract this, I decided to spend a day each week, putting on modern plays, even though it wasn't in the outline.

Although Clancy Junior High was one of the first to be racially inte-

grated in Sacramento, I was quick to notice that on the school grounds during lunch breaks, the students quickly segregated themselves into groups of
Anglos, Hispanics, Blacks and Asians. Often fights broke out between some
of the boys.

In Colville I had allowed my students to choose their own seats, but here
I decided it might be the better part of wisdom to seat them alphabetically.
All went well for several days, but in one of my ninth grade classes, where this
system brought two black boys sitting next to each other, I had a white girl
exchange seats with one of the boys, hoping to stop their constant chatter.
It stopped the chatter, but after the class, the girl came up in tears, begging
me not to make her sit next to that "dirty nigger". "He smells awful, Miss
Benton, really he does." she claimed. "So much for integration," I thought. I
spent a great deal of time that night working out a solution and finally, the
next day changed several students' seats, hoping that my reasons for making
the changes wouldn't be obvious.

The next time I visited with Margaret and John, he initiated the dancing
sequence again. This time Margaret got up, at once, to go to bed.

"Don't you want to dance, too?" I quickly called out. "Maybe that would
help me," I continued in desperation. However, she remained firm in her decision to retire.

This time John put on a Tommy Dorsey record and, again, began dancing with me slowly, holding me close as before. In my discomfort, I began
to stumble.

"Hey, relax!" John said, holding me closer, not trying anything other
than just swaying with the music.

Finally he released me, saying, "I have an idea. Let's go over to your
apartment." Did he think it would help getting farther away from Margaret,
I wondered. He helped me into my coat and led the way to his car. I went
along in a stupor, fearfully wondering what would happen when we got
there. After he had parked in my space behind the apartment building, he
suggested we sit in the back seat and "pitch a little woo."

It was not at all what I wanted to do, but I was afraid to make him angry
enough that he would break off my seeing Margaret. Doing as he said seemed
the lesser of two evils. This time he kissed me deeply, forcing my mouth open
and pushing his tongue inside. I was thoroughly repulsed, but unable to think
of what to do to stop it. By then, he was breathing in a way that I knew he
would be wanting to do the unthinkable. Did he forget he was married to

my sister? He seemed to hear my thoughts as he gasped, "Margaret doesn't care, honest," as he pushed me down on the seat and fumbled for my panties. My garter belt definitely got in the way. Suddenly he got up, cursing. "What do you say we go inside?"

I was terrified. Then I remembered that Marie would probably be home and in bed. I told him this and he gave up and silently took us back to his house so I could get my car.

While the discipline in my classes wasn't as bad as it had been before I entered the convent, it was difficult enough to take the joy out of teaching. In one of my ninth grade classes there was a boy who enjoyed being the class clown.

When I would discipline him by telling him to come in after school, Joey was Mr. Charm, himself, cleaning the chalk boards and doing anything I asked, including promising not to clown around again. But the temptation was too great. I began sending him to the vice principal, instead.

One morning, while I was correcting papers during my free period, the vice principal sent for me. I was certain it was about Joey, which was a relief. I hoped Mr. Brown could help us work out something, as I had helped my teachers and students when I had been principal in the Convent. Instead, as soon as I walked into the office, Mr. Brown abruptly fired a question at Joey.

"Joey, do you know what happens when you've been sent to me more than three times in a nine week period?"

"Yessir!" the boy mumbled.

"Then stoop over and put your hands on your feet," Mr. Brown commanded.

"Miss Benton, you will witness that I do not injure the boy in any way." With that the vice principal took up a wooden paddle made from a two by four and gave a resounding thwack on the boy's buttocks. The boy stood up, face red and tears burning at the edges of his eyes. He glared at me and left the room.

"That should do the trick," Mr. Brown declared and dismissed me.

In shock I returned to my room. I had never been told of the rule about a student having three chances to conform before getting paddled. In fact, I had believed that paddling was illegal. Had I known of the rule, I never would have sent Joey in. He may not have been physically injured, but I knew I had lost any respect he might have had for me, and could well imagine that the entire class would be down on me. I was right. Discipline problems in that class became rampant. They seemed to sense my own feelings of guilt.

From the beginning, I had forced myself to eat lunch in the teacher's lounge, hoping to get some ideas for maintaining discipline. I persisted, even though, after perfunctory greetings, we always ate in complete silence, looking glum and dissatisfied. The same week I had the encounter with Mr. Brown and Joey, one of the men teachers came into the lounge all upset because he had pushed a student into a chalk board. The teacher was over six feet tall and must have weighed close to three hundred pounds. He wasn't concerned if he had perhaps injured the boy, but was worried that he might be sued and lose his position.

I began shaking all over on hearing his story; I decided then and there that I simply could not remain at Clancy any longer. I put in my resignation after school that afternoon.

Before this occurred, I had made an appointment with a physician Margaret had recommended. I was out of Elavil and had decided to see what he would think of my going off psychotropic drugs all together, since they seemed to make me feel dead inside. While I was sitting in the waiting room, I was interested to see that he had a Ph.D. in humanities as well as his M.D. in internal medicine. He sympathized with my reaction to the psychotropic drugs and agreed with my assessment and plan. After quitting my teaching job, I regretted that I wouldn't be able to see him on a contining basis, being without medical insurance. My depression was replaced by severe anxiety attacks, keeping me awake at nights and destroying my appetite. However, I felt it was understandable, considering what was taking place in my life, and I decided that I would just have to bear with it..

At the end of the month I had to move from the apartment to one room, until I obtained another job. It was barely large enough to hold a single bed and a hot plate. There wasn't even a closet to hang my clothes.

In the meantime, Marie had gotten a job at a home for developmentally disabled children. She was a house mother for one of the groups, which meant she worked there for four twenty four hour days and then was off for three days. I was surprised at the responsibilities she had been given, but she seemed to do a good job of it. She had been offered a small room to stay in on her three days off, which certainly came in handy until I could get employment.

When Margaret learned that I had left my job, she told me she had seen want ads for government social workers in the Sacramento Bee. A person could prepare for the government tests which were a prerequisite for an interview, by checking out a book from the library and memorizing the material. After I had done this, Margaret took me around to several places in the northern part of the state, where they were seeking applicants. In Stockton, about fifty miles south of Sacramento, I was granted an interview with the head of the Social Service Department at the San Joaquin General Hospital. I was given the job late in November, but would not begin until December 23. In the meantime, I found a seasonal job at Weinstock's department store, which kept me from totally depleting my checking account.

On one of my days off, Marie coaxed me into coming to the group home and helping the children decorate for Christmas. I wasn't much into the spirit of Christmas, but knew that I would feel good helping these children experience some happiness. The children and I finished with the decorating and, after eating lunch, were sitting around a table playing checkers. Marie came by with a priest, who was taking a tour and giving out little gifts to the children. Looking straight at me, he asked in a syrupy voice, "And how are you, today?" It was some seconds before I realized that he had mistaken me for one of the inmates, gray hair and all. I looked at him steadily and replied with as much control as possible, "Why, I'm just fine thank you, and how are you?" asking the question in the same tone of voice he had used. He blushed profusely as he realized what he had done and quickly moved on. I enjoyed this brief humorous break from my many problems, without feeling guilty at all.

About a week and a half before I was to leave for Stockton, I came down with the 'flu and a high fever. Margaret insisted that I come to their place so she could take care of me and get me healed in time to begin my new job. I accepted with alacrity, also being relieved that apparently Margaret still loved me.

I was still pretty weak when I forced myself to get up in time to go to Stockton and find an apartment to rent. I finally found a vacancy in a complex at the north east end of town. It boasted of being an all electric apartment.

The twenty-third and twenty fourth of December, I spent at the welfare office in downtown Stockton, learning the basics of government social work and receiving a book of rules two to three inches thick. I hoped my job at the hospital wouldn't be as punitive as the book seemed to direct.

Miss Garrison, my supervisor and the head of the Social Service Department at the hospital, seemed pleasant enough and I felt I could work for her. All day long I interviewed prospective patients to determine their methods of payment or to deem them eligible for the state Medi-Cal program. The last half hour of the day, I filled out computer forms indicating changes of address and the method of payment for these patients.

My salary was close to the one I had received in Colville and it was going to be a tight struggle to pay my rent, buy groceries and come up with the $72.00 car payment. However, if my work was satisfactory, I would get a raise in six months and I would have medical insurance after three months.

When I telephoned Marie later to tell her about the new apartment, she persuaded me to come to Sacramento and get her so we could visit. I still had mixed feelings about Marie. I had hoped that I was beginning a new chapter in my life, as Marie was building a new life for herself in Sacramento. At the same time, I was feeling isolated and somewhat fearful of being so alone.

A couple weeks later, Margaret called me and invited me down for a visit on the weekend. I accepted with trepidation, wondering what would happen between John and me. Sure enough, a little after supper, a record went on the turn table and after Margaret left, as usual, the dancing routine was begun. This time, after a dance or two, John led me over to the couch and had me lie down. When he bent over to kiss me, I pushed him away and, with tears running down my cheeks, I exclaimed, "I don't want to do this," and tried to sit up. John pushed me down promising not to hurt me and assuring me of his love for me.

I pushed him away again and sitting up, exclaimed, "Maybe you think you're helping me by doing this, but you're only making things worse!" He sat back at once and got up so I could get off the couch. I grabbed my purse and coat, got into my car and left for Stockton. If this meant the end of my relationship with Margaret, I couldn't help it. I did not feel triumphant or even proud of myself. I simply felt afraid and defeated.

During those first weeks in Stockton, I was never really warm in my apartment and when I received my first electric bill, I knew I couldn't afford to stay there. The following day, as soon as work was over, I bought a paper and began seeking out a new place to live. I found a two bedroom furnished apartment in French Camp, about ten miles south of Stockton, but only three blocks from the hospital. The rent was about the same, but it had an extra room and was heated with gas, which proved to be more comfortable and less expensive. Also I would be able to go home for lunch.

It was shortly after this, that Marie took a bus down to Stockton from Sacramento and told me she had quit her job at the group home. The pressure had become too much. She took it for granted that she would be welcome, especially when she saw that the new apartment had two bedrooms. However, when it came time to go to bed, she decided to sleep with me.

Ever since Marie had arrived in Colville, I had been feeling guilty, because I felt I had been keeping my distance from her in spite of the occasional love making. I decided to make us be more like a family. One Saturday I prepared an especially festive supper and afterwards initiated making love. I had moved my record player into the bedroom, in order to play some music after the love making. However, Marie fell sleep immediately. In my heightened state I enjoyed the music, but in spite of myself, felt the gap between Marie and me widen. I determined that our being lovers must come to an end.

When spring introduced itself, Margaret telephoned again to invite Marie and I on a trip to the mountains. John would go fishing and the rest of us would hike and just enjoy nature. We would have a picnic and I offered to bring potato salad and soft drinks. I was most relieved that the last episode with John hadn't estranged me from Margaret. After we arrived, John offered to teach Marie and I how to fish. Remembering my pleasure of fishing at the Girl Scout camp, I accepted. John seemed comfortable with Marie and since neither of us had poles of our own, I was just as glad to go back to the picnic table and visit with Margaret.

A few weeks after this, Marie informed me that she had written to a boy at Boy's Town, whom she had met while she was still at the Good Shepherd Home in Omaha. He had answercd promptly and was inviting her to his Senior Prom. She made her own formal, choosing some lovely baby blue satin and some small artificial pearls, all of which I paid for, since Marie hadn't found employment. She cut and sewed the dress and laboriously stitched on the little pearls, one by one. I was proud to see how well she accomplished this.

It was also up to me to pay for a round trip air ticket, in order for Marie to get there. All of this took a toll on my limited income, but I was relieved that Marie would be doing something with someone her own age.

While Marie was gone, in desperation, I signed up with a dating service in order to fit in the "real world." I was determined to be heterosexual or die. One evening, I got a call from a man who lived in Angel's Camp in the Sierra Nevada Mountains. We arranged for him to come to Stockton to meet me. As soon as I opened the door, after Ed had knocked, he stepped back and said, "Well, you're really a tall one!"

I saw that he was at least as tall as I and found the courage to ignore the remark and invited him in. As we were getting to know one another, I noticed that he looked very much like the actor Raymond Burr. He was pleased when I spoke of it and admitted others had noticed the similarity. We enjoyed being together enough that we planned for me to drive up to Angel's Camp the following week.

In Ed's small home in Angel's Camp, after he assured me that he had had a vascetomy, we made love. It was short and quick and not a very satisfying experience. It didn't improve things when he got right out of bed and went to take a shower. I had read about the breaking of the hymen, but there was no blood on the sheet, nor had I felt any pain. Then I wondered if he expected me to take a shower, as well. He came back in the bedroom, crawled in bed, turned out the light and promptly went to sleep. I lay awake, quite disappointed and wondered if it would get better. It certainly didn't compare with my love making with Lynn or even Marie. I forgot to be concerned about not providing proof of my virginity and he said nothing about it.

However, Ed seemed satisfied, and wanted to repeat the experience on our next date. As if realizing I hadn't achieved orgasm, he told me he knew how to stimulate me and clumsily rubbed where he thought my clitoris was, but missed it entirely. It did nothing to help and the routine continued as before, including the shower.

Marie telephoned me from Omaha and told me that she wouldn't be coming home. She was staying at the Good Shepherd transition home, until Karl graduated from Boy's Town and she could be there for the occasion.

After Karl graduated from Boy's Town, he and Marie began living together, obtaining enough work to rent an apartment and, somehow, to purchase a new Chevy Nova. Then they drove it to Stockton.

Still, I was somewhat surprised when, one evening early in June, Marie arrived with Karl. Marie hadn't thought to tell me he was a black man.

I found Karl amiable and suggested that we drive up to Angel's Camp to meet Ed. I had told Ed about Marie and Karl, but hadn't said anything about Karl being black since I hadn't known either. Ed was a little taken aback, but soon pulled himself together and treated them well enough. Marie seemed pleased that I had also met someone and she and Karl decided to return to Omaha.

Soon after, Ed introduced me to his married son and his wife and to his younger, unmarried daughter. They both had nothing but praise for Ed, explaining that when they were young, their mother was rarely home, belonging to many different clubs and it was Ed who had seen to it that they were fed and clothed. I couldn't help being impressed and they seemed equally impressed with me.

I learned that Ed had been working for the Pacific Gas and Electric Company for twenty years, when his wife obtained a divorce. He had quit that job and moved to Angel's Camp, purchasing some land and having a small one bedroom house built on it with the retirement money he received from P. G. and E. as a down payment.

Now he was working as a night watchman, thirty miles from Angel's Camp, for minimum wage. When we began speaking of marriage, he agreed to quit that job and come to live in Stockton, where he could find something better paying and with more congenial hours. In my eagerness to conform with society's standards, I completely ignored the fact that I was not really in love with Ed. On some level, I felt he wasn't truly in love with me either. It would be a marriage of convenience for both, I rationalized.

In June, we drove up to Carson City, Nevada, where we could marry quickly and simply. I was most disappointed when I learned he hadn't purchased wedding rings, but I excused him with the thought that he probably didn't have that much money. However, I did beome angry, when, after the brief ceremony, he took us over to a casino and spent the next few hours standing in front of a one-armed- bandit, losing fifty or sixty dollars. Realizing it wouldn't help much to express my anger, I bought myself a sandwich, which I was barely able to eat. The vows we had just made were pounding in my head and I wanted to cry. Instead, I laughed at myself for having been so foolish, and finally insisted we drive as far as Angel's Camp that night. When we arrived, he was too tired to make love. I could only hope things would change when we began living together.

The next day I insisted on driving on to Stockton, where I took him to a department store and purchased wedding bands for both of us. I couldn't face going to work and breaking the news of my marriage, without a ring on my finger. At work the following day, everyone was enthusiastic about my marriage and planned a small shower for that Friday. After Beth Garrison left the shower, they began telling risque jokes, which they had never done before, being certain that I wouldn't have appreciated them. Already, I had noticed at my interviews that I received more respect being Mrs. Schultz, than I had as Miss Benton. While I experienced a feeling of belonging, at last, it was not exactly comforting, since the marriage already seemed to be deteriorating.

However, within a week, Ed had found a better paying job as a warehouse man in Stockton and we moved his clothes down to my apartment. His home in Angel's Camp would be for weekends and vacations. My hopes were raised significantly.

This helped me to decide it was time to break the news of my marriage to John and Margaret. They were surprised, but pleased to hear I was married and invited us down the following weekend.

When we arrived, it was a cool enough day that we could sit in the backyard to visit. John proudly showed us the fish pond he had installed and the deck he had built, where they had lawn furniture and a rotating burner for grilling meat. After talking a little, John spoke of the new Buick he had recently purchased, inviting us to go with him to see it. Relieved that John could be so friendly after our unpleasant experiences together, I promptly expressed enthusiasm about the new vehicle and followed him into the garage to look it over, expecting Ed and Margaret to follow.

John promptly lifted the hood so he could show off the powerful motor and point out its advantages. We had hardly been there a minute before the door leading to the interior of their house burst open and Ed and Margaret rushed through.

"What's going on in here?" Ed wanted to know.

Totally unsuspecting of his distrust, I invited him to come over and see the Buick.

"It's time that we're heading back to Stockton." he exclaimed. I was surprised at the anger in his voice and certainly didn't understand the rush to leave, but decided it was best to comply. All the way back to Stockton, he berated me for going into the garage alone with John, saying that Margaret had been equally upset.

"Why didn't you come, too, when he invited us?" I asked.

"Because it was obvious he just wanted you," was the quick retort.

"I think you're mistaken about that," I argued, but was upset that Margaret also hadn't trusted me.

Before he had married the first time, Ed had gotten a small jazz band together. He played the piano by ear. He dug out the sheet music he had saved from those days, *Tea for Two, Begin the Beguine, That Old Black Magic* and others. He enjoyed listening to me play them on my violin, but that was as far as it went, since neither of us had a piano. We planned to write a tune about how we had met, but each day brought out more ways we were incompatible, at least for me, and there was no energy left for any creativity.

If I had been living in a fog before, this change in my life brought about an even thicker haze. I was actually grateful for the routine of having to get up and go to work. However, coming home in the evenings became more and more difficult.

Ed had a full hour off for lunch and it was always from noon to one. I only had a half hour and since I was interviewing people all of the time, I couldn't take off for lunch at exactly the same time each day, but would wait for a lull in the number of patients waiting to be interviewed. Nevertheless, since I could be home in five minutes, we decided to try having lunch together. If I took off before noon, I would have to be back at work before he had hardly begun eating. If I was very late, he had to return to his job before I was finished. One night, as soon as Ed walked into the apartment, he began berating me about the fact that we rarely ate lunch together. When I suggested we give it up, even offering to pack a lunch for him, he became enraged and accused me of using my lunch hour to meet some man for sex. The ludicrousness of even the possibility for this struck me funny and I began to laugh. He quickly let me know that he was serious.

"If I can't even make it home to have lunch with you, how could I ever meet someone, come home, have sex and get back to work!" I exclaimed. "I think you had better come to work with me and find out from my boss that I really do have only a half hour for lunch and that I can't leave at the same time every day!"

Ed got red in the face, but of course did not act on my suggestion. By the time I had prepared supper, I was not at all hungry and when he suggested that we go to bed early to make love, it was the last thing I wished to do. The love making only got worse, rather than improving.

One day I got an ad in the mail with a sample of a Norform douche. I threw it on the night table, thinking that since I was having sex regularly, perhaps I should douche myself, something I had never done. Before I got around to it, Ed came into the kitchen one night, while I was preparing supper, with the sample in his hand.

"Now, I've caught you!" he crowed. "My other wife used this so she wouldn't get pregnant when we had sex."

"What do you mean?" I cried out. "That's a douche. Anyway it's just a sample and I haven't even used it."

"Well, if you'll read the small print at the bottom, it even says it can cause temporary sterility!"

I saw he was right about the manufacturer's warning, but the impossibility of my having an affair was the same. This time I did not laugh, but said, "Ed, when would I ever have the chance to have sex with someone else? What kind of a woman do you think I am? You're my husband and you're the only one I have sex with. Why can't you believe me?"

Then I began to cry in my fury and exasperation. To appease me, he led me to the bedroom to make love. I refused and said I thought we had better see a marriage counselor. I didn't realize that by getting angry and having a scene, he became aroused.

The next evening, I brought up seeing a counselor again and finally got him to agree to it. I could tell that he thought it was I who had the problem. After all, hadn't he been married for over twenty years? I made an appointment, but the day before we were to go, he backed out. I began to seriously consider divorce, but at the same time felt embarrassed at having to admit at work that I had made such a serious mistake. We had been married barely six weeks.

Ed and I were eating supper a few evenings later, when Marie and Karl arrived at the apartment. They hadn't had much luck at getting good jobs in Omaha and thought they would give Stockton a try. It was obvious that they expected to be taken in and I was relieved to have them around to put a halt, I hoped, to the evening scenes.

I quickly got up and prepared food for them and found linens for the bed in the spare room. I noticed that Ed was sullen and probably angry, since I hadn't asked him how he felt about it. I had previously told him Marie was like a daughter to me and felt that justified my action. That night after Marie and Karl had gone to bed, Ed informed me that *niggers* were not to be trusted and that, in fact, President Nixon was building a lot of new prisons all over the country and that he was going to round up all black men and imprison them. I had read about money being appropriated for new prisons, but not for the reason Ed gave. In fact, I had never encountered such rampant racism, and let him know I didn't believe a word he said.

Ed's anger intensified and a few days later, Marie called me at work to tell me that Ed had dumped all of her and Karl's things on the landing in front of our apartment and had told them they couldn't stay there anymore.

During the week, Karl and Marie had made friends with a black woman, who also worked at the hospital, and they had taken their things over to her house. Marie gave me Ellen's telephone number so I could let them know what was happening. I could hardly believe it, but when I went home that night, the second bedroom was empty. Ed was still at work.

An hour or so later, when Ed came in, carrying a bottle of wine and showed me the gun he had purchased, in case Karl and Marie tried to come back, I quickly grabbed my purse and ran out of the apartment, not feeling safe.

I telephoned Ellen, who insisted that I come over to her house and stay there for the night. The next morning I called Ed and told him he had no right to kick Marie and Karl out, that the apartment was in my name and that he had better get his things together and be out of there by the time I got home, since I was going to file for a divorce. Ellen had suggested that I get a restraining order. I informed Ed that I was going to do this. When I went home that night, none of Ed's things were in the apartment. I telephoned Marie and told her that she and Karl could return.

Before they arrived, however, I called Margaret and John to tell them what had happened. When John answered the telephone, I had barely begun to speak, when he interrupted me saying, "Margaret doesn't want to come to the phone. She doesn't want to speak to you. Ed called us last night and told us what happened. You've caused us nothing but trouble ever since you left the convent. We don't want to have anything more to do with you."

"I've caused *you* nothing but trouble!" I exclaimed, but John had already hung up. At first, I was going to call right back, to give my side of the story, but realized they wouldn't want to hear it. I was still sitting there, stunned, when Marie and Karl came in. I didn't tell them what had happened, but as I realized my own sister had disowned me, without even considering hearing my story, only taking Ed's story as the truth, feelings of despair engulfed me. I felt totally alone and rejected.

A few days later Ed's brother called me long distance to congratulate us. Embarrassed, I had to tell him he was too late, that I was about to file for a divorce. I told him a little of what had happened and he explained that

Ed had always been extremely jealous, even of his mother. He told me that Ed had chased one of his daughter's suitors with a gun. I thanked him for his frankness and, at least, felt I had done the right thing. However, the fact that I had gotten myself into such a situation was extremely depressing and I began having thoughts of suicide, feeling totally incapable of dealing with life *in the world*. Plans of suicide were to insert themselves into my thoughts for the next three years.

CHAPTER EIGHTEEN

SHORTLY AFTER, KARL got a job at KMart and I felt hopeful that he and Marie would be able to get their own apartment. However, I also felt that they had better get married, so no one could cause trouble about their living together. When I found out that Karl was only nineteen and would need parental permission to marry, we asked Ellen if she would go with us to Carson City and act as his mother. Ellen agreed.

Marie cut off her prom formal, making it into an attractive dress and wore that for the wedding. Karl bought a suit at work and we left for Lake Tahoe early one Saturday morning in September. I felt uncomfortable about having to lie about Ellen being Karl's mother, but since Karl had no idea where his own mother was, it seemed necessary. It was then that I learned that Karl had been in children's institutions from the time he was ten years old.

In the meantime, Ed had called several times asking if he could come back. I was tempted to tell him he had cut me off from my sister, but it was too painful to admit this. I simply said I didn't believe the marriage would ever work. He finally quit calling, but not without leaving his telephone number so I could call him if I should change my mind. He had rented a small garage apartment in Stockton, retaining his job at the warehouse.

Then I got a bill from Shell Oil and saw that Ed was using my credit card. He had even bought a couple new tires on it, his part of the bill coming to seventy-two dollars. I telephoned Shell, at once, telling them of the situation. They insisted I was still liable for the charges.

Remembering that Ed's birthday was the twenty-sixth of September, I called him and asked if he would like to have dinner together to celebrate. He was delighted, not having any suspicion of my real intention, which was to get my credit card back. He even agreed to eat at a restaurant, which he had refused to do before, because he felt it was very risky to eat out. He had cooked while he was in the Navy and believed all cooks were untrustworthy in keeping things sanitary.

Not wanting to make a scene in a public place, I said nothing about the credit card. After eating, we went to his room, where before I had a chance to ask for the card, he asked if I would like to make love. When I refused, he smiled and said he could make me if he wanted to. I was astonished at the threat and let him know that he could try but that there would be a struggle if he did. He got red in the face, but when I demanded my credit card, with some reluctance, he got it out and handed it to me. I left again, not feeling triumphant, but thoroughly ashamed that I had been so devious. Nonetheless, the next day I got an appointment with a lawyer to begin divorce proceedings.

When I went to pay the rent for October, the landlady told me she couldn't have an unmarried couple living together in her complex.

"If you mean Marie and Karl, they are married," I said." I can go up and get their marriage license right now and show it to you." I was relieved that I had insisted that they get married.

"That really won't be necessary, Anne," Mrs. Appleton quickly intervened. "My other tenants do not want a mixed couple living here. I really can't afford to lose renters and they will start moving out if Marie and Karl stay."

"But Marie is just like a daughter to me," I replied. "I can't just kick them out!"

"Well, you'll just have to move some place else," the woman firmly replied.

When I informed Marie and Karl that evening, I wasn't specific as to the reason we had to leave, but I realized they knew. Karl had lost his job at KMart and there was no way they could get a place of their own, even though Marie had begun working at a nursing home.

Fortunately, the three of us were able to find a small frame Victorian house with two bedrooms and a bath as well as a living room, dining room and kitchen. I was able to rent it in plenty of time to move in by the first of November. Actually, it felt more homelike than the apartment ever had, especially after we put up the two plaster cats. It was wonderful having our own yard, and we began planning how we would plant flowers and vegetables in the spring.

The three of us made detailed preparations for Thanksgiving. I was pleasantly surprised when Karl suggested that he go to a nearby park, where some"bums hang out" and invite one of them for dinner. I was pleased with the idea, but was a little concerned how it would turn out.

When dinner was nearly ready, we changed into our good clothing and Karl went out after our guest. When he returned, I saw right away that the man was pretty destitute, but he looked more pathetic than dangerous – I hoped.

The guest was more than happy to drink the wine, barely waiting for the toast. He swilled it down and quickly requested more. Karl grandly refilled his glass. Before he had drunk half of it, he suddenly got up from the table, asking where the bathroom was. We could hear him vomiting. He finally came out and said he wasn't feeling too well and didn't think he could eat anything. Since he was staggering badly, Karl helped him to the front door.

When Karl returned, we couldn't help but laugh. So much for generosity.

I assured them I was certain our guest had had some drinks before he had arrived at our place.

I stoically went to work each day, feeling as if the world had no place for me. Driving to or from work, as I listened to The Fifth Dimension singing "What the world needs now is love, sweet love, not just for some, but for everyone." I agreed with the sentiment, but even though I felt that there didn't seem to be much love in my world, somehow the song was a comfort. Being with Marie and Karl did not really feel like family. Whenever the three of us had a disagreement, I definitely was often outnumbered. Then I would realize they were all the family I had, since Margaret and John had disowned me. I hadn't even made any close friends with anyone at work.

After the three of us were somewhat happy in the comfortable old house. Karl began teaching me how to dance in the '60's style, not on my toes, as I had done in my youth, but grinding on my heels and swaying my hips. When Karl described it as "making love on your feet" I was somewhat puzzled, since we danced apart, although we faced each other. It was certainly easier for me than trying to follow a man shorter than I was. Strangely, Marie did not care to dance, which made me somewhat uncomfortable, remembering John insisting on dancing and Margaret not wanting to.

We discovered that we could go to the YMCA, which was close by, and for just a little money, play table tennis several hours on Saturday and Sunday afternoons. Karl turned out to be a good player and my competency soon returned. When she wasn't working, Marie would come along, but did not play. I began to wonder just what Karl and Marie had in common besides sex.

During some evenings Karl and I got into discussions about existentialism. He had read just a little about it and was glad to have me filling him in from my readings at Notre Dame. Again, Marie was not interested in joining in. Also, Karl had taken French while he was at Boy's Town and could recite page after page of the text. It was the first time I had met someone with an eidetic memory.

It was during one of these evenings that Karl admitted he had been offered university scholarships from all over the country. With such a display of intelligence, I had no reason not to believe him, but was very puzzled as to why he hadn't accepted any. I wondered again about his attraction for Marie.

While driving through Stockton on the way home from work, I had noticed the spires of a beautiful old church. I drove by one evening and found that it was a Catholic church and they had a Sunday afternoon Mass where the sermon was in Spanish and a Mariachi band provided the music. I very much enjoyed attending one of these Masses, although I was unable to follow the sermon. Picking up some literature in the vestibule afterwards, I discovered they had choir practice on Wednesday nights which I decided to attend.

I squelched the fact that I knew in my heart I was doing it in hopes of meeting someone. Nonetheless, I enjoyed singing the folk hymns and admired the director's ability on the guitar. The following Sunday morning I was so repulsed by the sermon in English, realizing it was not reaching the congregation, much less me, that while I continued to attend choir rehearsals, I could not make myself go to Mass the following Sundays. No one seemed to notice and I continued going for three more weeks.

At that rehearsal we prepared for an upcoming wedding, which I attended. I was pleased to see the changes which had been made in the ritual, giving the couple a more active part.

At the actual ceremony, a man, somewhat taller than I and about my age, whom I had never noticed before, asked if he could look on the music with me, since he didn't seem to have a copy. I became aware of his lovely baritone voice, which seemed to blend nicely with my own. After the ceremony he asked me if we couldn't get together some time. In spite of his attractiveness, I answered abruptly, "I don't think so," hardly knowing why. I saw the hurt on his face at the rejection, as he stammered something about excusing himself for being rude. I walked rapidly away, wondering why I had done it. I never returned to choir rehearsals.

Shortly after this, I came down with the flu and finally had to stay in bed for several days. Karl was very solicitous of me, bringing me ice water, fruit juices and aspirin and, later, light meals. I was most grateful for his concern. It was something I would not easily forget. Marie had always been unable to accept the fact that sometimes I was not the strong mother and needed some care, myself.

One evening when I came home from work, Karl had obtained a very charming German Shepherd puppy. He named her Cissy after the popular song, *The Cissy Strut*, Cissy took to me right away. Karl felt we needed her to be a watch dog, but I was dismayed with Karl's training techniques and was even more distressed that he teased her in a mean way. Soon Cissy was coming into my room to spend the night, out of Karl's reach as it were. In fact, as soon as I came home from work, Cissy was right by my side. Finally, Karl told me that I had ruined Cissy for a watch dog and from then on, Cissy was mine. I was puzzled by Karl's behavior with the dog, when he had been so attentive to me during my illness, but I realized he was a very complex person.

Karl gave me more concern when he and Marie asked me to purchase a trap drum set he had seen on sale in a music store window for $350.00. He assured me that it was a really good price. I didn't doubt that, but I didn't want to take on such a debt. Karl's desire to have the drum was almost palpable and the next day Marie convinced the salesperson to let her charge it with me as a co-signer. I wondered how Marie thought she could take on the payments with her limited salary, but I was also influenced by the intensity behind Karl's insistence and reluctantly did as they requested. After all, I speculated, they didn't help with the rent or utilities and only occasionally with food, so they probably could manage the payments. However, I began to feel uncomfortable with Karl's continued unemployment.

Karl amazed me when, after listening once to a tape of *In a Godda da Veda*, he played the entire piece, which lasted for fifteen minutes, without a hitch. I realized that I wouldn't have known if he had made a mistake, but it certainly seemed that he had played it just as it had been on the tape.

Karl remained steadfast to his promise not to play the drums after nine at night, so as not to disturb the neighbors, but not long after, he lost interest in the drums and he and Marie were able to sell them, pay off the debt and make a little profit.

One evening shortly after that, I had gone to bed and was just falling asleep, when Karl came into my bedroom. I was suddenly very awake, somewhat surprised, as well as a little fearful.

"Can we talk a little?" Karl requested, quite politely.

I sat up, grateful that I had a nightgown on. "I guess so," I answered reluctantly.

"I…I have these strange feelings towards you," he gulped. "I think I am beginning to love you, like…like I love Marie."

"Well, that's not such a good idea, is it?" I quickly responded.

"It's not an *idea*," he argued. "It's how I *feel*. I thought that maybe …you felt the same way."

"Karl, you have been very good to me, helping me when I was ill and I enjoy dancing with you and playing table tennis and talking about philosophy…all of those things, but that's all." I hoped he understood.

He sat still for a moment, as if trying to take it in. Then he said, "Well, maybe we could go and talk to Marie about it."

"You mean right now?" I asked, somewhat surprised and wondering what we would say.

"Please," he requested.

I finally got up, slipped on my robe and followed him into the other bedroom. Marie had fallen asleep, apparently unaware that Karl had left their bed. Karl sat on the edge of the bed and motioned for me to sit beside him. "Marie!" he called. "Marie, Anne and I want to talk about something."

"Right now?" Marie asked sleepily.

"Yeah, it's important," he insisted. When Marie reluctantly pushed herself up on one elbow, he continued. "Anne and I really like one another," he began.

"You mean you like her better than me?" Marie was fully awake by now.

"Not at all," I interjected. "There are things Karl and I like to do together and there are things the two of you like to do together, that's all." I hoped I sounded convincing. Marie didn't like to dance, play table tennis nor talk about philosophy.

"Well, I know that," Marie complained. "Why did ya have to wake me up to tell me that?"

"I just wanted you to know," Karl intervened.

"Well, I have to go to work tomorrow morning and so does Marie," I interrupted and got up and went back to my own room.

The next morning, while I was at work, Karl called to apologize for what he had done the night before, promising that it wouldn't happen again. I was surprised but pleased with his consideration and told him so. That wasn't to be the end of it, however.

A few nights later, some time after I had fallen into a deep sleep, I was awakened by the delicious feeling of having my vulva licked and sucked. Remembering my love making with Lynn, at first, I thought that was what was happening. I began moaning with pleasure.

Then I heard Karl saying, "You like that, huh?"

"Oh, Karl!" I exclaimed, wide awake. "Stop! Please stop!" But it was too late and he knew it.

"I know you don't really want me to stop," he laughed as he got up and entered me. Soon after, he achieved orgasm and lay beside me.

"Gosh!" I exclaimed in surprise, "I think I'm wetting the bed!" I pulled myself from his arms and ran into the bathroom. I found it was blood running down my legs. I quickly cleaned myself, found my sanitary belt and put on a pad. In the meantime, Karl was examining the sheets, quickly discovering the fresh blood on them.

"I think I've just broken your cherry," he laughed with pride. "Ed must have been some lover if he couldn't even do that!"

"Karl, we can't do this! You're married to Marie and she is my friend! In some ways she is like a daughter to me! I can't deceive her like this! Go! Get out of here and don't come back!" It was then that I remembered that Marie was working a night shift.

"Look, Anne. I know you love me," Karl maintained. "I tell you what. I'll ask Marie if we can't be a *menage a trois*."

"Right now, just leave! Leave!" I screamed. He took a close look at me and did just that.

A few days later, when Karl was able to be alone with me before Marie returned from work, he admitted that he had asked Marie and she had refused. "Then that's definitely the end of it, Karl, and I mean it!" I declared. Karl walked off.

It was shortly after this that the landlord informed us that he wanted to fix up the house and put it on the market. He gave us two weeks to be out, which was when our rent was up.

Marie and Karl finally found a strange apartment in a complex that must have been a motel at one time in the little town of Manteca. Since Manteca was southeast of Stockton and the hospital was due south, it was closer to my job, but that was the only favorable thing about it.

It consisted of three rooms and a bath, which were all in a row. The front room had a couch and chair with a hide-away-bed, where Karl and Marie slept. The middle room had a bed, a closet and dresser drawers, where I slept and the bathroom and kitchen were at the other end. Karl and Marie had to go through my room to get to the bathroom and kitchen. Besides that there were windows only at the two ends, so my room was completely without natural light. Even the kitchen and front room were somewhat dim since the windows were small. The linoleum on the floor was cracked and missing in places. It was cheap!

We were allowed to have Cissy and didn't even have to pay a cleaning deposit. I could see why, but I was determined to get out of there as soon as possible. I definitely preferred being at work to being at home. The relationship between the three of us had become strained to say the least.

We hadn't been there for two weeks, when Marie was permanently put on a night shift. She was glad to get more pay, but I was fearful at what this might mean to Karl, although he had promised Marie he wouldn't make love with me again. By then Marie had discovered she had been pregnant since some time in January.

After a few nights, Karl came into my room, wanting to make love. I refused, and began gathering my clothes. I determined to leave and get a motel room. He barred my way and promised he wouldn't hurt me if I cooperated. Knowing how strong he was, I relented. I decided right then that I would tell Marie that I was going to find myself another apartment and that they would have to remain there.

When I heard Marie get home from work the next morning, I motioned for her to come into my room. Karl had returned to their room after the sex and fortunately was sound asleep. When I told Marie of my plan, Marie exclaimed, "But why? Why don't you want to live with us anymore?"

I had hoped Marie would guess the reason. "Karl insists on making love with me and I'm afraid to stop him!" I answered truthfully.

Marie ran from the room and I could hear her screaming at Karl. I was fearful for Marie and since it was still early enough that I didn't have to leave for work, I went into the kitchen to wait and see what would happen.

When I heard Marie calling for help, I grabbed my purse and ran into their room. Karl was still naked, but as soon as he saw me, he yelled, "You shouldn't have told her! You shouldn't have told her!" I saw the fury stream-ing from his eyes. "I've got a gun, you know!" he yelled.

I ran out the front door and luckily found a telephone booth, where I called the police and then called Amy Garrison, my boss, to tell her why I would be late for work. By the time I finished talking to Amy, I saw a squad car pull up in front of our apartment.

What happened in the next few minutes was an unbelievable nightmare. By the time the police had arrived, Karl had dressed and fear had calmed him down.

The police could not arrest Karl unless Marie pressed charges. I could understand why Marie was afraid to do this. I finally asked the police to stay there until Marie and I had gotten in my car and left.

I drove to work to tell Amy what had happened and to get some advice as what to do next. Amy was very understanding and advised us to get a law-yer, a restraining order and by no means to return to the apartment without a policeman, assuring me that they could manage without me for the day.

The lawyer got the restraining order and called the police to get the help we would need to return to the apartment. We waited a block down from the apartment until we saw a squad car pull up and two policemen get out. We drove up behind the police car and joined the men. Together, the four of us entered the apartment, the police with drawn guns.

As soon as we got inside, Karl came out of my room wearing his best clothes and smiling as if nothing had happened. I wondered if he had the gun in one of his pockets.

By then, Marie was willing to place charges against him, but of course he denied having threatened us with a gun. The police began searching the place for evidence and Karl walked up to me and asked me if he could speak with me, alone, in the bathroom.

"Are you kidding?" I cried and pushing him aside, ran into my room where the police were. "He wanted to talk to me alone," I said.

One of the men took Karl by the arm and led him into the front room. "I think it's me you need to talk to," the policeman ordered.

Karl obediently followed him out to the squad car, while the other po-liceman covered his partner from behind. Karl got in the back and the first policeman got in the driver's seat, turning so he could speak with Karl. The other man got in the front passenger seat. Marie and I looked on from inside the apartment. We could see Karl hand over his gun to one of the officers.

After a few minutes the second policeman got out and came in, saying to me, "It's a good thing you didn't go into that bathroom with him, lady. He had a gun with a silencer on it and after shooting you, was going to leave before we discovered what he had done. He's furious at you for telling on him. He probably wouldn't have gotten away, but he might have well shot you before we could have stopped him. You don't need to press charges, ma'am," he told Marie. "We're taking him to a secure mental health unit for a seventy-two hour assessment. He's got to be crazy."

Marie and I spent the rest of the day seeking a more appropriate apartment. By the time we found one, it was too late to move until the following day. Suddenly, Marie was exhausted, not having slept since the day before. I called the nursing home where she worked, telling them Marie wouldn't be in that night. I then packed our dishes and linens until about midnight, when I finally went to bed so I could go to work the next day. I figured Marie could finish the packing while I was at work so we could move as soon as I was free.

When I went to my closet the following morning, I was shocked to find that Karl had systematically slit every piece of my clothing with a sharp butcher knife, which I found laying on the floor. I quickly put on the clothes I had worn the day before and went to work. As soon as Amy saw me and had heard what had happened, she told me to take another day off, in order to move and get some rest. Even so, it would be a long time before I could admit, even to myself, how close I had come to a violent death.

After we had our things in the new apartment, I took Marie to see Karl. I refused to go in. Marie reported that Karl said he was getting a lot of help. I could see that Marie was as doubtful as I was. Marie had also learned that after seventy-two hours there, it was up to Karl whether he would stay or not. Then Marie begged me to take her to Santa Clara to visit a friend. I hadn't even realized Marie had a friend there, but she had an address and directions and I could readily see how upset she was. I was afraid that she might lose her baby.

The directions hadn't informed us that San Jose and Santa Clara were not only next to each other, but in places their boundaries were like interlocking fingers.

We would be in one, when suddenly we would see a sign informing us that we were in the other for no reason that we could figure out. After stopping and asking for further directions, we finally found Marie's friend. I returned to Stockton alone.

The last day of the seventy-two hours was Friday. Saturday, I got a call from Karl asking me to come and get him, as he felt he had received enough help. I was afraid to go get him and be alone with him, but was just as afraid to refuse to go get him. On the way over I determined that we would go after Marie together. I did not even take him to see the new apartment. I was relieved that I remembered the way enough that I was able to drive directly to Marie's friend's house. Nonetheless, I could see that Marie was not too happy to see Karl. However, it seemed the three of us were a family, like it or not. I decided that perhaps having a family was not all that important.

Marie quit her job, which meant I would not be alone at night with Karl, although I would be bearing the full financial burden for the three of us. By then Marie's pregnancy was definitely showing and I could see that transferring people from bed to wheelchair, to showers etc. was not good for her.

I became determined that Karl begin to assume financial responsibility for his family. When I had worked at the telephone company as an operator, just before entering the convent, I had noted how efficient the repairmen were with the little bag of tools they wore around their waists. I also knew that they made good money and were able to work themselves up to responsible positions. When I suggested it to Karl, he was quite interested. We found out when the company would be giving the written examination for prospective workers. Karl was eager to take it.

When they saw the high scores he made, the company offered to put him into training at once. I cheerfully drove him up to Sacramento, where he was given a room and meals at a Holiday Inn. He would be there for a week of intensive training, after which he would return to Stockton and finish his training by going out into the field with an experienced man. At this time he would begin receiving a salary.

When Marie and I went to get him at the end of the week, he was in better spirits than I had ever seen him. He proudly showed us his kit of tools and described some of the things he was able to do with them. He had been outfitted with good work boots and a hard hat.

Two weeks later when he got his first paycheck, he and Marie found their own apartment. After I had helped them move over, I actually cried with relief and the feeling of being free at last. I determined, at once, to find a better place for Cissy. In fact I decided to try to rent a house with a yard, which I would be able to afford, since I was no longer supporting Karl and Marie.

I fell in love with an unfurnished old house in a rather old neighborhood, which felt very home-like to me. After work the next Friday, I went to a furniture store and obtained a couch and chair, a dining room set and a double bed with a simple Hollywood frame, which they delivered directly to my new home. Not only was there a nice yard in the back for Cissy, there was also a brick fire pit for grilling meat.

The dining room had two windows set close to each other and I decided to make a set of colorful, linen, traverse drapes. This necessitated adding a portable sewing machine to my credit card purchases. I enjoyed the challenge and the drapes came out to my satisfaction.

The dining room walls were badly in need of painting, for which I chose a golden yellow. There was a strange piece of furniture built right in the wall with drawers and a mirror on top, a kind of combination chest of drawers and hutch. It had been painted white along with the walls. I painstakingly painted it brown to look like wood. In some way all of this made my life more meaningful and I began looking forward to coming home at the end of the day.

I was delightfully surprised when Jaime, the Hispanic man who had sold me the furniture, called for a date. The first time we went to a movie on a Saturday afternoon, since he worked tending bar at night. He was working two jobs so he could pay child support for his two children. He assured me that he was in the midst of getting a divorce.

When we returned home after the movie and he saw my set up in the back yard, he told me he was good at grilling meat and we made a date to have a meal in the back the following weekend. I made potato salad and baked beans to go with the steaks. Along with the meat, Jaime brought a six pack of beer.

He told me stories of his childhood in a family of farm laborers, which I found most interesting. He kept insisting that they were poor but very close and happy, which I could readily believe. Because I was so interested in his stories and Mexican culture, he took me to meet his parents, which was an enjoyable experience, because they also had interesting stories to share. I realized that he was a good three or four inches shorter than I, but since it didn't seem to bother him, I forgot about it.

After he had returned from the War, he had passed the GED and had continued going to a Community College and attained an Asssociate's degree, of which he was very proud.

The first time we made love, for some reason, when I felt his firm body next to mine, I exclaimed in delight, "Oh, you are truly a man!" and snuggled closer, surprising myself. This strengthened my belief that one could choose to be homosexual or heterosexual. Naturally Jaime was pleased with the compliment.

One day at work, Jaime telephoned me, very excited because Jorge, a buddy of his, who was also a bartender, had invited him and me to his home for dinner. Jorge's wife would prepare it. I could discern that Jaime was happy, because they were accepting of his situation of having a girl friend, even though he wasn't yet divorced.

When he came and picked me up early in the evening, he was dressed up more than ever before and expressed his pleasure at the way I looked. Then we went bar hopping, his bartender friends giving us especially strong drinks in celebration. I was able to be friendly, but, after taking a few sips, was hiding my drinks behind plants, since I didn't want to get drunk.

At the last bar, we met up with Jorge, who gave us directions to his home where dinner was waiting. Jaime and I had taken my car and I was getting concerned over Jaime's ability to drive safely. I was very relieved when we finally pulled up in front of Jorge's house.

Belinda, Jorge's wife, was very pleasant and seemed relieved that I was sober enough to help with setting the table, while she took care of the finishing touches with the dinner. Belinda and I and their two children, who were around nine and ten, enjoyed the meal. Jorge and Jaime were too drunk to eat. I could tell this wasn't an unusual occurrence.

After supper, Jorge invited me to see the sun room, which he had filled with all kinds of herbs and exotic flowers. I was impressed but was also uncomfortable being alone in there with him. Jaime soon corrected this by coming in and informing me it was time to leave. I was barely able to thank Jorge's wife for the splendid meal, as Jaime rushed me out the door. When we got to the car, I insisted on driving. I was surprised and relieved when he agreed.

As we pulled up in front of my house where Jaime's car was, he was obviously too drunk to drive home, so I had to let him come in to spend the night. I was relieved when he went right to sleep. Nonetheless, a few nights later, I ended the relationship. Drinking played too much of a role in his life.

It was shortly after this that Karl came over unexpectedly one afternoon wanting to make love, even though ostensibly he was working. He told me he was losing his mind, because it had become too painful for Marie to have sex. Memories of the scene in Manteca flared up, especially of the ripped clothing in my closet, and I was afraid to refuse him. Afterwards, I made him promise not to come again. The baby would be due in less than two months.

In the meantime, I had received a letter from Sister Catherine, who had been in the juniorate when I had been the Directress. Sister Catherine's parents had both died and she was asking if she could spend her home visit with me. I was surprised, but delighted, since Sister was intelligent, a poet and we had much in common. I responded affirmatively right away. I was happy to have a pleasant home in which to entertain her. I could easily make up the couch into a bed for myself and Sister Catherine could sleep comfortably in my bed. Since Sister had lost most of her vision from diabetes, I was able to do this, leaving Sister with the idea that I had two bedrooms. I knew she would refuse to sleep in my bed, while I slept on the couch.

To my dismay, I began menstruating harder than I ever had before. In fact, I was practically hemorrhaging. I figured out I had not had a period since early July and this was late August. I had to refrain from taking Sister any place since the only way I could slow down the bleeding was to keep my feet up on a chair.

The second afternoon Sister Catherine was there, we were enjoying sharing stories of our lives, when I heard a truck pull up in my drive way. I got up and saw that Karl had come again during his work time. Since he came in the back, I was able to intercept him in the kitchen. I told him I had company, but he wanted me to make love anyway. Staring him down, I quietly but firmly said, "No!" and walked into the living room where Sister Catherine was waiting. I breathed a sigh of relief when I heard the back door slam and the truck drive away.

In the meantime, I had already invited Marie and Karl to go to San Francisco with me when it was time to take Sister to her return flight. Since the plane left in the morning, we would be able to spend some time at Golden Gate Park and eat at the Wharf before returning to Stockton.

On the drive down Marie and Karl laughed and talked all the way to the airport. The laughter was loud and somewhat invasive of any conversation Sister Catherine and I tried to have. What they were saying was said too low for Sister or I to make out and after a time it felt to me that they were making fun of us. I was relieved when they went off on their own, while I waited with Sister until it was time to board the plane.

Later when the three of us were walking in Golden Gate Park, Karl and Marie kept five or six paces in back of me, laughing and talking as before, acting as if I were not there. I was fuming at their rudeness, not having the slightest idea of the cause.

The hemorrhaging had almost stopped the day before, but when I felt moisture running down my legs, I told them I wasn't feeling well and that we would have to return to Stockton right away. They quieted down, saying very little during the drive back home. I dropped them off at their apartment and when I arrived home, I found that my seat was filled with blood clots. I cleared it out, cleaned myself and, feeling quite weak, propped my feet up for the rest of the day. I was feeling frightened by then.

The following morning I called in sick and telephoned my doctor for an appointment. Surprisingly he came on line and after I had described my symptoms, he said, "Sounds like a miscarriage to me. Is that possible?" I hadn't thought of that possibility but knew right away that it very well could be. I gulped and admitted it.

"We'll make arrangements for you to have a pregnancy test at the hospital before I see you. Even with all of the bleeding, you might still be pregnant."

Although I had often thought it would be wonderful to have a child of my own, I knew in my heart of hearts that I was in no condition to raise a child in a world I despised and felt apart from. While the sexual revolution had been going on for several years and unmarried mothers were becoming a common thing, this would not be true for a forty-four year old woman working as a social worker at a hospital.

Worse still, I had to admit the father was either Karl, who might be a sociopath (the first time I had ever admitted to myself such a thing was possible) or Jaime, who definitely had problems with alcohol. I wouldn't want to designate either of them as the father.

I was fearful as well as embarrassed to go in for the test, but it wasn't at the hospital where I worked and in their efficiency hardly anyone noticed me. Therefore, when Dr. Becker telephoned at work the next day to tell me the test was negative, I closed the door to my office and shed tears of relief, grateful that all I had to do was pick up a prescription for iron to take care of the blood I had lost.

When I came home that afternoon, I was surprised to find Marie waiting on the front porch. As soon as we were inside, Marie began sobbing hysterically.

"Oh, Mom, Karl's been accused of murdering a woman! They took him to jail today!" she burst out.

I was astonished but fearful that the accusation might be true. Howecer, Marie hadn't called me Mom for a long time. I took her in my arms.

"That's why we were acting so awful when we went with you to take Sister Catherine to the airport. He knew they were looking for him. He wanted to go down to Mexico, but I talked him in to staying, since he didn't do it."

"What happened that they think he did it?" I finally asked.

"He went to work last Friday and when he went to this woman's home to install a telephone, she seduced him into having sex with her. Afterwards, she was afraid her husband would find out and she went for him with a gun. As they struggled over the gun, it accidentally went off and killed her."

I understood right away why Karl had wanted to leave for Mexico, but knew Marie had done the right thing in convincing him to stay. It didn't occur to either of us to disbelieve his story.

"How could he be a sociopath, when he was so good to me?" I reasoned to myself.

CHAPTER NINETEEN

MARIE ASKED ME if she could move in with me, even before the rent on her apartment was due. She and Karl had become friends with another mixed couple, Jenny and Jose Sanchez. Jose had a truck and offered to bring her things over. They did it the next Saturday so I could help with the packing, since Marie was so close to her due date. We put Marie's things in my living room, where she would sleep on the couch. We also set up the bassinet for the baby. In the meantime Marie canceled their utilities and got their cleaning deposit back.

Marie and I were watching television in the living room one evening, when we heard loud screams coming from outside the front door. I jumped up to see what it was. "Has someone left their baby here?" I wondered, hopeful and horrified at the same time. After I opened the door, at first I didn't see anything. It was entirely dark. Then another scream drew my eyes down to a tiny black kitten. I quickly scooped it up and took it inside. It was hard to believe that such a loud scream could come out of such a small being.

It ravenously lapped down some milk and then was happy to lay in my lap and sleep. I was able to determine that it was a female and named her Green Eyed Lady, after a song I had been hearing on the radio. The next day I got some cat food and kitty litter. Green Eyed Lady had chosen the right place to howl.

When Marie expressed fear that the kitten might smother her baby, I promised her that would not happen. At night I would keep the kitten in my room.

Cissy's maternal instincts seemed to keep her from wanting to chase her new companion. In fact, as it grew colder my two familiars often shared the bed, Cissy curled up in my crooker (the bend in my legs) and Green Eyed Lady curled up close to the back of my neck, tangled in my hair. She must have thought I was her mother as she often tried to suckle.

A week later on Sunday morning, Marie ran into my bedroom to tell me she was having bad pains in her stomach. "Do you think I'm having labor pains?" she asked. I could see she was afraid, but talked her into waiting to see if the pains came closer together. I finally decided it was time to drive her over to San Joaquin General, where she had been going for her prenatal care. It was about eleven a.m. when we arrived. I stayed with her, grabbing a meal in the hospital cafeteria. I was allowed to remain with her even when they took her into a small pre-delivery room, around nine that night. The pains were getting quite intense by then. Finally, a nurse came in and after examining Marie, said it was time to go in the delivery room and told me to wait in the hall with the expectant fathers.

When a nurse called my name, she took me to see the baby through a big window. It was a boy and he seemed beautiful to me. I even thought he waved at me, although his eyes were tightly shut. The nurse assured me that Marie was asleep and I went home to get some sleep so I could go to work the next day. I went up to see Marie on my break the next morning, to find her nursing Karl Jr.

After hearing what had happened to her husband, the social worker signed Marie up for AFDC. When she was released, she was loaded down with diapers, corn starch, baby gowns, little towels etc. Karly was jaundiced and stayed in the hospital a few more days.

Although Marie was permitted to visit Karl on Wednesdays and Saturdays, she waited until Karly came home from the hospital. That Saturday I stayed at home with Karly, while Marie went to see Karl. Marie came home in tears.

"Oh, Mom, they shaved his head and he has to wear an orange jump suit because he's being accused of first degree murder. The others wear blue. They do have TV's though and get to go out in a yard once a day. I left money for him so he can get cigarettes and candy at their canteen."

We followed that routine until Karly was old enough to go with Marie. I would drive her to the county jail, while she held the baby. Marie said Karl actually cried when he saw his son. Jenny Sanchez took them on Wednesdays.

In the meantime I had tried out and had been accepted as an alto in the University of the Pacific's Community Chorus. I really liked the director and it was this that helped see me through a very trying year.

Just as we were settling into a comfortable routine, my landlord came over to tell me he had to sell the house. He was impressed with the way I had fixed it up and asked if I might like to buy it. He was asking eight thousand for it, but when he told me he would have to have cash, because the house wasn't good enough for anyone to get a bank loan on it, I had to pass. I had grown to love the house and wondered what was wrong with it, but knew I could never come up with that much money. However, it did help me to decide to try to buy a house. My boss had suggested I do that anyway and I was getting tired of having to move at the whim of landlords.

Ellen, the woman who had stood up with Marie and Karl when they got married, gave me the name of a realtor. After I told him how much I was earning, he told hme he could probably find a nice two bedroom house with monthly payments of around one hundred and fifty dollars. However, I would have to have a down payment of five hundred dollars and close to the same amount for closing.

When I had been working at the telephone company, before I entered the convent, I had taken out life insurance, which the Order had kept up. I decided to see about cashing it in, since I had no dependents. I was surprised to discover that after paying on it for close to twenty years, I only had a little over five hundred dollars coming. Nevertheless, I cashed it in and put the money in a savings account until I found a house, adding to it whenever I could.

In November I found a house with a large fenced-in back yard. It was in a twenty year old tract, but it hardly appeared that way, because the owners had made enough changes that the houses seemed quite different. The owner was living in California, having rented it out for the past year or so. After putting five hundred down, I was told that it might be several months before they could get the title cleared. Knowing that I needed to get out of my present home, they offered to let me move in and pay rent until that happened. My realtor had checked my credit and was certain I would get the house. The rent was just a little more than I was already paying, so I took the offer.

The walls were all the same color throughout the house, except for the paneling in the living and dining rooms. I decided I would like to paint the two bedrooms and the hall in between the same golden yellow I had painted the dining room in the rental. Marie surprised me when she offered to paint it for me. I bought a new single bed for Marie and a crib for Karly. Marie looked forward to having a room of her own. We were able to move in, December first.

We put up a small tree for Christmas, but Karly was really too young to appreciate it and Karl being in jail, put somewhat of a damper on our joy, but we took pictures anyway. I bought a small photo album called Grandma's Pride, which I could carry around in my purse. Nevertheless, it was early in February before anyone had the energy to take the tree down.

In January, I had bought a ticket to see Itzhak Perlman play the Mendelssohn violin concerto with the Stockton Symphony. I had played this concerto in college and loved it for its joyful spontaneity. At that time, Perlman was hardly known, but his sensitive playing won me over at once.

Marie surprised me again, when, late in February, she told me she wanted to get a place of her own. She said her case worker promised to help her find a place she could afford. I understood that Marie was mature enough now to want a home of her own, where she could have things the way she wanted. Marie promised to come and see me and bring the baby. As it turned out, I often took care of the baby on weekends, which I thoroughly enjoyed.

Nonetheless, it felt somewhat like a rejection and at times I became quite depressed, still feeling like I really didn't fit in anywhere, and wanting desperately to find compatible friends. Sometimes at night, when the pain was particularly intense I would imagine driving to the Oakland Bay Bridge, parking by the side and leaping over to my death. Knowing I probably didn't have that much courage, I would opt for a fantasy of a slower death, in which I would go to the state mental hospital in Stockton and demand they take me in. I finally discovered the radio station KPFA in San Francisco, which was totally run by listener support. At two or three in the morning, when I couldn't sleep, I would tune in to a program called Red Stockings. The woman who announced it sounded so friendly and the alternative music she played seemed beautiful to me. I would get up and dance to it and feel a little better.

Nonetheless, a gradual change for the better crept into my life. I finally began to make friends.

* * * * *

I had been promoted from doing intake to covering half of the medical ward. Gail Burnside had been taking care of that ward by herself, but it had become more than one person could handle. When my boss, Amy, told me about the new job, she had promised me that now I would get to do *real* social work. I wasn't quite sure what that meant, but it sounded promising.

To relieve the strain of trying to help comatose old men, homeless men and women and alcoholics, Gail and I would jokingly speak of "running off together to the beach" and becoming hippies. Gail had a husband and several children, including a son who was still at home, so I was acutely aware that it was, indeed, a joke, but the two of us were often able to arrange to have lunch together and became friends.

One noon, Gail got me to talk about my marriage to Ed. After hearing me out, Gail remarked, "Oh, Anne, no wonder it didn't work! It would be hard for a man to acknowledge that his wife was the better wage earner. And besides, it doesn't sound as if you had much in common."

"I guess you're right," I admitted.

"Listen, I know this doctor whose wife died about a year ago. He is really lonely. With all your education, I'm sure the two of you would have some lively discussions. Why don't I have the two of you over for dinner some time, so you could get to know one another. Just think! You wouldn't have to work any longer!"

The idea of not working at the hospital was promising, but somehow the roseate picture Gail had described didn't resonate with me. I thanked her and didn't refuse to meet him, nor express the fear I felt in my heart about being a doctor's wife or anyone's wife for that matter. I decided to just wait and see. A week went by with nothing more being said about it. One day at lunch, Gail described a symposium being held over a weekend at Mills College in Berkeley .

"It's my alma mater, you know. I'd give my eye teeth to go!" Gail exclaimed.

"Why don't you?" I quickly responded. "It's not far and you'd just miss a Friday at work. I'm sure I could get along for one day without you," I laughed. "I'm sure you could," Gail quickly agreed, "but my husband and son both had a fit when I mentioned it. It would mean they would have to cook for themselves for a few days"

"Couldn't you leave some meals in the freezer for them?" I suggested. "Of course I could, my dear, but they wouldn't be as good. I even offered to do that, but they weren't at all happy at the prospect."

"And…and you're letting that keep you from going?" I cried out.

"I'm afraid you're right, my dear," Gail admitted.

"If I were you, I'd just go anyway," I sputtered.

Gail's eyes grew large with understanding. "Oh, Anne," she said. "You'll never get married with that attitude!"

"You're probably right," I replied. Having dinner with the doctor was never again mentioned.

However, we continued joking about walking out on our jobs, driving to the beach and living on our beach combings.

Kathy Nakamura was hired to work in the Emergency Unit. Often her clients would end up on Gail's and my ward. When I discovered that Kathy liked to play tennis, I bought a racket and some balls (I hadn't played since college) and we began playing together on weekends. We often went someplace afterwards to assuage our appetites.

When I mentioned that I had gotten my BA from the Colorado State College of Education in Greeley, Kathy's face clouded over. "That's where my parents were detained in an internment camp during World War II," she said. "My two older brothers were born there, in fact."

"Oh, Kathy, I think what our government did was awful!" I exclaimed. "I remember walking by the high walls once. I could just feel the unhappiness from the other side."

"Some people just couldn't take it and committed suicide," Kathy continued. "Thank heavens my parents hung in there for the sake of my brothers. Also some of them formed a chorus, which also helped tremendously. My folks still belong to a Japanese chorus here in town."

"Really?" I exclaimed with excitement. "Do they sing Japanese music? I watched a Japanese chorus sing on PBS not too long ago. I really loved the music. Does your parents' chorus give concerts?"

"Yes, they sing Japanese music and they do give concerts once or twice a year. Would you like to go to one?"

"I surely would," I replied.

We went over to Kathy's house, where she introduced me to her parents and found out when the next concert would be. The concert was one of the high points of the summer for me. I was amazed at the high, clear tones of the women and loved the accompaniment of a koto (a Japanese plucked stringed instrument).

Later that summer Kathy got a bright red Datsun 240Z. She took me for some rides in it, but shortly after that Kathy met a Japanese man through some friends of her parents. The two fell in love and I didn't see much of her any more.

★ ★ ★ ★ ★

Being a large dog, Cissy hadn't come into heat until after I had moved to my own home. When she did come into heat, I thought my nice large fenced-in back yard would be sufficient protection against her becoming pregnant. However, one brightly moonlit night, I happened to look out my large back window to see a black Labrador jumping over the fence and out of the yard. I hoped that nothing had happened between the two dogs beforehand. I called Cissy to come in just in case...A few nights later, I forgot and let Cissy out into the yard. A little later, when I happened to look out, I saw a German Shepherd in the act of copulating with Cissy. I ran to the sliding doors and yelled. The dogs reluctantly parted company, but I knew I had probably been too late.

When Cissy's girth began to broaden, I mentioned to Joan, the secretary of the social service department, that I had a pregnant dog. The secretary was immediately interested and asked me if I was feeding her eggs. "She needs the extra protein," she claimed. The next day she brought in some lovely green eggs laid by her own chickens. "Give her two eggs a day," she instructed. I had never seen naturally green eggs before and wondered aloud what they would taste like. "They really taste pretty much the same," Joan assured me and then laughingly gave me permission to eat one myself.

By then, a year had passed since Karl's arrest and a date was set for the trial. A lawyer from the ACLU took Karl's case, feeling that Karl wouldn't have much of a chance with a public defender. Being a black man accused of killing a white woman was a definite disadvantage for Karl. Both Marie and I felt heartened that Mr. Carlson believed Karl's story.

The trial lasted two weeks ending with a conviction based on evidence that was entirely circumstantial. Being convicted, Karl was transferred to a prison for young offenders outside of Tracy, California, which fortunately for Marie, was not far from Stockton.

In many ways, the prison was a better place to be than the county jail, since they provided vocational, educational and recreational activities for the inmates.

However, the security was much tighter. First, visitors stopped in a small building just inside the grounds, where they were checked for contraband items such as drugs or weapons. Then they went over to the large complex, where their visiting rights were confirmed.

Karl was permitted to have visitors each weekend. Marie took Karly and visited with him three weekends and I took Karly for visits once a month. As soon as I parked in the parking lot, Karly would begin crying. We could both feel the tensions of the place. After comforting him, we would finally be ready to go through the screening process. When we were admitted into the visiting room and Karly saw his father, he would be all right. The prisoners and their visitors sat around card tables and there was an obviously armed guard at one side, sitting in a chair on a platform.

When I saw the glares we got, especially from some of the white inmates who apparently didn't approve of mixed couples, I was relieved with the guard's presence. These visits were primarily centered on Karly.

Meanwhile, San Joaquin General Hospital had a dormitory and dining hall in two remodeled army quonset huts where homeless men recovering from some illness in the hospital could be sent until they were well enough to be on their own again. When I felt I had a candidate, I would call Eunice, the matron, to find out if they had room and to tell her something about the man.

These telephone conversations soon led to some friendly discussions about the progress of certain patients and then the two of us began to meet for lunch.

This led to sharing stories about our personal lives. Eunice could tell that I was somewhat lonely and invited me to come to a sewing circle she had been in for a number of years.

"You don't have to sew if you don't want to," she assured me. "Some of us have been in it for nearly fifteen years, but most have been coming for only a short while. We meet every two weeks at different homes. Do you think you would enjoy that?"

"Why, thanks, Eunice," I responded. "I think I would. Most of my sewing is done on a machine, but I'm sure I would enjoy the conversations."

"I think you would, too," Eunice assured her.

The first circle I attended was at Eunice's home and I felt quite at home with the women. It proved to be quite a diverse group. The next meeting was held at the home of two women, who hadn't been able to be present at the previous meeting.

As soon as I walked in the door, I was quickly introduced to one of the hostesses, who was sitting on the floor making a wax model to cast a silver ring, using the lost wax method. I barely heard her name because when our eyes met, I found myself saying mentally, "She isn't afraid to be deep." I would ponder these words and somewhat discover their meaning over the next few years. By the end of that session, however, Troy and I had exchanged telephone numbers and promised to get together outside of the sewing circle.

Troy came over the following weekend and shared the rather amazing story of her adolescence with me. Her family was extremely poor, but Troy "pulled herself up by her bootstraps" determined to make a better life for herself. She obtained a position waiting tables at a posh restaurant and not only received very good tips, but learned good table manners by carefully observing how the rich ate.

Later Troy met and married Bill Peterson and by working as a clerk at a drugstore for seventeen years, managed to put him through college until he earned an MSW. During this time Troy's children, Katie, Lars and Brenda, were born. They were all in high school, by the time I met Troy .

Troy understood how unhappy I was with my job and dissatisfied with my life in general and encouraged me to play my violin more and got me to take a dream workshop, which opened me up to writing.

Catherine, Troy's next door neighbor who had co-hosted the sewing circle, had seven children, six of them by a brilliant, but physically abusive man, also a social worker. She had divorced him and had married a somewhat inadequate man, by whom she had a daughter. Her second husband, Bob Schmidt would insist that Catherine spend time with him alone and the older children were running pretty wild by the time Troy moved in next door. Right away, Troy helped pull the family together and encouraged Catherine to get a divorce from Bob, as well.

After the divorce, knowing how lonely I was, Troy introduced me to Bob, who was living on a houseboat by then. He liked to go out in the canals surrounding Stockton and fish. I enjoyed going on these fishing trips with him, as well as cooking in his little galley. I soon discovered how good catfish were, especially when they were eaten soon after catching them. Bob played the guitar and struggled to play along with me when I played my violin. I knew I wasn't in love with Bob, but we both seemed to be satisfied just getting together occasionally.

Early one Saturday morning Cissy came into my bedroom carrying something in her mouth. I quickly got out of bed and saw it was a puppy still in its sac. The poor mother didn't know what to do with it. Neither did I, or perhaps I just didn't want to do the obvious. I telephoned a sleepy Bob, who told me to break open the sac and hung up. I quickly found some scissors and did just that. At once, the puppy gulped in air and Cissy took over, assiduously cleaning it and managing, on her own with eight more puppies over a three hour period. Four of the nine looked like black Labs and four appeared to be German Shepherds like their mother. Only one looked like a mix.

As if that was not enough, two weeks later Green Eyed Lady had four kittens in my bedroom closet. Two of them were beautiful calicos, one was all yellow and one was black with white boots. Suddenly my house was like a menagerie. Fortunately both mothers cared for their offspring without much help from me.

By the time Christmas came, I had found suitable homes for the puppies and kittens. I obtained a large Christmas tree and made a real effort to have a wonderful celebration for Karly. He was over two years old and able to appreciate it. On the day itself, Troy and her children came over in the afternoon with some chocolate chip cookies Lars had baked. I felt like I was in a truly home-like atmosphere for the first time since I had left the convent.

However, unknown to me, Troy and Catherine became involved sexually and had less and less time for me. Perhaps Catherine was jealous of me, because when I would telephone Troy, Catherine always seemed to answer. After telling me that Troy wasn't there or was too busy to come to the phone, she would proceed to tell me about the good times she and Troy had going to garage sales and picking up wonderful antiques. She never seemed to think of inviting me to go along or to come over and see their booty and I was too shy to invite myself.

That spring, a young man, Tony Vitello, was hired into the social service department at the hospital. Since he lived out by me, we began car pooling and became friends. He had earned a B.A. in art and that was what he really wanted to be doing. However, he had married while still in college, and with two children, had to get a "serious job" in order to support his family.

I was sympathetic with his dilemma, but couldn't think of a way for him to find time for his art. I soon learned that he was a perfectionist and spent his entire weekends tending to his yard. He was also very critical of how his wife kept up the interior of their home. He couldn't seem to appreciate the time and energy it took to raise two small children. I tried to sympathize some, but also tried to point out the difficulties of his wife's role.

They had me over to dinner one weekend and I saw how harassed Betty Vitello was. However, to me, the house looked fine. Possibly Tony had helped bring it in order. He showed me some of his paintings, which I thought were quite good, but what intrigued me most was a small ceramic vase shaped somewhat like a cluster of mushrooms. It definitely had a humorous touch to it. I fell in love with it at once and Tony insisted that I take it.

When he would complain about being stuck as a husband and father, he would angrily point out to me that I didn't have any responsibilities besides myself and could be doing as I pleased. He had no idea of the seeds he planted in my mind.

Another MSW social worker, Corinne Smith, was hired to work with patients receiving dialysis in the newest unit in the hospital. She was also assigned to give in-service training sessions to the six social workers without MSWs. I found most of these sessions interesting, but still remained unsure as to what *real* social work was.

The three women with MSWs were all very interested in the teachings of Sigmund Freud, proudly calling themselves Freudians. When I happened to mention to Corinne that I liked the way Carl Jung had expanded on Freud's teachings, Corinne invited me to present this at one of the sessions.

I got out my notes from Notre Dame and carefully prepared my lecture. I had almost forgotten the pleasure I got from teaching. Afterwards, Corrine came up and told me she how much she had enjoyed the lecture and that she had no idea how extensive Jung's teachings were.

This experience got me to consider looking into teaching at a junior college, but I didn't see how a Masters in Theology would help me attain a position. I thought perhaps I could teach a class in Comparative Religions, but I didn't know where I would get the energy to study up on them. Finally, I knew I was still too raw from my religious experiences as a nun to do this. Also, while I suspected I wouldn't have discipline problems with older male students, I wasn't certain. Again, depression weighed itself down on me. Sometimes I would have to lock the door to my office, put my head down on my desk and sob. "Is this all there is to my life?" I wondered.

One Sunday afternooon, I found myself over at Troy's house Troy's husband Bill was home. I could hardly believe it when I heard myself complaining to the two of them about how I hated my job and life in general. Troy and Bill immediately became concerned.

"What would you rather be doing?" Bill asked.

"Oh, I don't know," I answered. "Something simple like…like managing a walnut farm. I think I could do that." Actually I knew nothing about walnut orchards. Although there were many right around Stockton and I had gone gleaning for some with Marie and Karl one fall, that was the extent of my experience with them. Perhaps it was thinking that it would be seasonal work that appealed to me.

Bill totally amazed me when he promptly offered to buy a walnut farm with a big house on it, where we could all live together. He was probably influenced by the back-to-the-land movement which was in vogue then. I looked over at Troy to see what she thought of the idea. Troy rolled her eyes and lifted her shoulders, but agreed that it might not be a bad idea.

I remained speechless, but quickly realized how ignorant I was about raising walnuts and even became more aware that I couldn't possibly live in the same house with Troy very long without expressing my true feelings for her. The subject never came up again.

Because of the frailty of the evidence brought forth in Karl's first trial, his lawyer was able to get a second trial, which was held that fall of 1972. This time Karl's lawyer achieved a hung jury, but the District Attorney was certain of Karl's guilt and started working on a third trial. Marie and I were profoundly grateful for our lawyer's solicitude, which also strengthened our own faith in Karl's innocence.

In the meantime, a Chinese girl, Patty Wong, who worked in the medical library at the hospital, began joining Kathy and me for tennis. Her family had been in the United States for several generations and Patty laughingly assured me that she was Christian. In May, when Kathy announced her wedding plans in San Francisco, both Patty and I were invited.

The wedding itself was held in a Buddhist temple. Somewhat incongruously, Kathy wore a traditional long white wedding gown and the bride and groom entered to the familiar strains of Wagner 's wedding march from Lohengrin. However, the ceremony itself was entirely foreign to the two Christians, under the smiling but watchful eyes of a large Buddha at the center, with gongs and other unfamiliar accompaniments. Later the wedding guests were to meet at the new Japanese Center in San Francisco for the reception.

It was at this time that Patty discovered that she had locked us out of her car. We could see her keys still hanging in the ignition switch. Fortunately I had a membership with triple AAA, so we found a pay phone and asked for assistance. While we were waiting for this, the two of us stood on a very windy corner in order to direct the mechanic to our car. Both of us had dressed in summer clothing (in Stockton, May was definitely warm), totally unprepared for the extremely cold weather in which we found ourselves. San Franciscans hurried by, bundled up in winter coats. We had both worn sleeveless dresses and I had brought along a short loosely crocheted shawl, which was totally inadequate, but I could tell Patty was most envious of it. By the time triple AAA got there, we both felt like statues made of ice.

When we arrived at the Center we were quickly seated for a sumptuous twelve course meal, served by waiters in tuxedos. When the bride and groom arrived, they had changed into beautiful, traditional Japanese clothing. During the meal their friends got up and toasted them in Japanese, amidst much laughter, which humor went entirely over the heads of Patty and me. Nonetheless, the food was perfectly prepared and dexterously served; the hot food was definitely hot and the chilled courses were bedded in ice. That was the last time either of us was to see Kathy, and I felt the loss of a good friend and tennis partner.

In spite of these friendships, I was increasingly dissatisfied with my life, having no ideas how to change it more to my liking, or rather, so that it was more meaningful to me. I had been invited by some of the people at the hospital to some weekend dinners or cocktail parties where the guests were paraded around the homes admiring the latest recently purchased "toys", usually expensive appliances. These were couples who had been married for years, their children no longer at home, enjoying the surplus of two incomes. I definitely felt out of place and was unwilling to invite them to my comparatively sparsely furnished home. I was often the only single person there and felt totally unable to contribute much to the conversations. Worse than that, I really didn't even want to, finding them somewhat limited.

One of the things I did to relieve my depression was to take trips up to Mt. Diablo which was near enough to Stockton to make an overnight feasible. There were wonderful vistas of the surounding territory. I had always felt spending time in the wilderness to be healing. The first time I did this, I only purchased a good sleeping bag, feeling safe enough to sleep under the stars with Cissy there to protect me. However, I felt a little too exposed and bought a small sleeping tent. Cissy got in with me the first time I used it, but wanted out right away. However, I could feel her pushing against me from the outside. Cissy had always been a good cuddler.

In the middle of that summer a new woman began doing the eligibility on the medical ward, freeing Gail and me to do *real* Social Work. I was still uncertain what this was, but I really liked Barbara. It turned out that she was a hippie! I remembered the girls in Seattle, encouraging me to go meet the hippies at the University. I smiled as I realized that at last, I was meeting a hippie. Although Barbara did dress a little out of the ordinary, having a proclivity towards clothing with bright colors; she was so naturally beautiful, she got by. Barbara invited me over to her apartment, where I saw my first hippie pad, complete with big bean bags on the floor, tie-died curtains on the windows and large psychedelic posters covering the walls. Barbara was also an art major and had made some beautiful woven "eyes of God" which impressed me. In the small kitchen I noted the pleasant aroma coming from various bunches of herbs drying by the window. Then I commented on the jars of sprouts by the sink.

"Sprouts have much more protein and vitamins and minerals than the mature plant," Barbara informed me.

"I didn't realize that," I said, "but I can easily believe it."

"Here, try a bite of these sprouted lentils," Barbara offered, as she pinched off a generous mouthful.

"Mmmm, they even taste healthy!" I exclaimed.

"Believe me, they are," Barbara assured me.

Suddenly there was a hoot outside Barbara's door, which Barbara answered in kind.

"Hi, guy," Barbara greeted a huge black man with an infectious grin. "Meet my friend Anne. She works on the same ward I do at the hospital."

Leroy showed me the special hippie handshake, after which he also shook hands with Barbara.

"I've got some primo stuff here. Wanna try some?" he offered, carefully taking a baggie of marijuana from a pocket of the huge shaggy vest he was wearing.

"Sure enough," Barbara agreed. "Let's use my pipe, though." She quickly walked over to an orange crate standing in for a bedside stand and got her pipe.

"Heavens," I thought. "I wonder what they would think if they knew I've never smoked marijuana before."

When the pipe came to me, Leroy immediately guessed that I was a neophyte and with twinkling eyes, carefully explained to me how to inhale, hold my breath and then release the smoke. Even though I did as instructed, I began to cough when it was time to exhale. The two hippies laughed in a friendly way and assured me I would get the hang of it. It only took three or four tokes and I was feeling relaxed and happy.

"We're going to make a hippie out of you, yet," Leroy grinned.

"I'm sure you will," I quickly agreed. I hadn't felt so close to people for a long time. The three of us had a wonderful conversation interspersed with much laughter.

A few weeks later, I invited them over to my house for supper. As soon as they entered, Barbara exclaimed, "But your place is so straight, Anne!"

"Well, what do I know?" I laughed. "Remember, I'm just an ex-nun not long out of the convent!"

"No! I didn't know that Anne!" Barbara exclaimed. By then Leroy and Barbara were in hysterics.

"And here we are teaching you to smoke and…and everything else!" Leroy said as he appropriately lit up a pipe.

"Yeah," I agreed. "I'm really going to the dogs," I laughed as I took a toke from the proffered pipe. I didn't even cough. "But then, I've always liked dogs!"

Later at supper, Barbara exclaimed, as she cut off a generous piece of the pot roast I had prepared for them. "Well, you sure can cook! Although I'm really supposed to be a vegetarian."

"Really!" I gasped. "I can fix you something else," having no idea what that would be.

"No way," Leroy interrupted, as he also helped himself to a large slice. "We can still enjoy a little meat every now and then. We've only been "veggies" for a little while. Meat really isn't good for you, though," he murmured.

"It's all the steroids and junk they feed the animals, not to mention all the cholesterol," Barbara explained.

"I see," I said. "You eat a lot of sprouts to get your protein, right?"

"That's right," Barbara said, pleased that I was catching on.

"I think I could learn to be a "veggie," I murmured.

"Sure you could," Leroy agreed. "But for now let's enjoy what's before us."

"You're going to make a hippie of me, yet," I said with a big grin.

"We do have something to tell you, though," Barbara continued. From the tone of Barbara's voice, I knew it wouldn't be good news I was about to hear.

"There's this wonderful commune of artists and musicians up in southern Oregon. We're going up there to live for awhile. I'm quitting my job in a week."

"That's really neat," I blurted out. "I will miss you, though."

"Hey!" you're a musician!" Barbara cried out. " Maybe you would want to come up some time, too."

"That really would be great!" Leroy exclaimed.

"Who knows, maybe I will," I choked out. By then I was fighting back tears. "You know, I always thought I was too old to be a hippie."

"No way!" they both exclaimed.

"We know a lot of older hippies!" Leroy assured me.

"Well, maybe not a lot, but you wouldn't be the first we've met," Barbara amended.

"Will you write and tell me all about it?" I asked.

Barbara quickly promised to do that.

Shortly after they left, Karl's third trial occurred, where he was finally and absolutely convicted of first degree murder. There would be no chance for any further trials. Karl told Marie she should go ahead and get a divorce, since he couldn't offer her much from prison and she decided to take him up on it. I continued to take Karly out for a monthly visit, but it was getting more and more difficult to make the time go by. What Karl told me about life in the prison was nothing but depressing to me. He did seem to enjoy seeing his son.

I desperately wanted to ask him the unthinkable question, "Was it really a mistake that you killed that young woman?" I simply didn't have the nerve, probably fearful of what the answer would be.

CHAPTER TWENTY

It was early November before I finally received a letter from Barbara. Almost two months had gone by since she and Leroy had left and I had just about given up ever hearing from them again. In the letter Barbara again extolled the wonderful commune of artists and musicians, describing in some detail their celebration of love on Halloween. She ended the letter by reminding me of my plans to visit the commune during my vacation the following spring. I responded at once, assuring Barbara that my plans were still intact.

On a dreary Monday morning early in December, I was returning to my office after seeing several patients on the medical ward, my arms full of records. I nearly dropped the entire pile when, upon entering my office, I saw Barbara sitting in my place behind the desk, smiling broadly. After setting the folders down on the desk, I took in the hiking boots resting on the opposite side of the desk, my eyes traveling up the tails of a man's long gabardine overcoat, the shoulders of which hung half way down Barbara's arms, topped by a floppy, stained fedora rakishly angled on her head. I noted right away that despite the odd garb, even for a hippie, Barbara was still beautiful, perhaps because she looked so happy.

"Barbara, what in heaven's name are you doing here?" I almost shouted.

"I dropped by to see you on my way down to Orange County to see my folks," Barbara replied.

"You…you aren't leaving the commune, are you?" Fear was evident in my voice.

"Not on your life!" Barbara assured me. "I'm going back in time to celebrate the Winter Solstice." Then she leaned forward in her seat and almost whispered, "Anne, have you ever tripped on LSD?"

"No,.. no I haven't," I answered truthfully. "Before I met you, I hadn't even smoked marijuana."

"Well, I have some really good, clean stuff with me. I know it's good, 'cuz I've already used some. Would you like to take a trip?"

I quickly remembered reading some articles by Timothy Leary describing his mystical experiences on LSD. I also recalled the peace loving revolutionaries at the Home in Seattle, but I also remembered those girls who had experienced *bad* trips.

"How much is it?" I asked, avoiding the issue suggested by my fear.

"Well, since this would be your first trip, one hit would be plenty," Barbara answered. "That would be ten dollars."

"Is that all?" I was surprised. "Well, I just might," I finally said. "Did you mean that you would be tripping with me?"

"Of course," Barbara assured me. "But I'll be leaving Stockton on Saturday, so we'll have to do it before then."

At first I thought it should be Friday evening so I wouldn't have to go to work the next morning, but I thought I would probably want Barbara around the day after. "How about coming over to my place on Thursday for supper?" I suggested.

"We should eat as early as possible," Barbara said. "It's better to take it on an empty stomach."

"Well, I can pick up a couple Mexican dinners at that restaurant on the corner so we could be eating by five," I suggested.

"That would be great," Barbara replied. "We could begin tripping around eight. You would probably be able to come to work the next morning."

"Oh, yeah…yeah, I'd want to be able to come to work on Friday," I quickly agreed.

"I'll see you then," Barbara said as she got up to leave.

That evening I decided to telephone Troy to tell her of the plan.

"Would you like me to come over? Just in case?" Troy offered.

"You mean you'd like to come and trip with us?" I asked, somewhat surprised.

"Oh, no," Troy laughed. "I think one of us had better stay straight."

That Thursday after Troy arrived, Barbara and I each popped a little purplish pill.

"Huh!" I said after a few minutes. "Nothing's happening."

"Be patient," Barbara chuckled. "It takes awhile to get from your stomach into your circulatory system."

"Oh, right," I conceded. Then Troy and I got into a discussion about a movie we had seen recently when suddenly I interrupted myself in the middle of a sentence. "My gosh! Look at that rainbow on the front window! I didn't know you could see rainbows at night! And it hasn't even been raining!"

Troy followed my gaze and asked, "You mean the reflection from the street lamp?"

"No! No!" I insisted. "It's a beautiful rainbow going across that bottom pane. Don't you see it?"

"That's what she gets for not tripping with us," Barbara interjected. "The world really becomes beautiful when you're on acid."

"Wow! It sure does!" I agreed, becoming more excited by the minute.

"Let's go outside and see the stars. Is the moon out tonight?"

"I don't think so," Barbara answered, "but you can see the stars better when it isn't." She led Troy and me out into the front yard.

"Oh my gosh, Troy!" I cried out. "Look at the stars! They're like pinwheels spinning. Wow! Van Gogh must have been on acid when he painted *The Starry Night*."

"Well, maybe something like it," Barbara agreed.

We began to get chilly and reluctantly went back inside. I had set some logs in my fireplace and asked Troy to light it. After it got a good start, I was totally mesmerized by the flames, dazzled by their enhanced colors. I began exclaiming at their exquisite beauty, laughing and crying in my excessive joy. Noticing Troy sitting there, I flung myself down by her feet and looking directly into her eyes, exclaimed, "Oh, Troy, I love you so much! I don't ever want you to leave!" I put my head in her lap.

"Well, I do have a family, you know," Troy replied softly, stroking my hair.

I sat right up. I was ultra sensitive to the rejection, in spite of the tactfulness with which it had been given. Quickly, I stood up and began to cry out, "I can't go back! I can't go back!"

"You can't go back where?" Troy asked, relieved but astonished at the sudden switch.

"I don't know!" I said. "I just know I can't go back!"

Barbara quickly came over and put an arm around my waist. "Take it easy, Anne. You don't have to go back if you don't want to," she assured me.

I began sobbing, repeating over and over, "I can't go back! I can't!"

Troy was puzzled and not a little concerned. "You can't go back to what?"

I answered impatiently, "I can't go back to a job I hate and a life I don't like much better!"

"You really don't have to go back, Anne," Barbara again asserted, looking deeply into my eyes.

"You're right!" I exclaimed. "I'll go back to the commune with you when you come back from Orange County!" Suddenly I shifted again. "What are your folks doing living there? I thought Orange County was ultra conservative!"

"It is!" Barbara laughed. "And so are my folks!"

Again I leaped forward in the conversation. "Will it be all right? Can I just decide to go live at the commune just like that?"

"I've already told them about you," Barbara assured me. "They'll love it when you play your fiddle! You can stay in the big house where Leroy and I live with another man."

"Wow!" I exclaimed again. "I'll go in tomorrow and quit my job!"

"Well, maybe you'd better sleep on it first," Troy advised.

"No, I've already made up my mind," I insisted.

Troy looked at her watch and stated, "It's already after midnight. If you're all right, I think I'd better head for home."

"Is it really that late?" I cried out. "Why, we've been tripping for over four hours! I can't believe it! Yes, Troy, I'm fine! In fact, I'm wonderful! Thanks so much for coming over. I hope I didn't scare you too much!"

"Don't worry," Troy said as she walked over to the door. "I don't scare that easily."

I turned to Barbara and asked, "Were you planning to stay here to-night?"

"If it's all right," Barbara answered.

"I'd actually appreciate it," I assured her. As soon as Troy was out the door, the two of us got into bed and quickly fell asleep.

The following morning Barbara woke up in plenty of time for me to get to work, but I was absolutely exhausted.

"I'll call in sick for you," Barbara offered.

"Oh, gee, thanks," I mumbled. Then suddenly I sat up. "No! Tell Amy I'll be in to see her this afternoon!"

"Well, if you're sure," Barbara said.

"I am! I am!" I said, quickly falling back on the bed, practically asleep before I hit the pillow.

That afternoon Barbara went with me to the hospital. I wore the only pair of jeans I owned, along with a plaid shirt and a pair of boots. When I told my boss of my intention, Amy suggested that I take a six month leave of absence. This reminded me of Mother Provincial's suggestion that I remain in the Order for another year before making a final decision to leave.

"Well, thanks for the offer, Amy, but I know I won't be returning. My mind is firmly made up."

"All right, Anne, we'll miss your good work, but it does seem you need to go on to other things," Amy said. I then had to sign a form on which I stated my reasons for leaving.

Early the next week, when I returned to sign papers releasing my retirement funds, while I was still waiting outside Amy's office, I could hear the man in charge of hospital personnel read my reasons for leaving. "I no longer believe in what I am doing." He laughed and remarked, "Who lives by their beliefs?"

After I had signed the papers, I went over to Gail's adjoining office and seeing she wasn't in, called on the ward, asking to speak with her. When Gail came on the line, I asked, "Guess what I'm going to do?"

"I have no idea," Gail replied.

"I'm going to the beach!"

"Oh, Anne, be careful!"

I laughed giddily, said goodbye and hung up.

Then I met Tony Vitello in the hall and gave him a hug, saying, "I'm doing what you told me! Remember? I'm leaving to go live the way I really want."

I was shocked when I saw his eyes fill with tears. "Anne, Anne, please don't! You don't know what you're doing!"

I became serious at once and replied, "Oh yes, Tony, I do! I really do!"

While I waited for Barbara to return to Stockton, I learned that Leroy, whose mother lived in Stockton, had taken advantage of the ride to come down with Barbara and would be in town the whole time. When he learned that I had quit my job and planned to go back to Oregon with them, he was delighted to initiate me into the pleasure-loving ways of hippies. In a few days we became lovers.

The two of us drove down to Berkeley and spent a day and most of a night on Telegraph Avenue. As we were walking away from a snack bar where we had enjoyed a thick sandwich of avocado and sprouts, I suddenly heard a most amazing sound. I could pick out a flute, piccolo and congas, but the main sound remained a mystery to me.

"Hey! Let's go find out what's happening," Leroy said, guiding me towards the music.

By following our ears, after walking a couple blocks, we came upon a steel drum band in a little triangular shaped grassy island in the middle of the Avenue.

There were two men playing steel drums, a man playing piccolo and flute and another on congas. There was no need for amplification whatever. It was the first time I had heard or seen a steel drum used as an instrument. I was mesmerized by the sound and by the way it was being produced with the use of snare drum sticks.

During a break between songs, I went up to one of the men.

"How are you getting all of those tones out of that?" I asked.

He showed me the many indentations in the sides of the drum. "You have to know just where to hit it," he explained. "But the whole chromatic scale is there."

"It would be hard to believe if I hadn't heard it," I said in amazement. "You must have to be really good to be able to make one."

"That's right," he acknowledged. "I didn't make this one. It came from Jamaica. I've tried, but I could never make one this good."

'Well, you certainly can play it good," I assured him, "which must take no little skill in itself." He could tell that I was sincere and gave me a brief demonstration as to how the tones were placed and let me hit out a few myself.

Later, as Leroy and I walked among some booths, I saw some bolts of material from Guatemala. I realized that I could make myself a long hippie skirt with it and with encouragement from Leroy bought a few yards. It was black with a band of bright colors embroidered around the bottom. The price was definitely right.

Late that night we were sitting, pleasantly stoned, on a bench on the edge of the commons on the campus of the University, when a man with bagpipes took out his instrument and began to play. In no time a crowd had gathered, in spite of the hour. I had never heard bagpipe music like this. I found it thoroughly enjoyable and eagerly dropped some change in his case to show my appreciation.

Afterwards, Leroy wanted to play some of his compositions for guitar. I found them quite innovative and told him so, pleasing him immensely.

I decided to sell my house offering it for a thousand dollars in cash and arranging for the buyer to take over my loan payments. Since there were only two weeks before we were to leave, I decided to rent it in the mean-time. A couple of men answered my ad and rented it on the spot. I arranged for Marie and a friend to come and give the house a good cleaning the day Leroy and I were to leave. Since I had given the extra bed to Marie, I bought a second hand bed for the second bedroom, asking Marie to pick it up at the store, the first thing. I paid Marie well feeling good that she would have some extra money for Karly's Christmas.

Then to my surprise, just a few days before Barbara was due to return, Corinne Smith, the social worker from the hospital, telephoned me and told me she had heard that I was trying to sell my house. When I told her that I hadn't sold it yet, Corinne said she was definitely interested in buying it, es-pecially when I told her the terms. We had a contract drawn up and Corinne gave me five hundred dollars, promising to pay the other five hundred when the deal was finalized. She was glad that I had rented it, since she already owned the house in which she was living and wanted this one as an extra income.

On the twenty-second of December, Barbara returned and we planned to leave for southern Oregon the following day. The commune was twelve miles inland from the coast town of Sixes. The next morning as we headed out for Oregon in my car, along with Cissy and Green Eyed Lady, the fur-ther we got from Stockton and the closer we came to Oregon, I became more and more apprehensive. Just before we arrived at the commune, Leroy proudly announced, "We've built all our own houses on the Eighty Acres. Some people would call them shacks, but they aren't."

"Oh yes they are," I said to myself as we drove up to the first one, which was the one in which I was to live with Leroy, Barbara and Jason, the man who had built it with Leroy's help. It was an octagonal building with ply-wood walls and windows of varying sizes all around. As soon as we stepped inside, the first thing I saw was two tall metal cans with garbage overflowing out of both onto the floor. It reminded me of a cartoon depiction of cornu-copias, but I didn't find it at all amusing.

There was no one at home, but there was a note on the door telling us that everyone on the commune had gone into Sixes for a Solstice party where we were all invited and that we should come as soon as possible. Bar-bara quickly showed me where I would be sleeping in the loft, which turned out to be as large as the main floor. She helped me take my essentials up to my bed and, after shutting Cissy and Green Eyed Lady in the cabin, we left for the party.

When we arrived, everyone there was thoroughly stoned and I suddenly felt very straight and not a little afraid. Leroy and Barbara were catching up on old friendships. Introductions did not seem to be a part of the culture. I wandered into a bedroom where a group of women were complaining about living on land with a bunch of men. As I listened, I became terrified as I realized that was just what I would be doing. As I slowly became aware that the most vocal of them all was Sarah, the owner of the Eighty Acres, the woman's shining stoned eyes and tightly curled, uncombed black hair did not reassure me. I wanted to run clear out of the place and go…where? It staggered me to realize that I had no place to go. These people were home like it or not. Finally after what seemed like eons later, Leroy sought me out to take me back to the commune.

The following day, I took Cissy for a walk up torrential Elephant Rock Creek that ran through the land. I breathed in the fresh mountain air and slowly became aware of the beauty surrounding me. Two of the men who lived on the land stopped by and the three of us talked about the beauties of the land, which helped me to feel more at home. I walked back to the cabin, emptied the garbage cans into a compost pit outside and prepared supper with Leroy. I would stay, for awhile anyway. It didn't take long for me to agree with Leroy that the owner-built cabins with their humorously placed windows were definitely not shacks.

I had not been there long before I discovered the musicians on this commune of "artists and musicians" were mainly of the three chord variety of guitarists and an occasional singer. Leroy was definitely the most versatile guitar player. Men definitely outnumbered the women on the commune. Sarah, the owner of the Eighty Acres, was the only woman besides Barbara and me. A few women came up with other hippies from Corvallis on week-ends. The octagonal house seemed to be the meeting place for music jams, probably because there was a piano there, although no one seemed to play it. I soon noticed that the women's role was to sit and stare adoringly at the male guitar players. It didn't encourage me to get out my violin.

In the middle of January, Barbara showed me a little valley up above our land, where for some reason, the spring wild flowers were beginning to come out and the blackberry bushes were already blooming. We took another acid trip there which inspired me to write this poem.

Unanswerable Questions
You've been here all along — and I'm just seeing you!
You've always worn so many hues of greens and blues?
Why, the blue violet of the blackberry bushes' brambles is glowing!
Is my seeing, you being?
Or is my seeing being you?

I lie face down to feel the pulsing of the breathing
The breathing of the mountainsides of trees!
Through the earth, I find I am breathing with the trees!
Is my breathing, you being?
Or is my breathing being you?

I hear your singing ringing through the cosmos
All round my ears sound waves are quavering!
I find myself joining with the singing.
Is my singing, you being?
Or is my singing being you?

Strangely enough, when I would stop to exclaim over the beauty of the glowing of the blackberry bushes, Barbara seemed bored with it all. I wondered if the effect of acid diminished with frequent use.

Cissy had come along on the trip, staying close to me as if to protect me. It seemed that not only did she experience some of the effects of the LSD, she also seemed to realize that I was especially vulnerable. Once, while we were sitting and enjoying the enhanced beauties of nature, I caught Cissy's gaze and felt I was looking deeply into pools of wisdom. I suddenly realized how much I could learn from my four legged companion by becoming more aware of her as a conscious being. (Green Eyed Lady had not fared as well. Shortly after arriving, she got out of the cabin one night and was never seen again.)

Later that evening, when Barbara and I returned to the Eighty Acres, I found myself feeling paranoid when we joined the others who had not been tripping. I became extremely self conscious, fearfully asking myself again and again, "Can they tell I'm stoned?"

Leroy came up to me when he saw me leaning against one of the supports in the middle of the room. "What am I going to do with the rest of my life?" I asked him querulously. He found it extremely amusing, but put an arm around me, sensing that I needed reassurance.

At twilight I went outside to use the hole dug in the earth, with a board on each side for footing, known as the shitter. As I squatted there relieving myself, I glanced up at the octagon to find it looked like a gingerbread house all out of proportion to what I knew it really was. I could barely wipe myself and pull myself together to return for supper. By then, I was definitely feeling very hungry, or as it had been explained to me, I was having the munchies.

After supper, I went up to my bed in the loft feeling safer there. When I closed my eyes, I saw strange and varied images. Some of them were of persons I had known from my past, but some were unrecognizable. Sometimes I simply saw beautiful, glowing, brightly colored paisleys slipping by. I suddenly understood what was meant when certain colors were called psychedelic. Even more strange were the cartoon-like figures that would sometimes fill my mind. When it became too intense, I would open my eyes to enjoy the more familiar realities of the wooden beams holding up the roof over the loft.

When I woke up the next morning, I called over to Barbara, "It's not going to be like it was before, is it? The trip yesterday really changed things... didn't it?" I wasn't certain, especially when Barbara failed to answer. For the rest of the day I stayed off by myself, my only companion being Cissy. I was busy thinking over what had occurred the previous day. "Which is the true reality?" I asked myself over and over. I finally decided that both could be real. I also felt that I had experienced a very sacred event the day before. I decided I would only use acid for very special occasions.

A few weeks later I met Barry, a man who lived on a mining claim nearby. He had studied engineering and had built an amazing three storey tree house between four Douglas Firs forty feet in the air. With the use of cables he had built the house so that it wouldn't be pulled apart by the wind blowing through the trees. He also played the piano and with the help of his best friend Glen, who built pianos as well as tuned them, they pulled up an upright piano, piece by piece to the second storey of the tree house where they put it back together. The first storey had Barry's cook stove, which also heated the house, plus cupboards and a table and four chairs. The top storey, where Barry slept, had a glass paned pyramid for a roof, which he claimed kept his razor blades sharp.

I had only heard of this wonder, when one day Barry appeared on the land inspiring us to throw a spontaneous party where the primary entertainment was playing music. Someone mixed a batch of electric Kool Aid (Kool Aid enhanced by some tablets of LSD). At first I was hesitant to partake of this because no one could tell me how much acid had been put in. After observing a number of them drinking it with no noticeable bad effects, I drank a shot glass full. Barry sat down at the piano and began improvising. I got out my violin and joined in with him, as did some of the guitar players. Without warning, he began playing a game of "follow the leader" in which he would suddenly change keys (i.e. from the key of G to C etc.). The guitar players began to drop out one by one as it became too difficult for them to keep up. Somehow I seemed to know when and into what key he was going to modulate. I stayed with him until we were both exhausted.

"That's the first time anyone's been able to do that," he said staring deeply into my eyes, suspicion dripping in his tone of voice.

Suddenly feeling defensive, I quickly admitted, "I don't know how I did it, but I just seemed to be able to sense in a split second what key you were going to go into. Wow! It was really exciting!" I suddenly sensed that Barry had not found it so and in fact seemed angry with me.

Feeling Barry's hostility towards me, I quickly put my violin away and climbed up to my bed in the loft, only to find Glen giving someone a massage on my bed. I sat down by him to watch, definitely feeling unsafe. His calm demeanor kept me from panicking.

"Would you like a massage?" he offered, after he had finished the one he had been giving.

"Why…why I guess so," I answered reluctantly, not wanting to offend him. "I've . . .I've never had one before," I quickly admitted.

"I can guarantee you'll like it," he assured me.

He had skillful fingers and quickly loosened the knots in my shoulders which I hadn't realized were there. "Ouch!" I suddenly exclaimed and then laughed. "It hurts and feels good at the same time!"

"When I get the knots out, it'll just feel good," Glen promised, which is exactly what happened. He could see my eyelids were drooping and left so I could get into my bed.

The following morning Barry seemed in better spirits and invited us all over to see his tree house. I truly wanted to see it, but knew I wouldn't be able to climb a rope that long. When I expressed this fear, Barry told me he had a winch with a rope on it and they could pull me up to the house on that. In fact that was how they had gotten the piano up there and how he got his supplies up there even now. He also offered to do this for the young woman who had just come onto the land and who was pregnant.

I felt wonderful flying through the air towards the tree house. After touring the three storeys, we ate a light lunch and it was time to exit by sliding down the rope. For some reason the winch wasn't available for going down. The rope was outfitted with knots about every eight feet so one could stop for a rest by planting their feet on the knot. I felt a flash of anger that I hadn't been told before I had gone up that this was the only way to get down. I could see that Patti, five months into her pregnancy, was frightened, also. Soon we were the only ones who hadn't descended. Patti bravely took her place on the rope and started down. I was horrified when I saw Patti's hands slip, when she was about a third of the way down. She shot down to the next knot, where she was able to stop her fall, unharmed except for some rope burns on the palms of her hands.

This made me very determined not to do the same thing. I let myself down very slowly, but without incident. However, the next morning I found the insides of my thighs were badly bruised from gripping the rope so hard. Nonetheless, I felt experiencing the wonders of the tree house had been worth it.

Leroy and I had not made love since we had arrived at the Eighty Acres, perhaps because he slept down stairs, not being able to climb the upright ladder to the loft, since he was so large. I had enjoyed our love making, but still knew I was not in love with him. I realized he was not making love with anyone else and wondered about his celibacy. I didn't feel inclined to approach him, however. When he invited me to take an acid trip with him, I intuited that love making went along with the offer. I wondered what it would be like making love while tripping.

I remembered Timothy Leary's injunction not to do so lightly, but trusting myself and Leroy, I accepted his offer.

The acid Leroy provided must have been laced with amphetamines (speed). We began leaping goat-like from rock to rock over the creek. I had never experienced such surefootedness before and was exhilarated by it. When it came time for the love making, however, it was disappointingly tame by comparison. Perhaps we had become too fatigued. We slowly returned to the cabin and fell into Leroy's bed falling asleep at once, even though it was still afternoon.

In the middle of the night we awoke with the munchies. We got up and by lamp light made ourselves humongous sandwiches and after consuming them returned to bed.

Finding us in bed the following morning, the others assumed that we were a couple. I knew better. Leroy always said he liked his women wild, which meant that they didn't want to be tied down to one person, just as he didn't. This was fine with me, but I winced when I overheard two of the other men referring to me as Leroy's old lady. Also I was beginning to realize that if I was in love with anyone it was with Barbara, who was totally unavailable to me. Slowly I was coming to admit that I was really a lesbian, like it or not.

One evening I decided I would like to bake bread in the wood cook stove in our cabin. I set aside a whole day for the event, first collecting smaller pieces of wood for the stove, then going down to the common house and hand grinding enough wheat berries and steel cut oats for the flour. The use of the oats was to lighten the loaves. I made my sponge, mixed in more flour and kneaded the dough until it seemed ready to put in covered containers to rise. It was then I realized how drafty the cabin was and I had to take time out to cover some of the windows so the dough would rise. It never did rise to my satisfaction, but I didn't want to waste the materials, so I put the mixture in loaf pans and into the oven, in which I had already prepared a good fire with many coals.

The finished product was very much like what I imagined hard tack would be, but both loaves were rapidly consumed with the soup Leroy had prepared. As I lay in bed that night I felt the day had been a good one for me in spite of the bread not being that good. Going through all of the processes of grinding the flour, making the fires etc. was somehow healing for me. It had seemed like a day long meditation.

About that time, Barbara returned from from spending a couple of weeks alone at a cabin on some land a day's walk from the Eighty Acres. Together, she and I began to plan a greenhouse for planting starts. Barbara had read of an experiment where people had dug out trenches in the form of a cross, had built up the soil between the arms for the beds and had put up a dome roof over it made of saplings and plastic.

The two of us cleared a small space near the garden and measured out a circle about twelve feet in diameter. Then we marked off the cross and began digging the trenches. Leroy got interested in the plan and helped with the digging. When the trenches were completed, Barbara and I left early the next morning to look for suitable saplings for the frame of the dome. It would take eight saplings of nearly the same length. It took all morning to find and fell the saplings. After lunch we painstakingly peeled the bark off and stacked the poles near the trenches. We waited a few days for the poles to dry out and then, after digging eight holes around the perimeter, we buried the thick end of each sapling about a foot deep in the holes and fastened them together at the top of the dome with twine. All that was left to do was to get some seeds. Again, I felt healing taking place in myself from having done a project from start to finish, as it were.

Barbara had traded her sports car in for a utility van for the commune. At the beginning of each month, everyone on the commune would pack themselves into the van and take off for North Bend, a little town just north of Coos Bay, where we did our monthly grocery shopping at a large hippie co-op. We all chipped in enough food stamps to pay for the staples kept in the common house, such as wheat berries, steel cut oats, oil, tamari and rice and beans. The different households bought fresh fruits and vegetables for their own use. If there was anything left over, an individual could indulge her or his own tastes.

During the March trip, I telephoned Corinne Smith at work to find out why she hadn't paid the final $500.00 on the house. Corinne told me that Marie and her friend had not only *not* cleaned the house, they hadn't picked up the bed for the extra bedroom. When the men went to move in, they were not too happy with the mess they found and the lack of the promised bed. Corinne claimed she had to take a day off work in order to get a bed and hire someone to clean the house. She felt this had cost her the $500.

When I questioned this, she asked me if I wanted to come back to Stockton and take her to court. I hung up, unable to even consider this.

Besides, I was flabbergasted that Marie had done such a thing, but understood more what had occurred when I got bills in the mail from Sears and Weinstocks. Apparently I had left credit cards in the drawers of my desk and the two women had spent the day shopping instead of delivering the bed and cleaning the house. I recognized the description of Marie's car on the Sears bill for four new tires. The cards had been sent to me in the mail unrequested and I had barely opened them. I simply put them in a drawer of my desk wanting to think over the possibilty of using them. I wrote to the stores reminding them that I hadn't applied for the cards and that I had not made the purchases and did not intend to pay for them. They wrote back asking me if I had any idea who the person might be who had done this. Because of how it might encroach on Karly's life, I did not feel I should give them Marie's name or address. However, I was deeply hurt and felt Marie had betrayed me. I never wrote to her again, although I often wondered how Karly was doing.

Also during that eventful trip into North Bend, I overheard someone remarking that the coming Sunday was Easter. When that day arrived, I took the *Liber Usualis* Sister Catherine had sent to me from the convent and went up to the little valley where Barbara and I had tripped on LSD. There I sang my favorites from Holy Week and Easter. I became very high *sans* drugs. I felt I had experienced the death and rebirth of the entire world, but most real to me was my own rebirth.

I wrote to Troy trying to share this experience which had been so meaningful to me. Even when I discovered later that that Sunday had really been Palm Sunday, the validity of the event remained the same.

Later that same month when the check covering my retirement from the hospital arrived, out of gratitude to the commune for providing me with a home, I bought a second hand flat bed truck which was badly needed, as well as a dozen fruit trees to begin an orchard. This left me with three thousand dollars from the check of a little over four thousand.

Reluctantly, I decided it was time to return to Stockton, pick up the things I had stored in Troy's garage, have them shipped to Sixes and, in that way, finally close the door on that chapter of my life.

CHAPTER TWENTY-ONE

WHEN I HAD found a copy of *I Never Promised You a Rose Garden* in the commune's library and had recommended it to Barbara, I was shocked a few days later, when she returned it, saying she couldn't read it because the woman's experiences were too much like her own. She also quietly admitted that she had an older sister still at her parents' home, who stayed in a room on the top floor of the house, refusing to come out of it.

Upon hearing this, I quickly averted my eyes, not having any idea of what I could say. Barbara quickly walked off before I could think of something.

Later, when I told her that I was planning to return to Stockton to pick up my things, she was more than willing to help me with the driving, although she didn't tell me then that she would not be returning to the Eighty Acres. Leroy promised to take care of Cissy, so Barbara and I took off the next day.

We decided to take highway 101 down the coast, beach hopping, until we arrived at San Francisco and then go over to Stockton. It was during that trip that Barbara told me she was going back home, maybe to stay. When we arrived in San Francisco, Barbara asked me to take her to the Greyhound Bus depot. Barbara's going home didn't seem like a good plan to me, but I didn't have a better one to offer. I was still dismayed at Barbara's self revelation. She was not only outstandingly beautiful, she seemed normal in every way.

Tears blurred my eyes as I blurted out, "Barbara, can't you get help?"

Tears of frustration filled Barbara's eyes, as she answered. "I…I've tried so many times. Actually the best help has been LSD and marijuana, but they don't seem to be helping anymore. You saw me take seven hits on that trip we took together. You didn't realize the danger I was putting myself into. But as you know, nothing at all happened, good or bad. Schizophrenia is a tough one to treat, believe me!" By the end of the narrative there were no tears in Barbara's eyes. She did not want pity and hastened away to get her ticket to Los Angeles.

Upon arriving in Stockton, I told Troy that I was going to leave my car in the parking lot outside Family Finance, since they were holding the title as security and I couldn't pay off my debt. I had planned to ship my things to Sixes and take the bus back. I had already asked Leroy to pick me up. Troy was amazed at my plan, but had to agree it was the right thing to do.

As I watched the ten o'clock news that night with Troy, and Bill, her husband, I had to get up and leave to stifle my amazed laughter. "Are they really still doing that?" I asked myself. "Why, all they're doing is talking in balloons. And the way they keep smiling while reporting all that bad news!"

This was the first time I was aware of what I termed "talking in balloons", which came from the balloons used by cartoonists to carry what the characters had to say. Just as the characters had the words put into their mouths by the cartoonist, it seemed to me that many people seemed to speak only in cliches, or at least only what they felt they were supposed to say whether they agreed or not, or at the very least, with very little thought. However, I had to admit there was some use for this. I knew I sometimes spoke in balloons myself, but I also knew that since my trips on LSD I did this less often.

Before I returned the car, I decided to make one last visit with Karl at the prison in Tracy. Since I didn't want to see Marie, I went without Karly, although I wanted to see him very much.

After only a few minutes in the visiting room, Karl gripped his hands together and I saw perspiration gathering on his forehead.

"I've...I've got something I have to tell you," he stammered.

I just looked at him, waiting to hear what he had to say.

"I...I did kill that woman after I...I raped her!"

"Oh, Karl," I gasped. "Why? Why?"

"I...I don't know," Karl gulped. "But I knew something was going to happen. I took the gun with me to work that morning."

"You knew you were going to install the phone for her and then kill her?" I asked incredulously.

"No! I just knew that something was going to happen," Karl maintained. "Are you...does that make you afraid of me?" he asked. His voice was actually trembling.

I looked him in the eyes as the truth of my own feelings came to the fore. "Karl, I guess I have been afraid of you for a very long time," I said, as I got up and left.

After Troy drove behind me over to Family Finance where I left my car in the parking lot, she took me to the bus station and got me to promise to keep in touch. As we got out the cartons with my things, taking them to the baggage department, I again felt like I was walking in a nightmare that would never end. But I felt certain that this feeling would go away when I got back to the commune.

As soon as I saw Leroy in his shaggy vest waiting for me by the bus station, I did feel much better and felt like I was returning home. This was even stronger when I saw he had brought Cissy along. After we loaded my packages in the van we drove over to Port Orford for a big bowl of clam chowder to celebrate my return.

Afterwards we went to Bandon to get some cheese and finally headed out for the Eighty Acres.

It was only when we were just a few miles from home that Leroy finally said, "I'm afraid I've got some bad news."

A lump quickly formed in my stomach. "So, tell me what it is," I said.

"Well, Jake took the flat bed out to get some booze and ran it into a tree."

Of course I was angry. I took in a breath, knowing that the commune's belief was that one shouldn't be overattached to material things. I finally spoke up, saying, "I don't see why he was permitted to use the flat bed to go get booze! We don't have that much money to spend on gas. The flat bed was just to use for heavy hauling, right?"

"Nobody gave him permission," Leroy reminded me. "He just took it upon himself."

"Well, I guess that's what we get for leaving the keys in our vehicles," I said bitterly. The subject had come up before in regard to the van. When visitors came up for the weekend they often took the van for the eleven mile trip over bad dirt roads to get some booze at Sixes. Everyone on the commune complained about it, but not to the offenders and no one wanted the responsibility of keeping the keys, including me. "Well, I guess it's too late to worry about that," I concluded.

"Frank thinks he can fix it enough to get it running again," Leroy said hopefully. "Then we'll have to take it over to George's for some body work."

Frank was a Navaho man on the land who would quietly sit in the driver's seat of the van when anything went wrong with it, and after a half hour or so would climb out, raise the hood and make the necessary repairs. I had a lot of confidence in him and it did raise my spirits.

We drove on in silence for a time, when Leroy again tried to lift my spirits. "I do have another surprise for you," he said and then laughed. "This one's a good one."

"Thank heavens," I exclaimed.

Leroy pulled off to the side of the road. We'll have to take a little walk down this road so you can see it," he said as he climbed out of the van. I followed after him until we came to an abandoned cabin. It was not only abandoned; about all that was left of it was the foundation and the floor.

"There's a lot of good lumber underneath the plywood floor," he explained "Come over here where I've pulled off a little of the plywood and you can see."

When I stooped over to see, I was surprised to find the joists and braces looked like new lumber. "You're right," I exclaimed. However, I was unsure of what this meant for me.

"I thought you might like to build a little place of your own," Leroy said. "You could start out by pulling out this good lumber."

I couldn't remember speaking of a desire to have a cabin of my own, but in fact, I had been thinking about it. One of the other men had a beautiful cabin near the creek, and I thought I would like to have a similar one for myself and Cissy.

"I'll help you get started," Leroy promised.

This project was indeed interesting to me and it took my mind off the somewhat childish ways of the commune dwellers. They spoke of becoming self sufficient some day, but had often left the chain saws and other necessary tools out in the rain. I had to admit that the main energy I had noticed was when some primo marijuana, LSD or alcohol appeared on the land. Frank had returned to the Navajo reservation only for a while, he claimed, but no one really expected him back soon, so that the flatbed sat glistening in the sun, unable to be driven.

However, Leroy stood by his word, and we began dismantling the floor of the abandoned cabin. It was not on the Eighty Acres and I wondered what would happen if the owner came by. Leroy thought it highly unlikely, since it had been over two years since anyone had seen him.

As I hiked along the creek to choose my site, I realized I was dreaming of a companion, besides Cissy, who would live with us. It was always an amorphous woman. What would Leroy think of that – or the others, I wondered.

When I showed the site to Leroy, he said I should move it farther from the creek because in the spring, when the snow from the higher altitudes began to melt, the stream grew a fair amount. I took his advice and a week or so later, he helped me stack the reclaimed lumber in the van and drove it as close to my site as possible.

It was around this time that Sarah, the owner of the Eighty Acres, and I had a good talk, during which Sarah told me that Hannah was the Hebrew for Anne and didn't I like it better than Anne?

I was somewhat taken aback, but when I recovered myself and thought about it, I realized that I not only liked the sound of it, but it felt entirely right. From then on I asked everyone on the commune to began calling me Hannah.

It was on a Monday, when the father of Patti's baby arrived on the commune with some sensemilla he had grown himself. The knowledge of the arrival of the sensemilla soon spread around the whole commune and the octagonal house was quickly full of people toking away. It didn't take any time and I was flat out in an easy chair unable to move, but being absolutely contented not to have to. At first I thought it was just because of my inexperience, but then I noticed everyone else was occupied in the same way. Finally, that night we began to have the munchies and laboriously dug out food to eat. Anything would do! After eating, everyone returned to their own homes for the night.

When I finally awoke the following morning, I quickly promised myself that I wouldn't smoke any more such powerful stuff. I was unhappy with myself for having lost an entire day of working on my house. When I went downstairs there was a bunch already standing in a circle waiting for a roach to come around. I naturally went over by them greeting them for the day. The next thing I knew I had toked up some of the sensemilla without thinking of what I was doing, and again, we were all stretched out, happy and contented to remain that way for the rest of the day.

The next morning I resolutely grabbed a couple apples for breakfast, wended my way between lounging bodies and walked over to my building site after picking up a claw hammer to remove nails from the lumber. Soon after, Leroy joined me, laughingly asking if I had had enough sensemilla.

"You bet!" I answered. "We're not going to become self sufficient very soon that way!"

"You're probably right," he agreed as he began cleaning nails from the lumber.

Soon after this, I walked into the octagonal house one afternoon to hear Leroy and some of the other men on the commune laughing because one of them had stolen a cake Patti had put in a window to cool before frosting it. He willingly shared it with the other men, but Patti had none of it.

I was furious. "You guys make me tired! Do you realize how much work it is to bake a cake here? You have to cut wood small enough to put in a wood cook stove, then you have to grind your flour and finally mix all your ingredients together. I think you have your nerve just taking it on yourselves to eat any of it, much less the whole cake, without leaving any for Patti!"

Then I noticed Patti sitting in a dark corner. Patti sat up straight and said, "It's all right Hannah. It was just a cake!"

I recognized the pseudo detachment the commune praised and replied, "Oh, of course. You're absolutely right, Patti. It was just a cake." I tried not to sound sarcastic, but I went on up to my space in the loft knowing full well that none of the men were that detached.

I was becoming more and more depressed at the way things were going on the commune. Since Barbara was gone, I, myself, hadn't gotten any seeds for the greenhouse she and I had built together, nor had anyone else planted anything in the garden. I finally decided that I really could not be a part of such a way of life. I had noticed the hippies in Corvallis had little businesses of their own and in this way earned enough money to live on, not depending entirely on food stamps as many on the commune did.

The next day I pulled Leroy aside. "Leroy I've decided to leave the Eighty Acres and go to Corvallis. I don't understand the way things are done here. I want to go there and get a job before all my retirement money is gone."

"You know Hannah, I've been thinking about the same thing. I'll never get to be a rock and roll star here! But what about your house?"

"Someone here will make use of the lumber. All I have to figure out is how to get there with Cissy and all my stuff. I sure wish I still had my car."

"Why don't we go up on the bus?" Leroy suggested. We can find a place to live and I know some of the people there, who would probably bring us back to get Cissy and your things."

I hadn't really considered that Leroy would want to go to Corvallis also, but I was relieved, since I really didn't know anyone there very well. I went over to Sarah's and told her of my decision and asked her if she would take care of Cissy until Leroy and I would come back for my things.

Sarah seemed somewhat hurt that we were leaving, but promised to take care of Cissy. "Maybe you'll decide to come back and stay," she said hopefully. I thanked her but couldn't give her much hope about changing my mind.

When everyone went over to North Bend in the van early in May, Leroy and I caught a bus from there to take us up the coast to Newport, where we would then head east for Corvallis.

When we arrived in Florence, we stopped to spend the night with some friends of Leroy's. Some hippie entrepreneurs had renewed the old part of the wharf with restaurants, arts and crafts shops and even a food co-op. Leroy's friend made and repaired canoes, sailboats and small motor boats. His workshop was the downstairs of an old warehouse. The upstairs, where he lived with his wife, had been a dance hall. Nelly had put up dividers for rooms and since she made cloth sculptures and wall hangings, the decor of the place was beautiful. She had also made the ceramic tiles around the kitchen sink, decorated with some gnome-like figures dancing on them.

Late the following morning found Leroy and me in Newport, where we spent some time at the Marine Laboratory of Oregon State University. I was fascinated with the information about high and low tides and their relationship to the moon. I was amazed at the wide variety of fish and eels in the display tanks. We finally watched a short film on how the practices of industries and tourists were slowly destroying the bay.

After a very late lunch at Mo's, Leroy suggested that we go on up to Tillamook before heading over to Corvallis.

"I've never been there," he admitted, "but it's supposed to be beautiful. Also they're even more famous for their cheeses than Bandon and I thought maybe we could go visit and get some samples."

It was definitely out of the way, but the name Tillamook stirred my memories just enough that I felt a strong desire to go there. It wasn't until we were on the beach just south of Tillamook that I again saw the rock formation of the Three Sisters and remembered the retreat I had made there over seven years before, when I was still wearing a habit. Tears stung my eyes and I told Leroy I would like to take a long walk.

"Would you rather be alone?" he asked, sensing something was awry.

"Well, let me think," I replied. "No. I think I'd like your company, but I might not want to talk much." I knew he would understand. We had spent time together before, without saying much.

As we walked, I was thinking, "A little over seven years ago I was walking along this beach wondering what I was going to do with my life and here I am still trying to figure it out," Leroy knew I had been a nun, but I didn't feel like sharing this with him yet.

"Well, at least I realized that the Eighty Acres was not the right place for me and I'm trying to do something about it," my mind went on. "I know I have never regretted leaving the convent nor quitting my job in Stockton. I guess I just didn't realize it was going to be so hard finding myself."

Having Leroy walking silently beside me helped me to have hope in my future in Corvallis. "I am finding myself, though," I thought, realizing it was probably a lifelong job.

After walking close to a mile, I began to run into the edges of the ocean, yelling at the coldness of it. Leroy rapidly joined in the play. We finally found a sand dune that protected us from the wind. We made love and spent most of the night there. It finally got cold enough that we had to walk into town and take refuge in the bus depot.

When we arrived in Corvallis the following day, Leroy took me over to some friends who lived in an old Victorian house. We were assured there would be room for us for a few days. In the meantime I had gone back to going by Anne, because a woman living there was named Anna and people were always confusing us. By the end of the week, Leroy and I had rented a small apartment.

Quickly I felt the need of some kind of transportation, since Corvallis was large enough that it wasn't feasible to walk everywhere. There was a small bus company, but it mainly helped the college students and was very irregular. So Leroy and I went to a bicycle shop where I bought ten speed bikes for both of us. We thoroughly enjoyed riding them together although I noted with some dismay that Leroy always managed to be in front. A few times I strained myself to get in front of him, but not for long. I finally realized it was not chauvinism on his part, but that his self esteem would not allow him to ride behind a white person, although he never expressed this.

A few days later, I bought a sewing machine. I hadn't made my hippie long skirt with the material I had bought in Berkeley. I decided to make more of my own clothes.

Leroy had brought some marijuana from last year's crop at the Eighty Acres to sell. It wasn't long before word got around the hippie community that he had some primo stuff and people began coming to our apartment to buy some. It was one of these customers who decided he would like to go to the Eighty Acres to check it out. He was happy to take Leroy and me with him, and since we offered to pay for the gas, he promised to bring us back along with Cissy and my things.

Joe had a big old station wagon, but by the time we had loaded my things, even with some of them on the luggage rack on top, it was pretty crowded, especially with Cissy being an extra passenger. However, we made it in record time, taking a more direct route than Leroy and I had by bus.

There was hardly any yard for Cissy to be in, so we began to look for another place to stay. Leroy discovered a house that was going to be for rent at the beginning of June. It not only had a large fenced yard for Cissy, there was plenty of room for the garden Leroy and I wanted to put in. As soon as possible, but before we were able to move in, I paid to have the sod turned in preparation for the garden.

A young hippie couple lived next door and we decided to become a commune in the city. About a week later, when we moved in, we found the man next door had gone ahead and planted seeds and starts in the prepared soil.

"How could he have done that without even finding out what we wanted to plant there, Leroy?" I asked, eyes flashing with anger.

"I don't know, Anne," Leroy answered, not really knowing what to say. It really didn't make me feel better when he continued. "Well, anyway, now we have a garden to take care of, and…and we are part of a commune with them."

The young hippie woman could play blues on the piano pretty well. I asked if I could try and improvise with her, but when we did, it confused her and she would have to stop playing. Also when I brought up the garden fiasco, the woman wasn't sympathetic at all. Perhaps that was because the young man was her "old man".

There were a number of alternative businesses in Corvallis, but none of them were large enough to have much of a staff, nor were they hiring anyone. The Food Co-op gave a twenty percent discount to volunteers who put in four hours a week, so I began to cashier on Wednesday afternoons. While this helped with the grocery bill, it was far from sufficient. As my retirement money grew more and more scarce, my anxiety level grew proportionately. I felt guilty because I couldn't seem to make myself go apply for a *straight* job. The thought of being locked into something that had little or no meaning in my life made me depressed as well as anxious and I knew this would only become worse if I did get such a job.

Leroy's drug dealing, which was his way of dealing with the problem, was making me more and more uncomfortable because of the people who came to make the deals. Yet, if I couldn't work a regular job, what was I going to do instead?

The musical ability of a few of our friends was not enough to be pleasureful for me. Whether I worked or not, life was again becoming meaningless, and my former suicidal tendencies returned. Instead of fantasizing throwing myself off the Oakland Bay Bridge, I thought of throwing myself in front of one of the huge logging trucks going through Corvallis.

Finally, I got the energy to call the twenty-four hour Crisis Counseling Service in Corvallis. The person with whom I spoke persuaded me to call the Corvallis Mental Health Department and tell them I was suicidal. Right away they offered me a session of counseling. I requested to see a woman, if possible. Fortunately, there was a woman on their staff who offered to see me that very afternoon, even though she wasn't on emergency call at the time. It was then that I met Linda Lewis.

As soon as I walked into the office, I realized that the woman before me was in need of help herself. This jogged me, somewhat, out of my own self pity. However, it did not occur to me to believe that she could not help me. In fact, Linda came right to the practical points of being able to pay the rent and buying groceries. She offered to get me on temporary disability, until we worked out a better plan.

Linda also liked music and encouraged me to try to find people with whom I could enjoy playing. She told me about the annual fourth of July picnic at the park and of all the music that would be happening there. I decided then and there to go check it out.

I was relieved that Linda didn't suggest medication or any other therapy than our own counseling sessions, which she offered to continue *gratis*. Because I still had a little of my retirement money, I took a rain check on the disability, but gratefully set up another appointment.

I went to the park on the fourth and it turned out to be quite a hippy event, but there were some really fine musicians there. I was pleased to run into Linda there and realized that she identified with the counter-culture in many ways. I was grateful to have found a friend with whom I could talk.

The new house only had one bedroom, and it was getting more and more difficult for me not to have my own private room. Also the young couple and I were not too compatible. I began getting irritable and decided to begin again to look for another place to live.

About this time I met a young woman fiddler named Clara, who was looking for a house mate. She and her boyfriend were renting a four bed-room house and were looking for room mates to help with the rent. I would have a room of my own and the use of the living room, kitchen and bath-room. It impressed me at once that Clara took her fiddling seriously in that she realized she had to practice. She was taking fiddle lessons from an elderly man, who had been trained by his father and had fiddled all of his life.

Clara dreamed of starting her own group playing old-timey music. I was extremely pleased when she offered to teach me some fiddle tunes and invited me to join the group.

Clara and I enjoyed each other's company from the start. We not only enjoyed fiddling together, but on several occasions we went to a bar down town and as we shared a pitcher of beer, would shoot some pool and laugh and laugh over everything and nothing. However, I had scarcely been living there a month, when Clara spoke several times of being a feminist, but as-serting that she could never make love with a woman.

"Well," I thought to myself, "at least I know where I stand." I wondered if Clara suspected that I was a lesbian. I also wondered what would happen if I brought a woman over for a night. Since I was entirely without prospects, I didn't think about it much. In fact, occasionally Leroy still came over for the night, but making love with him was becoming more and more difficult. I would find myself fantasizing that he was a woman. Still, I didn't have the courage to be honest and *come out* to him. I couldn't risk losing one of my very few friends, especially a good one like he was.

In the meantime, Troy, her lover and their children had left California for a visit with Troy's friends in Minneapolis, Minnesota, which was Troy's home town. I had written to tell her of my move to Corvallis, but I never got a reply. Then I telephoned the number she had given me where I could leave messages, but, again, I didn't hear from her. In the meantime, Linda Lewis had taken a three week vacation and I had no one to talk to on a personal level. I felt extremely isolated.

One night the pain of loneliness and feeling of alienation became so great, that I felt I could no longer bear it. My room was a second storey at-tic room in an old house with high ceilings. The window looked out over a cement driveway. I thought of leaping out head first and thus being killed instantly. Suddenly I found myself crouched on the window sill, ready to jump into oblivion and painlessness.

Just as suddenly I was on the floor of the room, as if I had been forcibly thrown back from the window. My mind became flooded with visions of sunsets, waterfalls, mountains, streams, flowering fields, beautiful vistas that had previously led me into mystical contemplation of the unity of all things. I came to realize the wondrous value of the gift of life, even when it was so painful. I got up from the floor and climbed back onto my bed, from which I could see the stars out the window. Pain continued to flow through me in great waves, but it was interspersed with feelings of relief and immense joy at still being alive. I fell asleep just when the sun began to rise, knowing that I would never again consider taking my life.

CHAPTER TWENTY-TWO

MY RETIREMENT MONEY was really getting low, when Leroy told me he was going to the local cannery to apply for a seasonal job and asked if I would like to try out for one, too. We went together. I felt I could do anything for a short time. They didn't ask for a resume, but I did have to join the union, although I didn't have to pay my dues until I received my first pay check. I was hired as a corn husker (putting unhusked ears of corn on a machine which did the actual job). Leroy was hired as a fork-lift operator for a dollar an hour more. He didn't have any more experience or training as a fork lift operator than I did as a corn husker and he was seated most of the day, while I stood the entire time. I realized I wasn't offered the job because it was felt a woman couldn't handle a large piece of machinery. However, I was too desperate to complain and possibly not be hired at all.

I loved getting up early in the morning and riding my bicycle to work by myself. It took a few days before I discovered that instead of fighting the corn husker, if I became a part of it, I could think about whatever I wished. It was wonderful not to have to think about the work after I left, except when I went to bed, as soon as I closed my eyes, I would see ears of corn going by on the conveyor belt. I worked at this job six days a week for six weeks, earning enough for a visit to a dentist, and still have enough for rent for a couple more months.

Shortly before I had started working at the cannery, Clara told me about her business making a high protein candy bar for a variety of people, including hikers, backpackers, tree planters or others needing protein. Actually the man who had put the recipe together wasn't interested in making and distributing them himself. He had talked Clara into making enough to provide the Food Co-op with some. Clara asked me if I would like to help. We decided to call them Moose Brownies, although they weren't baked and were more a candy bar than a cookie. Of course they didn't contain any moose meat. Moose Brownie was a nick name given the inventor, Bruce Barney, by a child of one of his friends.

Clara and I rented a booth at the county fair and entered the Moose Brownies in the food competition under the division of *other* (other than pies, cakes, cookies etc.) The bars won first place over fourteen other entries. This, along with good sales at the co-op encouraged us to spread out to the other alternative businesses in the community. They proved popular and the business grew rapidly. By the time I had finished at the cannery, Clara had gone back to work at the Montessori School nearby. She no longer had time nor need for the Moose Brownie business. In December I bought her out and found I had discovered a way to support myself.

We had been limited to selling the bars in Benton County, by putting a required warning on them that they had not been produced in a licensed kitchen. I looked into finding out how to license our kitchen, because I wanted to expand the business to other counties and I felt that the warning probably lost some business. To have our kitchen licensed would have meant keeping the others who lived in the house out of the kitchen when I was working on them and Cissy and Grover, Clara's dog, could never go in the kitchen. The only way we could let them out into the fenced back yard was through the kitchen.

About this time, I heard of a new alternative bakery that was going to open in March. My business had already grown to the point where being able to use a large commercial mixer would definitely be an advantage. I went to one of the meetings of the fledgling bakery and asked if they would consider my renting time and space in their facility. After determining my storage needs, as well as the use of a stove and mixer, they came up with a rent which was most acceptable to me and would help them in their beginning stages. The distributor for the Food Co-op also worked out an arrangement with me to take Moose Brownies to Eugene, Newport, Salem and later even to Idaho.

In the meantime Leroy and I were occasionally making love, but when he expressed a desire to move into the communal house, I felt I had to refuse him. We would have had to share my room and I was trying to face up to my lesbianism. I didn't have the courage to *come out* to him, partially because I feared that if Clara ever found out, she would ask me to leave. Fortunately, he met and fell in love with another woman and he and I could continue our good friendship in peace. I had determined to stop trying to be heterosexual, even though in Corvallis, at that time, it meant being asexual.

In Corvallis there was an alternative adult education program with low cost classes. I began taking a psychic self-healing class as well as a class in tai chi. In the psychic class we tried to see each others' auras, but I simply didn't have the ability, although I could feel prickles of heat or cold emanating from the person. We were never told how to interpret these findings, however.

I really enjoyed learning tai chi. The instructor was a young and friendly man, who wasn't put off by having an older woman in his class. I preferred it to yoga because I liked the way it flowed from one movement to the next, almost as if I were dancing, whereas yoga seemed more like exercises to me.

I also began playing first violin in the Corvallis/OSU community orchestra. I admired the conductor very much, but found the concert master arrogant and difficult to work under. After a season, I decided to form my own chamber ensemble. It consisted of Linda Lewis, who I had discovered played marimba, an orthopedic surgeon, who played clarinet, a woman at the bakery, who played flute and recorder and later a newcomer to the bakery, who was a jazz pianist. We played jazz, folk and a little classical music, for some of which I made arrangements to match our instrumentation. We played at a local coffee house and at a hippie restaurant on the west bank of the Willamette River. We were known as Anne Benton and Friends. The restaurant always had a full house when we played there. We were treated to a vegetarian meal and always got enough tips so each of us went away with a few more dollars in our pockets.

Slowly I obtained four violin students; two were men attending OSU, who couldn't afford to pay the rates of the college instructor. Clint was from New York City and was pursuing a PhD in Marine Biology. He was also married with two small children. In New York, while attending undergraduate school, he had worked at being a life guard at the city pools. Unfortunately, for his wife and children, his real passion in life was partying and being high on marijuana or LSD. At his wish, we concentrated on fiddling and he did become pretty good. After I had known him for about a year, his wife finally left him. He had realized even before he was married that he was not the fatherly type and not a very good husband either. Besides that, he was extremely homesick for the Big Apple. Sometimes he would unload on me for almost an hour before we got around to the lesson. He was a very likable person, but I did feel sorry for his wife and children.

Apparently he had an excellent memory because he got very good grades with very little studying. I was to learn that theirs had been a shot-gun wedding, but he simply could not change himself into being a responsible father and husband. I hoped he would be able to find good paying employment, in which case I was certain he would provide for his family. I wasn't at all certain, however, that he had the discipline to keep a good job.

My other student from OSU was a younger man, who had transferred from Evergreen College just outside Olympia, Washington. He wanted to learn to play classical music and, in spite of carrying a full load of classes and being a mentor at his dormitory, he must have practiced a good deal as we were playing fairly complicated duets by the end of the year. We taped some to send to his mother.

I had another fiddle student, Jerry, who worked construction by day and did auto mechanics on the side. His *old lady* had given him ten lessons for his birthday. After the ten lessons, he was interested enough to continue on his own. He really got to be pretty good and began playing with a group in town.

My fourth student was a boy of nine. He had been studying under the OSU violin professor, but after the prof had rapped the boy's head with his bow a few times, his parents changed over to me. Of course I was also quite a bit cheaper, but his father was an emergency physician at one of the hospitals, so cost was not really a consideration. Charlie had taken lessons for only a few months, when his father became bored with his job in the emergency room. They moved to a larger city, where he could establish a private practice.

One day I found myself walking over to the philosophy section of the public library. It was right next to the religion section. I stumbled on some books about Edgar Cayce, which introduced my mind to the possibility of re-incarnation. It was also at this time that I read all of Albert Camus' books. There were some things about them I didn't care for, but I especially liked *The Plague* and his tenacity to awareness of the present moment and tried to bring this more and more into my own life.

I met an ardent Sikh, a young man, who taught me to do some Kundalini yoga. I got up very early in the mornings to practice sadhannas with him. I was always energized by them, but at about two in the afternoon I would be overcome by fatigue. Shortly after, he moved to Eugene and joined an ashram there. I continued to do a few of the sadhannas, but didn't really wish to become a Sikh. I did enjoy what I called the bodily meditations.

In time, I became known as the Moose Brownie Lady about town, often delivering my wares on my ten speed bike, my silver pony tail flying behind.

I had become a member of the co-op board and checked out and closed there one night a week. I exchanged work and goods with the people at the bakery collective and became considered one of the pillars of the counter culture community in Corvallis. But I was not contented. By now I was really wanting to meet some lesbian feminists and I also wanted to live in the country again, a desire firmly implanted from the four months I had spent on the Eighty Acres. I began to wonder if these two desires were incompatible. When I discovered Country Women Magazine, I had hopes they were not.

In June of that year Clara moved from Corvallis to study to become a Montessori teacher. Another male student quickly filled the vacancy, making me the only woman in the house. I really didn't mind, especially as I had already made it clear that I was not the house cleaner, dish washer nor cook. One of the men had been a marijuana dealer before he had decided to return to college. He still received samples in the mail tucked in between the pages of magazines.

One morning after he had received such a package, I was invited to join him and one of the others in trying out the sample. It only took two tokes to put me in an altered state of consciousness. We were sitting around the kitchen table and I began to wonder how the two of them could go on talking about such mundane things as their classes and assignments, while I.... I longed for silence to absorb what was happening to me. Feeling extremely vulnerable, I finally got up and decided to take a bath, where I could lock the door and feel I wouldn't be interrupted.

As I luxuriated in the warm water, I suddenly found myself standing at one end of a huge barn. At the other end I could see young people putting torches in sconces situated on the walls. Some musicians arrived and I saw they had been preparing for a dance. From their clothing I was able to determine it was around the time of the American Revolution. Then I noted the clear air which I was breathing and it came to me that this was how it had been before electricity had become harnessed.

With a start I partially returned to the the bath tub and the twentieth century. I sat up, somewhat frightened and began saying my name, address, present age etc. striving to re-establish myself totally where I had left. It took effort, but I finally got out of the tub and seemed fairly normal once more. However, I was amazed at the strength of the marijuana that could produce such a vision of the past.

One of the men living there, who was quite a bit taller than I, took a liking to both Cissy and myself. He was one of the many men who had come to OSU because of the good reputation of its forestry school. He was quickly disillusioned when he found out that the degree would not enable him to work out of doors, as he had thought, but would undoubtedly put him in an administrative position, where he would determine how many board feet of lumber could be had from such and such a stand of trees.

One afternoon, we took Cissy and drove out into the country to take a leisurely walk. Out of nowhere, a car came speeding around a corner and before we could realize what was to happen, Cissy was struck.

The woman driving the car slowed down, looked over her shoulder, and then sped on, seeing that we had no way of stopping her. Clint ran to where we had left his car and drove back. He helped me get her in the back seat with me holding her and drove us straight to a veterinarian he knew.

The vet suggested that I leave her over night so he could treat her for shock before determining if she had any broken bones. He told me that often animals died of shock if it wasn't treated right away. He would be able to X-ray her in the morning to see about broken bones.

It turned out that her pelvis was cracked and he outfitted her with what looked something like a corset without stays to help hold it in place and relieve the pressure and the pain. Probably because of Clint, the vet let me pay the bill in installments.

Cissy could hardly manage to eat and drink and since she weighed seventy-seven pounds, Clint offered to take her out in the mornings and evenings to relieve herself. It would have been next to impossible for me to do this without exacerbating the problem He was most appreciative of the Moose Brownies I gave him in return.

In the spring, the land lord decided to sell the house to some developers, who would tear it down and build an apartment complex. I answered an ad seeking "family members on a farm ten miles south of Corvallis". The farm was owned by a couple, but the other man and woman living there were not a couple.

In the meantime I had purchased Clara's old station wagon that was in good condition, so I drove out to see about living there. Of course I took Cissy along to check it out. We were hardly out of the car, when out from nowhere a cat zoomed in on us, attacking a very surprised Cissy. Marlene, the owner ran out and rescued Cissy, apologizing profusely. She explained that the cat had just given birth to a batch of kittens and was being overly protective. Cissy learned at once to stay clear.

We were given a tour of the farm, which included two horses, three goats, several kids, a flock of geese and a lovely little pond that watered a huge garden.

The garden was primarily comfrey, because Marlene had a great faith in its healing powers. When I saw the nice little attic room, which would be Cissy's and mine, I arranged to move in with Cissy a few days later.

It was here I learned to work with goats, including milking one of them, and came to admire their independence and intelligence. I established a particularly close relationship with the nanny I was assigned to milk, a beautiful brown and white Nubian, called Valentine. When I would be walking near the pasture where she and her companions were situated, I would bleat out a greeting and she always responded, coming over to the fence for a treat.

Alas, even though there was an electric wire at the top of the fence, Valentine could not resist leaping over it to try out the greener grass (actually our neighbor's garden), on the other side. I watched several times as she beautifully leaped clear of the electric wire and began to munch contentedly on the vegetables. We tried to tether her and even to hobble her, but to no avail. Somehow she would manage to free herself. I hated to see such a free spirit held in like that anyway but was saddened when they finally had to sell her in order to keep peace with the neighbors.

Later in the summer, a blue heron came to fish in our pond over a two week period. I had never seen one before. Staying discreetly on my side of the pond, I would watch her wade and then suddenly plunge her long curved neck into the water and get a meal. It was when she would take off and amaze me with the span of her wings and the grace of her flying that I really fell in love with her. As I watched her I began to feel a bond between us. When she stopped coming by, my memories kept her fresh in my mind.

Marlene introduced me to Jane Roberts' Seth books. These gave a very convincing account of the possibility of reincarnation within an evolutionary context. However, it was Seth's teachings that we create our own reality that intrigued me most. Of course one could take this too simplistically and deny it out right, but I had lived long enough to see how, in many ways, this had been true in my life. The problem was that most of us do not take on this responsibility and allow ourselves to be overly influenced by events, which determine many of the decisions we make. It was a complex idea, but it helped me to take more charge of my life, even as I discovered that some times events did more or less determine my choices. I strove to make this less the case than more.

Indeed, it was a series of events that finally determined me to move from the farm after only five months. My attic room was right above Marlene's and Jerry's bedroom and I could not help but hear them arguing and even fighting at night. It got so that I finally would get up, dress and take Cissy for a long walk, hoping they would have desisted by the time I returned.

It was then that I discovered a beautiful stand of virgin Douglas furs. They must have been sixty to eighty feet tall. I found a ring of them and would lie down inside of it with Cissy and gaze at the stars. When I went there one day to contemplate their daylight beauty, I realized I had been trespassing on some one's land, so I kept my visits nocturnal.

In the meantime, Marlene gave birth to a little girl at home with the help of a midwife. I had heard hippie women rhapsodizing on the sacred beauty of giving birth in this way, but Marlene's cries of pain somewhat diminished the picture. For some reason this addition to the family increased the fighting that would go on at night. I actually didn't hear their words, but the tone of their voices told me more than I wished to know.

I inadvertently mentioned this to Marlene and we both decided that I should try to find another place to live as soon as possible.

I quickly found a trailer for rent in the little town of Philomath, just west of Corvallis. Of course I missed the country setting of the farm and Philomath turned out to be a bastion of hippie-hating red necks. Nonetheless, the trailer was in the back yard of Irma, who had come almost directly from the Haight and most decidedly dressed a la hippie. The mother of two sons, she had given up any use of drugs and lived a somewhat straight life. She was attending OSU hoping to eventually earn a PhD in philosophy and psychology in order to help her be a more effective astrologer. This was amazing to me, but admirable at the same time. She explained the difference between humanistic astrology and mechanistic astrology, which raised my opinion of the art considerably. Also I remembered Jung gave some credence to astrology, as well.

For a couple of boxes of Moose Brownies she did my chart. After explaining the signs and their relationship to the planets and some about the houses and the aspects, she exclaimed, "You're lover relationships are not of the usual type." Then she paused a few seconds, while I stiffened in my chair. "You may have difficulty in finding a suitable partner, because of your over trusting nature. Tauruses in general have this problem. But don't give up. You will finally find the right person."

I breathed a sigh of relief and realized what she had said was somewhat true. I was particularly pleased that Irma had never used the word *man* nor a masculine pronoun in her advice. I was a little dismayed that my lesbianism was right there in my chart, although Irma had been too tactful to use the word.

When I had rented the trailer, it was with the understanding that I was looking for a more appropriate place and she let me pay weekly. After three weeks I discovered that Hester, the woman with whom Leroy had become involved, was looking for a room mate in her home in north Corvallis. She and Leroy had broken up and he had moved to Eugene. I went over to see her and Jackie, her six year old son. They both accepted Cissy and me right away.

I had been living there about three weeks, when one Sunday Hester asked if I would stay with Jackie for about three hours while she went out to Grandma's farm for the weekly Sunday morning meditation. She was not Hester's grandmother, but a psychic called Grandma by her followers. "I promise not to ask this of you often," Hester promised.

"Well...I had planned to go to the bakery to work, but, oh well, if it's just for a few hours, I can go later," I replied.

"Gee, thanks, Anne. I should have found some one earlier, but I just decided I would really like to go this morning," she explained. "Jackie really likes to go to the park, if you'd be into that."

"Sure thing," I quickly replied. I had been wondering how we would spend the time together. However, my curiosity was peaked as to what went on at Grandma's and a few days later I asked Irma.

"Well there's usually seven or eight of us and we sit around her dining room table for about a half hour and then we share whatever we saw during that time," she explained. "It was really neat last Sunday. About three of us experienced the same vision, except that we each had a different perspective on it, naturally. That's the first time for me that that happened. It was really exciting to be a part of it."

"I can well imagine," I replied. "Do you suppose I could go some time?"

"Well, I'd have to ask," she replied. "I'm planning to go next Sunday and I'll ask then. Jackie will be going over to spend the time with a friend of his, so I won't be asking you to take care of him."

The following Monday, Hester informed me that she had asked Grandma and had received permission for me to go to *circle* with her. "That's what we call it," she explained.

"Thanks, Hester. I would really like to see how it is." I had been feeling the need of some spiritual companionship and hoped this would provide it. Grandma had married and had two daughters. Her own parents, her husband and now her daughters never acknowledged that she had any exceptional psychic powers. In fact, they disapproved of them. When Hester and I arrived the next Sunday, her daughters and a grandchild were just leaving for church. They felt that the people who came to Grandma's circles were heathens. It was especially painful for Grandma, because one of her daughters was dying from cancer and she wouldn't let Grandma try to help her with her healing powers, although she had helped many others during her lifetime.

The rest of us arranged ourselves around the big oval dining room table with a small glass of water in front of each of us. This was supposed to help concentrate our psychic energies. After Grandma spoke a few prayers, we sat in silent meditation. When Grandma felt that we were ready, she would begin by sharing her vision. Then we went around the circle, each sharing his or her vision.

The first few times I went, my mind went blank, probably from my fear that I would have nothing to say when it was my turn. I did begin to see faint auras around people's heads, but that was all I had to report. Nevertheless, I continued to go, as the visions the others had were most interesting.

Finally, one Sunday, I envisioned myself in the virgin forest I had visited when I was living on the farm. I felt myself being healed and loved. Grandma confirmed this by saying she had seen me standing in front of one of the trees, which changed into a knight in shining armor blessing me. "He seemed to be forgiving you for something," Grandma explained. "Perhaps it was Christ."

I had never mentioned to Grandma that I had been a nun, nor had Hester, but I recalled the nun in Dante's Inferno, who had needed forgiveness for having left the convent. I certainly was not seeking such a savior figure. Actually I felt that Grandma's vision of me had been distorted by her own cultural bias. However, I respected her integrity and continued going to her circles.

During another Sunday, Don, who was Grandma's biographer and was considered by the others to be the most psychic person there, next to Grandma, had a vision of me as a blue heron standing in the middle of a stream, calm and poised, while a coyote barked noisily on the banks. This reminded me of the heron I had seen at the pond on the farm the previous summer.

Don's vision seemed right. The heron seemed to exemplify some power and strength in me.

On yet another Sunday, during the meditation period, I went into a place of great light and love. I was enjoying this unexpected gift, when, as if from a distance and below me, I heard Grandma begin to share her vision. As each person around the table told of their vision, I became more and more uncomfortable. I definitely did not want to come down and listen to the others. Even more, I did not want to talk about what was happening to me. Inexorably my turn came. I had opened my eyes earlier to check out my spatial relationship with the others. I found myself seated with them around the table, but their voices still seemed to be coming from a distance and beneath me. Tears of frustration began to stream down my cheeks, as I felt forced to speak. Don, who happened to be sitting next to me began firing questions at me.

What are you seeing? Who do you see? What do you hear? Is some one speaking with you?" He hardly gave me time to answer. I was only able to shake my head in confusion.

"Is he suspicious of what is happening to me?" I asked myself. "Why is he so hostile? Why can't he leave me alone?" I began to weep.

At that, Grandma told Don to speak his vision and to leave me alone.

In spite of all this, I was still in that place of light and love. When the circle was finished, and people were preparing to leave, I wondered if I would be able to drive myself home. For some reason Hester had not come that day. Not wanting to draw any more attention to myself, I walked on out and got into my car. As I started down the road, I realized that I was even more than usually alert and aware of what was happening along the way. Yet, somehow, I remained above it all in that place of light and love. I continued in that state for the rest of the day, keeping to the solitude of my room.

Reflecting on the day's events, I was shaken by Don's attitude and negative behavior towards me and I did not want to be exposed like that again. Pearl, who was a year older than I, had been present that day and later telephoned me to tell me that she, too, had been distressed by Don's behavior and hoped that it would not keep me from returning to the circle. I admired her for doing this, since I knew she was Don's lover.

I returned the following Sunday, but found myself unable to open myself to any psychic experience. I definitely still felt hostility coming from Don. I decided I would not return.

In the meantime Pearl and I had become friends. She was a therapist and had just learned how to do rebirthings. We decided to do an exchange, where she would give me a session based on deep breathing in return for some voice lessons from me. As a child, she had been ridiculed for her singing, but had never lost the desire to sing. I was reminded of my work with the young sisters and after some time was able to release Pearl's voice.

During the breathing sessions, I never regressed to the time of my birthing, but I did go back to when Mama died, just seven years before, and during that session, I wept copiously, crying out, ""Mama, I'm sorry, but I just couldn't leave the convent when you wanted me to come home because you were lonely. I was too scared to go back into the world. Really, I was just too scared! I hadn't made it in the world before I entered the convent, and even though I did have people's esteem in the convent, I knew, somehow that if I returned to the world, I would fail again! Oh, Mama, I loved you and do love you so much! Can you ever forgive me?" I had unconsciously been feeling guilty about this all that time. During the session Pearl helped me realize I had probably done the right thing, but what was most healing was at the end of the session, I actually felt Mama's presence and her forgiveness. I also realized this was the first time I had wept about her dying since the funeral.

At another session with Pearl, I went back to my fifteenth year, when I had had a dream that my sister Margaret had shot me with a machine gun, filling my abdomen with gun shot wounds. In the dream I knew the doctor and Mama were just outside of my room speaking of my chances of surviving, but I was unable to understand what they were saying. My hand unconsciously went down to my stomach and when I felt a wetness there, I awoke and scrambled to turn on the bedside lamp. I discovered that the wetness was only perspiration, not blood. However, this had such a terrifying effect on me that I never shared the dream with anyone.

At our last visit with each other, Mama had told me that Margaret had been very jealous of me. I imagined that there were probably times she wished I were dead and that somehow I had picked up on the energy. It wasn't a pleasant thought.

About this time, however, an event propelling me towards a change in my life happened with the discovery of Kate Millet's book, *Flying*. It told me that there were defienitely other lesbians out there. I just needed to find them.

CHAPTER TWENTY-THREE

ON THE BACK cover of the winter issue of Country Women magazine, was an advertisement about a group forming for older women wishing to live an alternative life style. I was already living an alternative life style, but most of my associates were much younger and of both genders. I took more interest in the fact that it was signed by two women living at the same address. Perhaps living alternatively with women my own age would be an improvement, but primarily I was looking for lesbians.

I took the chance and wrote them a letter requesting more information about their organization. Almost by return mail I heard from Elizabeth Freeman, who invited me down to her home in Wolf Creek, Oregon. I called them long distance to confirm the invitation and to set the date. Both she and Elana Michels enthusiastically renewed the invitation, told me Cissy would be more than welcome and that I should plan to stay two or three days.

After arranging my Moose Brownie business so I could be gone that long, I packed a few clothes, Cissy's food, a box of Moose Brownies and took off for Wolf Creek. It would be an easy two hour drive mostly on I-5.

When I arrived they came walking down their long drive to greet me. The atmosphere was somewhat strained at first, while they were trying to determine if I were a lesbian and I was trying to find out the same about them.

"We…We're a couple you know," Elana finally blurted out. "We're lesbians."

"Oh, yeah, well…I guess I'm one, too. I mean I <u>am</u>…definitely." By then I was blushing furiously at my awkwardness. Then I briefly told them about my relationship with Lynn, how I had entered the convent and some of what I had been doing since. "Lately I've been looking for some lesbians, it seems for a very long time." By then I was laughing and crying from embarrassment.

"Well, you've found some," Elizabeth said and gave me a hug.

"Yes," confirmed Elana. "Here we are!" and also gave me a big hug.

They took me up to Elana's room, where Cissy and I would be staying at night. Then they each shared how they had come out. For Elana, it had been many years before when she was still in her teens. Elizabeth had only been out a couple years. The two of them had been together for only a little over a year.

"Gosh," I exclaimed, looking around at Elana's room. "This place is beautiful. Did you build it yourselves?"

"My nephew built the main part," Elizabeth explained. "I've been living here about three years. Elana had a group of women build this room."

"Yes, I like to surround myself with women's energies whenever I can," Elana asserted. "I helped some, but women younger than I did most of it. I had built an adobe home in New Mexico years ago."

"Really," I exclaimed. "I'd like to build a home for myself some time."

"Then you probably will," Elana laughed, giving me encouragement.

Next they told me about the group of women they were gathering together with the purpose of forming lesbian communities in the country.

"But that's just what I'm looking for!" I exclaimed.

"We've only had one general meeting so far, but the second one will be happening next month. It will take place at Nourishing Space, about twenty miles east of Tucson, Arizona. The owner rents it out to groups of women. Do you think you could come?" Elizabeth invited.

"I'd really love to," I replied, "but that's pretty far." I had already told them about my Moose Brownie business. "I don't know if I can squeeze that into my budget." My disappointment was evident in the tone of my voice.

"Why, you could come along with me," Elizabeth said. "Elana is going on ahead to help set things up. I was dreading going down by myself anyway. It won't cost me anymore if you're along and it seems that Juniper and Cissy are becoming fast friends." Juniper was Elizabeth's dog.

Before I left Wolf Creek, Elizabeth and Elana took me over to the ten by ten foot cabin, on the same land as theirs, where Ruth and Jean Mountaingrove lived . The two of them were the founders and publishers of *WomanSpirit Magazine*. Elizabeth and Elana went on and the two women received me warmly. The three of us quickly fell into an animated conversation as we lay comfortably on the bed, which nearly took up the entire cabin. They described their magazine to me, since I was unfamiliar with it.

Suddenly Jean confronted me. "Anne, what about your spirituality?" she wanted to know.

I was stunned. "My…my spirituality? Why…why, I don't know," I stammered. "I…I guess I'd have to think about it," I admitted. I really hadn't thought about myself as a spiritual person since I had left the convent. "Can lesbians be spiritual, too?" I blurted out and then began blushing at the foolishness of my question.

"I certainly hope so," Ruth laughed. "I consider myself a spiritual person and I am certainly a lesbian."

"Yes, of course," I quickly agreed, tears coming to my eyes. "Of course," I repeated. Then I told them about having been a nun for seventeen years, the circumstances of my conversion and those leading to my departure. They were most supportive of my discovering my own spirituality.

"You don't have to belong to a church," Jean assured me. "But women's circles are very inspiring." Then she described what often took place in these celebrations. "Here, take this complimentary copy of *WomanSpirit Magazine,*" Jean said, handing me a copy. "I think you'll come to like our magazine very much."

"Oh, thanks, a lot," I replied, taking the magazine. "I'm sure I will." Then I gave them some Moose Brownies, which they immediately loved.

"Say," Ruth said, "these would be great when we're putting out an issue and don't have much time for cooking."

"They really would," Jean immediately agreed. "If you would like a subscription, we'd be happy to do a trade."

"That sounds great," I said, taking her right up on the offer.

In February, when Elizabeth and I arrived at Nourishing Space, I discovered for the first time the beauty of the Sonoran Desert. This was even before the first rains which I was told would draw out wild flowers in abundance. Then I was treated to deep full bodied hugs from everyone there. It was fantastic to see women going around without shirts. I was amazed at the beauty and variety of women's breasts.

"And to think," I exclaimed. "I had to wait until my fiftieth year to discover this!'

The next day, Shelly Arendt taught us all some basic massage strokes and then had us massage each other. "Anne, you really have a lot of healing in your hands," Shelley assured me. "You ought to study massage." Since I had admired Shelley's manner and expertise, this made me feel wonderful. As I became more aware of my own body in such positive ways, I wanted to learn this art to bring other women to the same positive body awareness. What could be more healing?

One morning, Sheba, one of the younger women living on the land, took me on a long hike up in the lava covered hills surrounding Nourishing Space. I was filled with energy and began climbing rapidly, leaping from rock to rock, climbing higher and higher. I was celebrating my wonderfully long and strong legs as they stretched farther and farther out, leaving my young friend farther and farther behind. No indictments here for being so tall. I shouted and laughed in exultation.

I came to the top of the first peak and saw one just a little higher up and immediately started out to climb this new goal. When I came to the top of the second one, I was, by then, somewhat breathless, myself. I could understand how mountain climbers could become addicted as long as there was another peak still higher to climb. I looked longingly at another still higher peak, but knew that when the exhilaration had worn off I would be stiff and sore. Reluctantly I turned and started back down only to discover that Sheba had given up and had returned to Nourishing Space. Embarrassed that I had left her so abruptly, I sought her out and apologized. She laughed and had understood what had happened to me. In my heart, I continued to celebrate my height and agility.

I was soon initiated into the feminist political process. There was a class struggle going on between the owner of the land and some of the regular dwellers. Instead of the planned workshops on forming women's land communities, we tried to help with the struggle. I quickly learned of the painful differences between women of working class background from those with middle class connections. I had more or less assumed that I was from a middle class background. It would be another year, when I enrolled in a classism workshop in the San Francisco Bay Area, that I discovered that I was from an upwardly mobile working class background. I had a sudden understanding why at times in the past, I could feel so uncomfortably alien in a group of middle class women. However, I had also felt out of place in groups of working class women, as well.

Martha Courtot was living at Nourishing Space at the time. She and I discovered that we both missed the beautiful liturgies of the Catholic Church. Together, we celebrated a Mass with orange juice and bread. Martha read a poem she had written about her mother and I spoke of Mama. Then she read a few more poems she had written and I read from an old favorite of mine, *The Blessed Virgin Compared with the Air We Breathe* by Gerard Manly

Hopkins. I was quite dismayed at some sexist passages in it, which I hadn't seen that way before.

Later that week Elana declared the evening of the first new moon after Clara Barton's birthday as a Woman's New Year. It provided a healing time after the class struggles. Martha guided us in a group tarot reading. This was my first contact with a tarot deck. I was fascinated by the images and admired the way Martha encouraged us to interpret them for ourselves.

After the reading Elana formed us into a circle and suggested that this might be a good time for anyone who wished, to change her name. I had noticed that some of the women had taken other names to replace their patriarchal names, but until that moment had not considered doing so myself. At once, Hannah Blue Heron came to my mind, as I quickly remembered Sarah of the Eighty Acres telling me about Hannah being the Hebrew for Anne and then my experience with the blue heron at the pond. I noticed how neatly they came together. After I expressed my wish, the women began chanting Hannah Blue Heron after telling me to stand in the center. As they chanted they side stepped around the circle. It was as if all the sound waves surrounding me were filled with my new name. Then they stood still and asked me to come to each to be greeted personally by my new name and to receive a hug with each greeting. I was ecstatic and happy that the name had come to me. It was a most empowering experience.

I had somewhat fallen in love with Shelley Arendt, who, while she liked and admired me, could not return the compliment of being in love. This was painful for both of us. She continued to encourage me to become a healer through my hands and gave me a copy of Christina Ismael's *The Healing Environment*. The book proved to be very inspiring to me, encouraging me to take a massage class when I returned to Corvallis.

The last night at Nourishing Space, Martha and her companions living in the A-frame nearby, invited us all down for supper and an evening of entertainment. Martha read some of her poetry. I was totally enchanted by it, being touched in a very deep place. Then Martha asked me to play some fiddle tunes, which I had promised to do earlier. Now I felt it would be the ridiculous following the sublime, but I played anyway. I would have preferred to go off with Martha and listen and listen to her poetry.

The next morning when I had packed up and was walking towards the small parking lot to stow my things in Elizabeth's car, I was surprised to see three black limousines parked there. I was even more stunned to see men in black suits, white shirts, black string ties and gun holsters obviously going across their chests walking around the grounds. Nourishing Space was being investigated by the FBI.

Astonished, I thought to myself, "Just like on TV!"

It turned out that they were seeking an ex-Weather Woman, who was reportedly working with the construction crew building a large summer house on the land. Elizabeth and I were wondering if we were going to be able to leave as we had planned. The men quickly determined that neither of us was the woman they were seeking and allowed us to drive off.

When Elizabeth and I pulled into Wolf Creek two days later, it was late afternoon and the sun was beginning to set. In spite of Elizabeth's invitation to stay overnight, I felt compelled to continue on to Corvallis. I needed to be alone as I came down from that wonderful high of being with women. I dreaded returning to the heterosexual world to carry on my business, to live again in very alienating surroundings. But I had a new name to sustain me and a dream of some day living in the country with a group of women.

Cissy and I pulled out of Wolf Creek just as the sun completed its setting. After barely a mile, we ran into cloud burst after cloud burst as we climbed up and over three mountain passes. Cissy became so frightened that she kept trying to climb into my lap. The rain and the heavy wind made it next to impossible to see the road and extremely difficult to keep from veering. I was afraid to keep going, but even more frightened to try to pull over to an edge I couldn't make out. For awhile I was able to follow the tail lights of a truck in front of me, but this also forced me to go faster than I felt was safe. I began chanting, "I am Hannah Blue Heron" over and over again as I crept on, soon without the help of any tail lights. The storm continued for nearly two interminable hours.

By the time I pulled into Corvallis I was totally exhausted from the strain of driving under such conditions, but jubilant from the ceaseless chanting of my new name, my new identity as a lesbian feminist.

I did not *come out* to anyone in my music group besides Linda Lewis, whom I trusted implicitly. Nor did I speak of my lesbianism to anyone in the bakery collective or the food cooperative. I officially changed my name and discussed feminine politics with my women friends and some of the men. They fully respected my change of name and my espousal of feminist principles.

I finally came out to Hester, who plied me with questions about lesbianism, but ultimately became threatened by it. Again, I felt it necessary to find a new living situation. I was delighted to discover a dilapidated cabin in a beautiful forest at the foot of Mary's Peak. In fact, it was my friend Irma, the astrologer, who told me about it. I paid my fiddle student, who was a carpenter, to help me put on a new roof as well as put in some windows and doors. I was able to put on the siding and insulation by myself. The owner bought me a new wood stove from Montgomery Ward and when she saw the results of my labors, she told me I could live in it for as long as I wished, rent free. She also gave me permission to run a water line up from the well and I paid another friend to install electricity.

I had been living in the cabin for a little more than a month, when I received a letter from Martha Courtot, along with a copy of her first book of published poetry. It was a rainy and chilly evening as I sat huddled by my wood stove, reading Martha's poetry, seeming to hear her voice as she had read them at Nourishing Space.

> On that other side of Madness
> Rivers flow upstream
> Women make love without hands
> Everything vibrates in nine primary colors
> And the roads we take
> Sometimes disappear between one footstep
>   and the next.... *

I was especially caught up by this poem. I felt deeply moved by it and wanted to respond to it from that deep place it had touched me. I picked up my soprano recorder and began blowing into it. I enjoyed the feeling of my warm breath pushing against my fingertips through the holes of the instrument. This, too, seemed a part of the music. One fragment of a tune kept repeating itself in my mind, through my finger tips and out into the sea of sound waves.

> And when we love,
> We love in threes. *

---

* From the poem A Woman's Place: Summer 1976 from Tribe , by Martha Courtot, by Pearl Child Press 1977

This was as far as it went that night, but I knew that I would come back to it, that I would be writing music from this poetry. I was extremely excited. I had not written any music since I had left the convent, almost eight years before.

It was after I had moved into my cabin that I came out to Pearl, with whom I was still doing therapy. Now we were exchanging therapy sessions, since Pearl wasn't interested in developing her voice further. Pearl was still lovers with Don, who by now, was stepping out on her and treating her in such a way as to cause a break up. It was obvious to me that he wanted Pearl to leave his home, but it was not so to Pearl.

Finally during one of her therapy sessions with me, she began crying out, "No! No! I won't take this! You can't treat me like this and get away with it."

This was the beginning of her painful pulling away from Don and establishing her own home and office in Corvallis. She still loved him and needed much support and encouragement, which I willingly gave. However, soon I was feeling increasingly attracted to her. Ultimately, during one of our therapy sessions, I spoke out, "Pearl, I can't help it. I am becoming attracted to you. It is really hard to become so close with you during these sessions and then not even feel we can exchange a hug at the end." I had already described the loving, full bodied hugs I had received at Nourishing Space.

"Well, Hannah, I'm certainly not adverse to hugs," Pearl replied, opening her arms wide.

One beautiful spring day around my fifty-first birthday, Pearl and I had gone to a lovely little meadow behind my cabin to do our therapy sessions. Afterwards Pearl told me that she would like to make love with me. At least that is what I heard. I could hardly believe it. In spite of the hugs, I hadn't expected Pearl to go any farther.

I centered myself and slowly began to kiss Pearl's face and lips, putting as much caring into it as I could. I began stroking and caressing her arms with my magic hands, while I moved down and began caressing her breasts with my tongue. Then I suckled her nipples, which by now had hardened appreciably. I continued to fondle her breasts with my hands as I pushed myself down further, licking Pearl's navel, her stomach, and finally her mons. By then, Pearl was moaning with the pleasure of it.

When I gently separated her labia, Pearl cried out, "You won't find everything there. I had to have some surgery for cervical cancer."

"Believe me," I said, "it is beautiful all the same." I began to stimulate Pearl's clitoris with the tip of my tongue.

"Oh, Hannah, it is more than I can stand," Pearl cried out pushing me away.

"I'm sorry, Pearl! Did you find that offensive? Surely I didn't hurt you, did I?"

"No, it was beautiful. Really, I don't think I realized how much you loved me, and . . .well,. . .it's just too soon after Don."

"I understand," I replied through my own pain.

"Maybe we'll try it again a little later," Pearl stammered.

"Whatever," was all I could manage to say.

After Pearl left, I found myself walking around in my cabin in a stunned state. As I went to wipe away my tears, I caught the musky odor of Pearl's yoni. "My God, I did make love to her. It did happen. But what an ending. I should have known better than to approach her so soon after she broke up with Don." Then I remembered that it had been Pearl who had approached me. Next, I remembered the suggestion of a promise to possibly try again later. I couldn't stop myself from falling in love – hopelessly.

We did make love several more times, when I began to notice that Pearl never made a move to make love to me in return. When I finally said something about it, Pearl broke out crying, "I can't! I can't!" she sobbed.

"Am I repulsive to you?" I asked.

"It's just that. . . that I'm a mother of seven children and a grandmother to eleven more. It just doesn't seem right somehow. How could I ever admit to them that I. . .that . . .I make love. . .with another woman?"

"I see," I answered, absolutely shattered. "Well, I think we'd better not see each other for awhile. This is extremely painful to me. I. . .I'll call you if and when I am ready to resume our friendship."

"I'm really sorry, Hannah. I guess I didn't realize how much it meant to you.

I certainly hope we can remain friends." she said.

"Only time will tell," I replied, tears brimming my eyes.

I hadn't learned yet that many straight peoples' idea of lesbians and gay men was that we are just into sex. Love isn't an issue.

In May, Elizabeth and Elana had a third meeting of OWN (Older Women's Network) at their place in Wolf Creek. Before breakfast one morning, shortly after I had arrived, I took a long walk down Wolf Creek which ran across the road from their property. I came to a place where some rocks had formed a miniature waterfall. Liking the energy I felt there, I sat by the side of the creek to do a chakra sound meditation. I was still following the Sufi method, which has a person go up the major scale, each tone of the scale assigned to one of the chakras. They used the syllable *ma* to take the place of *fa* (the fourth tone of the scale). Since that syllable was assigned to the heart chakra, the chakra of altruistic love, the open vowel sound of ah permitted me to open my mouth and throat wide and relaxed. I intoned freely and loud, feeling protected by the crashing of the water on the rocks.

As I toned, I thought lovingly of Mama and then I recalled my own years of mothering in Good Shepherd convents. Suddenly a great and painful wave of anger filled my chest and I began to cry copiously, even before I was aware of the reason.

When awareness came I felt the pain of being childless, because I would have had to have a man, to *catch* a man, in order to have a child of my own. I toned even louder to help release the pain.

"So I was not good enough to be the mother of your children! You were afraid of me. You thought I was a freak because I am so tall. Not only because I was tall, but as tall or taller than you. Also I frightened you because I knew my own mind. So I couldn't be the mother of your children. I was a freak! A freak! Even some women have smiled at my height and befriended me because I would not be competition in the race to *catch* a man.

In this way I howled and cried by the waterfall. Finally I stopped howling and wept silently. Slowly I came to know in my heart that I had never wanted to marry a man. I realized that I was better off childless and unmarried. I recalled my childhood dream of "living on a ranch with six kids, dogs, cats, horses and cows" but no man was ever in the picture. I felt healed from the anger I had held all these years from having been ignored by boys in my youth.

It was at this workshop that I got to know Baba Copper, who lived in Berkeley, California. Baba had also done meditating with some Sihks and we began to meditate together in the early mornings before breakfast.

The final afternoon of the workshop we held a workshop on sexuality. I had taught the others the few basic massage strokes I had learned and then we massaged each other in a loving but non-sexual manner. Afterwards some of the women spoke of their experiences of love making with other women. During this time two new women appeared and somewhat took over the work shop, because of the struggle they were having with their own relationship. One of them wished to open their relationship by becoming non-monogamous and the other wanted to remain monogamous. For most of us, it was a very uncomfortable discussion.

That night we planned to hold a dance over in the barn after supper. A group of us were standing on Elizabeth's porch, when Baba brought out some sinsemilla she had grown herself. Baba passed her little pipe around and after the first toke, I knew it was powerful stuff and was wondering if I ought to take a second toke, when the pipe was handed to me again, I automatically toked once more.

The two women who had come that afternoon had volunteered to carry the record player and speakers over to the barn and I followed after with a pile of records. Suddenly I heard them speaking of their stormy relationship in very private ways and I decided they had forgotten I was right behind them. I tried not to listen but it was impossible not to hear most of what they were saying. I began to cough to remind them I was there. They kept right on talking. I noticed they were not listening to one another very well.

When we finally walked inside the barn and went over to the table to put down our burdens, they kept right on talking even though I was in plain sight. Then I noticed that they weren't talking at all. Their lips were immobile and they weren't even facing each other. Quickly I realized that what I was hearing was their thoughts! Shocked, I dashed out of the barn and came across a young lesbian who had crashed this party for old lesbians only. I exchanged greetings with her and as we passed I heard her say, "It sure was nice of these old biddies to let me stay for the dance." I realized that she wouldn't have said that to me out loud. I was hearing her thoughts, too.

Two other women came along and I heard them speaking, but not to each other and not saying anything making sense in the context of the situation. I really began to freak out. I ran back over to the ladder leading to the loft I was sharing with another woman for a sleeping space. I hoped she was not there. I didn't want to hear one more woman's thoughts. My own thoughts were more than enough to keep me busy!

I had promised to play some fiddle tunes for some square dancing at the beginning of the dance, and when my loft partner came up to see where I was, I told her I was not feeling at all well and absolutely could not come down. All I heard from her was what I knew she actually said aloud to me. What a relief! As I lay there on my sleeping bag I had to wonder if I had really been hearing the thoughts of all those other women. I simply couldn't explain what had happened in any other way. I quickly fell asleep and the following morning, when I awoke, all was normal. During the workshop Elana, Elizabeth, Baba and I decided we would like to find some land and live together. I had thought Elana and Elizabeth were pretty settled where they were, but I guess they wanted the company of other women, as did the rest of us. The others knew that I would have nothing to contribute to a down payment, but they seemed eager to have me on the land with them. This was such a healing experience for me that I felt able to resume my friendship with Pearl when I returned to Corvallis.

Not long after I returned home, it became apparent that Baba wanted to live in California and the other women wished to remain in Oregon. I loved Oregon, but northern California was entirely acceptable to me. Baba invited me to her home in Berkeley for a visit. Since we were both vegetarians and agreed on most political issues, as well as the sharing of our spirituality, Baba thought we ought to get to know each other better, while we looked for others to live on land with us.

I had reconnected with Pearl and discovered that she was driving down to southern California to visit her mother. When she heard Baba had invited me down for a visit, she offered to take me as far as Stockton, from where I could catch a bus to Berkeley. I wrote to Baba telling her of the opportunity and found that it would be a good time for her as well.

While I was waiting for the bus in Stocton, I wondered if by chance, one of my former co-workers from the hospital would happen by. I realized that it was quite unlikely and quietly observed my mixed feelings of wantng, yet not wanting this to happen.

Baba lived in one of the beautifully restored cedar-shake houses Berkeley is noted for. I was amazed at the feminist library she had, as well as an immense collection of records and tapes.

One evening Baba brought out her pipe with some of her home grown sinsemilla. After we each took a few tokes, Baba placed herself in the lotus position and prepared for a meditation. I lay down on one of the couches looking at Baba. After a bit I saw her change into a small child, laughing and playing and calling to her mother. Next I saw her as she must have been about the time of her marriage. Then I saw the more mature woman admonishing her children. Finally, she became, once more, the older woman I had recently met. Again, I was astounded at the strength of her marijuana, but feeling somewhat strange, I decided to retire.

At the end of the week we decided I should sell my Moose Brownie

Business and come down to live with Baba, while we formed the women's community we envisioned together.

In the meantime I had met a lesbian couple who lived in Philomath, of all places! They had each been married before and between them had three children, two boys and a girl. When I met Nellie and she discovered I had just met some lesbians, she not only showed me how I could change my name by simply filling out a Social Security form stating my new name and that I was not changing it for purposes of fraud, she invited me over to meet Dottie and the children. We got along so well that she invited me to become a part of their family. It was a tempting offer. I really liked the children and we began spending a lot of time at my cabin.

Unfortunately Dottie and I fell in love. Nellie was too threatened to form a threesome. Dottie still loved and felt loyal to Nellie and we spent less and less time together. I began to firm up my plans to join Baba in Berkeley.

At a business meeting of the bakery collective, I spoke of wanting to leave and offered to sell them my Moose Brownie business. In the library I had found a formula to determine the assets of a business in order to come up with a fair price for it. The collective was surprised at my decision, but were most happy to buy the business for the price I was asking. They made an offer of a down payment and we worked out a schedule for paying off the rest. With the down payment, I got my station wagon in good repair. I decided to take only what I could get into it. The rest I would give away. It reminded me of when I had left home for the convent and had given away my few possessions.

A few days before I was to leave for Berkeley, I was lying awake in my cabin, making plans for the trip down, when a car drove up into my drive. I looked at the clock and saw that it was midnight and suddenly realized how isolated I was without even a telephone. I got out of bed and grabbed my hammer out of my tool box as I heard footsteps approaching my cabin. Finally I couldn't stand it and called out, "Who is it?"

I almost collapsed with relief when Dottie answered. She had come to spend the night with me. At once, I realized that we would make love and that it would be the first and last time. We did just that, for fifteen hours! It was a very beautiful experience, the expression of withheld desire and the knowledge that it would be the only time.

CHAPTER TWENTY-FOUR

I LEFT FOR Berkeley and moved into an upstairs room at Baba's. We soon discovered we had quite a psychic connection. One afternoon I thought it would be nice to have baked potatoes for supper. I went downstairs and on my way to the kitchen, called out, "How would you like to have some baked potatoes for supper?

"I just put them in the oven." Baba replied.

One evening two other women came over for a visit. Baba painted all of our faces in amazing ways and we decided to go out on the town and see how people would react. First we went to the Bacchanal, a lesbian bar in Albany. Most of the women at the bar studiously avoided looking at us, but when a few of them began to react with hostility, we decided it was time to leave.

People on the street would sometimes gape at us and then look away in embarrassment. Everyone's sense of humor seemed to be locked up for the night. However, I had been surprised at the way Baba did me. When I looked in the mirror after she had finished I saw a very strong and powerful woman from a very ancient past looking back at me. My visage really wasn't very funny at all. We finally went to a hippie restaurant for some sweets. There we were more appreciated. One man came over to our table and began going into long and detailed explanations about what our faces represented – as if he could know. Baba did not appreciate his autocratic descriptions of her art, nor did the rest of us. We quickly consumed our desserts and left.

On our way to Baba's car, a group of five walked out of an alley. Not only were their faces made up, but they were in full costume, as well. Both groups broke out laughing.

"Are you coming from a party?" Baba asked.

"Wel l l l l l," one of them answered sheepishly, "we just felt like dressing up for fun."

"Us too! Us too!" I shouted. "Hope you've gotten a better reception than we have."

"We've just started," a woman replied.

The four of us told them of our experiences, so they decided to begin with the hippie restaurant to be assured of a good beginning. We wished them luck and went on our way.

Baba painted with oils and other media. She also threw ceramic pots, having her own kiln, large enough to make vases three feet high. I admired the way she used her art to enhance her home. She had five or six paintings she called *Paintings for Stoned People.* She explained to me that she had taken plain white paper and randomly swished on some acrylics in pastel colors. Then she got stoned and took a black magic marker and drew in what the swatches of pastel colors suggested to her. At the time, I was not stoned, but I could appreciate the gargoyle type figures she had outlined. Some were laughing, some were terrified, others, it was hard to tell. There were also fanciful animals, plants and trees.

One afternoon Baba, a mutual friend and I were sitting out on Baba's back patio enjoying the lovely fall weather. Baba had passed a pipe and we were all satisfied to just sit and not have to keep a conversation going. Suddenly I sat up and cried out, "They're moving! They're moving!" I was pointing to one of the *Paintings for Stoned People,* just inside the kitchen door.

Baba laughed and laughed. "I told you they were for stoned people."

I got up and out of my chair and went closer. "They...they're moving!" I exclaimed again. Then I had to go all around the house to see if the others were doing the same. My intermittent laughter could be heard out on the patio.

Baba had an editor friend, who was also a devotee of Baba's marijuana. Pat came over one evening and we all settled in for a good time being stoned together. I was beginning to discover that instead of stimulating me, sinsemilla made me passive. I enjoyed what the others were doing in a heightened way, but I never felt the urge to play my violin, for instance, nor, as in this case, to enter into a stimulating and highly intellectual discussion. Neither Pat nor Baba seemed to notice or care, when I lay down on a couch to listen.

"I wonder where they get all that energy," I thought to myself. Then I found myself responding to what they were saying with derision. "Who cares?" I asked myself. "Who really cares?" I had noted lately that I was breaking away, somewhat, from the charm Baba had put on me. I didn't believe Baba was a witch and had put me under a spell, but I had been totally impressed by the woman's quick mind and wonderful talents in creating beauty. Now I began to see Baba as a fallible human like myself. It was like

I had been in love with her, without feeling sexual. It was admiration I had felt, but up to then, the admiration had hidden Baba's weaknesses.

One fateful morning after this, Cissy wakened me, because she wanted to go out. I let her out of my bedroom and was pulling on some clothes, when I heard Baba screaming. I ran down stairs not having any idea what to expect. The screaming was coming from the living room.

I ran in finding Baba sitting on the floor. As soon as she saw me, she began sputtering, "Your dog! Your dog!" as she pointed an accusing finger at Cissy.

"My God, did she piddle on your rug?" I asked.

"Piddle on my rug," Baba cried. "Might that have been the case. I was in here lying on the floor meditating and out of my body, and she…she licked my face!"

"Oh!" I replied, totally mystified and not understanding the tragedy that it apparently was.

"Do you realize, Hannah Blue Heron, that she could have caused my soul never to return to my body?"

"Well, no, I guess I didn't," I answered defensively. "Probably Cissy didn't either.

From that day forward our relationship deteriorated. I promised never to let Cissy out of my room again, unless I was with her. Baba seemed to accept the apology and the solution, but the next thing I knew Baba was accusing me of leaving the doors unlocked when I left the house. The first time this happened, I thought I might have been careless and determined to be more aware in the future. The accusations continued and I finally wondered aloud, "It feels like some genie – or someone – is following me around unlocking the doors as soon as I lock them. I clearly remember locking the back door when I left this morning."

"Well," Baba concurred, "there is a ghost in this house. Probably the woman who owned the house before me. Maybe she doesn't want you around!"

I realized instantly who didn't want me around. A few days later I met a young woman at the Pacific Center who was looking for a roommate and was accepting of the idea of having a dog. When I went home, there was Baba waiting up to tell me I hadn't locked the back door again.

"Well, if I didn't," I answered, "you won't have to worry anymore. I'm moving out tomorrow."

"Can't you understand that I have valuable things in my home? This just can't go on," she exclaimed as if I hadn't spoken.

"Baba, listen to me," I said trying not to return the anger. "I just said that I'm moving out tomorrow. You won't have to worry anymore."

"Tomorrow! You're moving out tomorrow? You don't have to do that! Where will you go?" I was surprised and nonplused at her concern.

"I just met a lesbian who is looking for a roommate. As far as she knows there is no ghost in her apartment to haunt me by unlocking the doors."

"You…you told her that," Baba was close to shouting.

"Well, I thought I should check it out," I laughed and went on up to my room.

I had enjoyed Baba's intelligence and the wit she expressed in her art, but I realized she did not trust me. I wasn't sure why, in fact I had no idea. Both of us were downwardly mobile, but Baba had come from an upper class background. What was clear to me was that I could not live with such distrust.

My new home was an apartment complex surrounding a small court yard. There wasn't sufficient room to let Cissy out without my taking her on a leash and going beyond the court yard. I realized I would have to move again, but not until I had obtained some kind of job. I had been trying to get assistance through the federal government program, CETA, to study massage and diet at the Berkeley Holistic Health Center. After three and a half months I was denied because of my academic degrees, i.e. I had had my chance.

I had met an older lesbian who told me of a job taking care of a woman eighty-four years old. Lizzie was bed-ridden but had staunchly refused to go to a nursing home. Her social worker had arranged to have someone go in for four hours in the morning to prepare Lizzie's meals and bathe her.

I was challenged with the idea of helping someone stay out of a nursing home, so I took the job for four days a week. I was shown how to transfer Lizzie from her bed to her wheel chair by her former aide. That was the sum total of the training I received. Through the Center for Independent Living, I got a few more similar jobs, which enabled me to take classes at the Berkeley Holistic Health Center as well as pay my rent and buy food. By working at the BHHC for four hours a week, I got to take classes there at a discount.

Shortly after I began doing attendant care, I found a lesbian in her final year at law school, who had a large garage in the back of her home, which

she did not use. Maureen also had a huge fenced yard where I would be able
to have a garden as well as providing Cissy with space. I persuaded Maureen
to let me remodel the garage into a living space. Maureen agreed, happy to
have someone who had the time to put in a garden. She let me use my first
three months of rent money for the remodeling and we signed an agree-
ment that I could live there for at least a year. I referred to it as my cabin in
the city.

By now I had enrolled in a class on deep tissue body work. The instructor was a Lomi affiliate. At the first class we learned about the Lomi tradition
and what he would try to cover in the course. I felt I would learn much
from him.

At the second class, Tom, another teacher from BHHC attended, although not as a student. Since this was the first time Greg had taught at the
Center, apparently Tom was there to see how he would do. I thought Greg
did a good job of pretending he wasn't there. During the second half of the
class Greg asked for a volunteer to pose for some body reading. This meant
that the volunteer would stand before the class in the nude. I felt safe enough
with Greg, that I finally volunteered. While I was standing there naked, Tom
began making some remarks about my character. According to him, he could
tell from my legs that I had a hard time making decisions and even more difficulty in sticking by them once I had made them. In other words, according
to him I was a pretty wishy-washy person. I was tempted to tell him about
the difficult decisions I had made in my life and give my record of staying
with them, but I knew it wouldn't change his opinion.

"Your diagnosis, if it can be called that, is most simplistic and made from
insufficient data, Tom," I finally said with tears in my eyes.

"Look," he replied, "you shouldn't take this so personally. It's all right to
be indecisive."

Greg could see the anger welling up in my eyes and quickly brought the
body reading to a close. He showed us some massage strokes for the soles
of the feet and had us practice them on each other for the remainder of the
class. My feet had always been very tender and when my partner began the
strokes on them, I let out loud and long howls, which had been the recommended way for dealing with pain from the strokes. I knew I was also releasing anger and frustration from the body reading. Did any of the others guess?
I didn't even care.

Sherry, an R.N., who was taking the class came over to my "cabin" so we could practice some of the strokes on each other. I asked her what she thought about the body reading session.

"I thought it was gross, Hannah. I was so relieved when you finally spoke up," she answered.

"Well, I'm still not satisfied with Greg's response," I protested. "I don't feel at all safe that something like that couldn't happen again. He should have interceded for me rather than changing the subject after the humiliation."

"You're absolutely right, Hannah," Sherry quickly agreed. "You should say something to him. I'll back you up all the way. How can any of us really feel safe in there?"

At the next class it was Sherry who brought it up at the beginning, and we spent the first half of the class discussing it. Nearly all of the others agreed that it hadn't been fair and even admitted that they would be loathe to volunteer to do anything similar. Greg was somewhat impatient with the proceedings and still seemed hesitant to take a firm stand.

In the second part of the class, when Greg was doing a demonstration, Tom flatly contradicted one of Greg's techniques. This time Greg didn't hesitate. "Tom, I'm teaching this class in my way, which is the way I've been trained. If you want to teach your methods, ask the collective, but I would really appreciate it if you would stop coming to this class. You've caused us nothing but trouble." Tom left without a word.

I finished that series of classes with Greg and signed up for a second. I liked what I was learning from him and no further incidents occurred that were offensive to me, although I did feel a certain uneasiness about him, which I couldn't explain.

After the second series of classes which he taught under the auspices of BHHC, Greg told us about some weekend workshops he would be giving at his own home on the coast. The prices were much more than the classes at BHHC, but I was determined to learn as much from him as I could.

At the second weekend Sherry and I were the only ones present from BHHC. There were three other women there, who lived nearby and had also taken previous classes from Greg. At this workshop it became increasingly obvious to me that Greg was ignoring me. He wasn't even giving me opportunities to practice the new strokes he was teaching. I finally got up the courage to complain.

"Greg this is the third time I haven't gotten to practice on someone. Please don't teach us another stroke until I've had a chance to try out the ones you've already shown us.

"Hannah, are you sure? I can't believe…"

"She's right, Greg," Sherry intervened. "You have been ignoring her."

"I'm really sorry Hannah," he sputtered. "Believe me, it wasn't intentional."

For the rest of the afternoon he was very solicitous in seeing that I got a turn. When we were going to practice doing the last stroke of the day, it was my turn to practice on Sherry. I centered myself and did it with utmost awareness and care.

"Wow!" Sherry cried out. "It feels just like it does when Greg does it."

I actually felt hostility coming at me from in back of me. I turned around and realized it was coming from Greg. Then a huge bit of insight came over me. One reason I had not gotten along with men in general was that they were threatened by me. By throwing myself into learning all I could from Greg, he felt threatened by my growing ability rather than being proud he had taught me so well. I realized that it would not be safe for me to be so vulnerable in his classes and decided, with regret, that this would have to be the last class.

In spite of this interruption in my training I felt I was ready to get a good massage table and began saving for one. I also began looking for other Lomi affiliates, in the hope of learning more of their techniques.

Instead, I discovered that Pauline, a woman I had met in OWN, had studied Jin Shin Do. We decided to trade lessons with each other on the two disciplines. Pauline would teach me the Jin Shin strokes for the head, neck and shoulders and I would teach her the deep tissue strokes I had learned from Greg.

It was about this same time when I was finally able to overcome a creative block on composing. I set aside Martha's *A Woman's Place* and wrote a lovely third mode melody to the untitled first poem of *Tribe*. I began calling my song *Crossing a Creek* from the first line of the poem. Soon after that I set *Women of the Dream* to a melody with a simple but powerful maraca accompaniment. Then I composed melodies for *Women That I Love* and *Under a Mushroom*, both of which were also from Tribe. From the volume *Night River* I composed a melody for *Gift*. By then I was ready to return to *A Woman's Place*. I didn't use a Gregorian mode but retained the free rhythm of the modes.

After a year of doing attendant care for various people, I strained my back transferring a man with multiple sclerosis from his bathtub to his wheelchair. I had been finding the work increasingly difficult and took this for a sign that I should find something else to do. I still didn't feel prepared enough to set myself up as a masseuse, although by that time I did have my table and had taught a series of classes with a woman who was an herbalist. I was also wanting to return to the country. The noise of the city was making me nervous, especially the traffic control helicopters flying overhead. Living in the country didn't seem an option right then, so I found some house cleaning jobs to keep me going until something more permanent would turn up.

It was during that year of 1979, that quite by chance, I recognized a Good Shepherd Sister as she was coming out of her apartment in Berkeley. We were both astonished at running into each other.

"What are you doing in Berkeley, Sister Eugene?" I gasped.

Sister Eugene laughed and said, "Believe it or not, I'm here with Sister Margaret studying theology at the Union Theological Seminary. It's an ecumenical seminary with instructors from many different faiths."

"Amazing!" I cried out. "How long have you been here?"

"This is our second and last year here," Sister answered. "I...I"m sorry, but I guess I don't know your name. It...it isn't Teresa, is it?"

"No," I laughed as I told her my name. Then I told her how I had come by it and in the process, *came out* to Sister Eugene.

"Hey, that's all right," Sister Eugene assured me. "Sister Margaret and I have been campaigning very hard against Proposition #6. Do...do you know about Dignity?"

"Vaguely," I replied. "It's wonderful that you're helping us fight Prop #6." I hoped to get Sister off the subject of Dignity.

"Listen," Sister Eugene continued, "I know Sister Margaret will want to see you. Will you come over to our apartment tomorrow for lunch?"

I felt hesitant about renewing these friendships, but couldn't honestly think of a good reason not to, especially since they were so open to my lesbianism.

Proposition #6 was a proposal that would have been very discriminating against lesbians and gays in the areas of housing and jobs, but especially in the field of education. I was sincere in my appreciation for their campaigning against it, even though the official Church still regarded homosexuality as a mortal sin. Dignity was a kind of underground organization in the Church, not recognized by the hierarchy, but there were priests who would say Mass for them. Those priests felt that homosexuality was an illness, and that gays and lesbians shouldn't be kept from the Church any more than other ill people. These two sisters encouraged homosexuals to attend Dignity meetings and the special Masses for them.

At that first luncheon with them, I remained firm about my decision not to attend Dignity meetings. "The Catholic Church is just too patriarchal and anti-feminist for me," I said, knowing that they would be disappointed. However, they seemed quite understanding and wanted to keep up the contact.

One afternoon, I was very surprised to receive a letter from Troy. I wasn't even certain how she had learned where I was living. She and her lover, Catherine, had moved to St. Paul, Minnesota, where the two families had bought an old mansion. Actually, there were four families living there, since two of Catherine's older sons had married and had some children. Troy wanted me to see their home, consider living there with them and even offered to send an airplane ticket for this purpose.

I had to pause and consider my feelings towards Troy. Was I still in love with her? I felt not, but knew I was somewhat vulnerable, not having found a lover during the two years I had been out. However, I was feeling somewhat at loose ends about my future and decided to give it a try. It was possible I could move there. Probably the competition for being a masseuse wasn't as heavy in St. Paul as it was in the Bay Area. I decided to go and wrote Troy telling her so.

During one of my visits with Sister Eugene and Sister Margaret, I mentioned my upcoming trip to St. Paul.

"Oh, are you going to visit the mother house?" Sister Eugene asked.

"Well, I don't know about that," I replied. The thought had crossed my mind but I had more or less decided not to.

"Oh, Hannah, you really should," Sister Margaret said. "You've told us how hard it was leaving the order without even saying goodbye. There were a lot of sisters who found that as difficult as you did. They would love to see you and hear what you are doing now. I'm sure it would be a healing experience for all of you."

"I hadn't thought of that," I admitted. "Perhaps I will."

"Mother Francis is back there, you know. She'll definitely be happy to see you."

"I didn't know she was back," I replied, feeling a little lurch in my stomach. "Maybe I will go visit. It would be nice to see the new convent, too."

When I arrived in St. Paul, and walked into Troy's spacious dining room,

I was totally amazed to see one of the choir stalls from the old convent there.

"Where did you get that?" I cried out.

"Oh, so you recognize it," chortled Troy. "Catherine's friend, Mary Beth, went to the auction the Good Shepherd Sisters had just before they demolished the old convent. She fell in love with it and got it for next to nothing, I guess."

I walked over to it and knelt in it. Undoubtedly I had spent time in it, assisting at Mass, chanting the office and meditating. It seemed a definite sign to me that I should go visit the sisters at the new convent.

Then Troy took me to the elevator, which took us to the third floor, from where we went on up to the unfinished attic. Here she suggested we could put in an apartment for me.

Later Troy drove me over to the site of the old convent. All of the buildings had been demolished except for the novitiate, which was occupied by Catholic Social Services. I was truly surprised to see the old summer house still standing. Memories of the many good times I had enjoyed there came flooding in my mind's eye – the picnics, roller skating, playing tether ball with the young sisters under my charge.

When we returned to Troy's, I telephoned the mother house right away, asking for Mother Francis. When she came on the line, it was as if all the pain between us had never been. Mother Francis was delighted that I was in town and warmly extended an invitation for me to come out and visit.

"We're having our annual province-wide meeting for a few days, so there are sisters here, who knew you, that wouldn't have been here otherwise. You came just at the right time," Mother Francis assured me.

The following morning, after Troy dropped me off, as I walked towards the modern yet monastic looking building, I remembered how I had felt twenty-nine years before, walking towards the old convent for the first time, wondering about my future there, filled with happy expectations. Now, I wondered again what I would find in this new place. I felt only a slight hope that it would be a healing experience for all of us.

As Mother Francis approached me, I noticed the pure white hair showing under the small modernized veil. After we hugged, we smiled at each other, remarking on our mutually graying hair. Then Mother Francis showed me the new chapel, which she had helped to design. It seemed quite severe, at first, but I could honestly exclaim, "It's really quite beautiful, Mother. I love the beautiful inlaid woods in the ceiling, walls and on the floor. A lot of love was put into the planning of this."

"I'm happy you like it, Hannah. We did put in a great deal of time planning it," she replied, smiling. Then Mother Francis took me to the parlor where the others were waiting. The first person I saw was Mother Mechtilde, my former novice directress and superior in Omaha. The dark chestnut colored hair showing from under her veil seemed entirely unclouded by any gray.

None of the sisters, who had entered with me, were there. Sister Louise, my red headed friend, was unable to get away. There were a few sisters who had been in the juniorate when I had been their directress. Many others had left.

As soon as I saw her, I went right up to the smiling Sister Philomena. She had been the older sister in charge of the laundry, whom I had always admired. There had been mutually warm feelings between us.

After we hugged, she said, "I hear you've been having it hard out there in the world."

Surprised, I became defensive and replied, "Well, life is hard anywhere,.... but, yes, it has been hard for me out there."

After I sat down, they began telling me where some of my old friends were, who had died, and all about the new mother house. None of them asked me what I was doing, but I told them about my studies in holistic health, of what the feminist movement meant to me and that I had begun to compose music again.

"I guess you don't know that I composed some music while I was still among you. I usually did it during meditation. It was in celebration of being with Jesus and of being with you, too," I added shyly. I hoped they would understand. "So, I'd like to sing two of them for you now. They seem to belong to you somehow."

As I sang *Tree*, the poem by Robert Lax I had set to music, I let my eyes travel around the room, trying to meet each one's gaze, at least for a second. In seeking their eyes, I was hoping to meet their hearts. At first I saw loving recognition as they listened to my voice.

"Yes, this is the voice of Sister Teresa," they seemed to say. I was swept back immediately to the old chapel, hearing again, all of our voices filling the space with our love and devotion.

Then I began singing the second of the two songs.

I am your reed, dear Shepherd,
Glad to be, glad to be.
And now if you will
Breathe out your joy in me
And make bright song . . .*

Suddenly I noticed pain in their eyes. Now, it seemed as if they were saying, "How could you have left us, you, who loved us so much, and we, who loved you in return?"

How would I ever be able to answer that burning question? I broke off, unable to finish the song. I apologized and thanked them for taking the time to visit with me. Quickly, I walked away. I knew there had been healing, but I also knew that there would always be some pain from being apart from them, that I would always miss *that strange intimacy* which had been ours.

---

*from *The Reed of God* by Caryll Houselander.

AFTERWARD

HANNAH DID NOT move to St. Paul, but listening to her urges to live in the country, she and Cissy, with her violin, moved to southern Oregon in August of 1980. She had dreams of creating a secret cooperative network among women's lands and in this way undermining patriarchy and beginning a feminist revolution. They would fight sexism, racism, ageism and the ravages of classism.

That December, she invited the poet, Martha Courtot, to come up to conduct a writer's workshop. From its success, she and Tangren Alexander began a writer's group which became known as The Southern Oregon Women's Writers Group, Gourmet Eating Society and Chorus. The half day meetings every three weeks attracted women from all over southern Oregon, and is still meeting today.

This writer's group became the 'family' Hannah had hoped to find in a woman's land commune. While living in the third trial community, Golden, she acquired a feline familiar, Purr Purr. Her friend Troy appeared, only to take the opposite side in some contentious disagreements in the group. Hannah sorrowfully concluded that women had to learn to live together amicably before anything like the revolution she had dreamed of could take place. Nonetheless, it was while she was at Golden that she wrote a fictitious novella, *Stories from the Other Side of Madness.* inspired by a poem of Martha Courtot. She made a musical based on the novella which has been produced in three different places. Music continued to be an important part of her life, performing, composing and teaching.

It was also while she was living at Golden that she learned of a search for submissions for a proposed anthology, *Lesbian Nuns Breaking Silence.* Hannah began writing and writing, ending up with a complete work in itself. A selection from *That Strange Intimacy* appeared in the anthology.

In June of 1982 Hannah discovered a wonderful cabin for rent and decided that it would be good to live outside of a woman's group to assess her recent experiences and plan for her immediate future. While living at the cabin, she began reading books on Zen Buddhism and started to sit (Zen term for meditating) almost daily, which she has continued up to the present. Unhappily, it was while she was living there that she was forced to have her beloved Cissy put to sleep.

After eighteen months at the cabin, Hannah was invited to join a group living at Rainbow's End, just outside of Roseburg. They did not attempt to be a commune with rules and regulations. She lived there for nearly two years, but after a time, she began suffering from muscle and joint pains, often requiring her to spend two or three days a week in bed. Later she wrote in her journal, "Arthritis and what I now perceive to be the poorly defined 'fibro myalgia' made me decide that the damp, foggy weather of southern Oregon was not healthy for me." She had already learned about Arizona's dry climate while helping an arthritic friend move to Adobe Land, a woman's land just outside Tucson.

At Adobe Land she experienced an amazing, almost miraculous rejuvenation, and over the course of a couple years, beginning at age sixty, she built her round earth home almost single handed. The seventeen feet in diameter 'kiva' is five feet deep with a three foot wall of adobe bricks, which she made from the dirt from the hole. The vaulted roof measures nine feet from the floor. Many a wonderful celebration of the pagan circles, musical happenings, private mediation and counseling sessions as well as healing massages have been witnessed by those walls as Hannah has become a locally revered crone.

During her seventeen years at the kiva, Hannah gave music lessons, worked at WomanKraft, a local art gallery and performance center and participated in the Civic Orchestra of Tucson, as well as starting a string quartet. And, of course, she continued composing and writing on her newly acquired Mac computer. As she transferred *That Strange Intimacy* onto that marvelous machine, she destroyed the chapters covering the six very difficult years right after leaving the convent, deciding that "no one would want to wade through those terrible, depressing years with me." She also wrote her only novel, *The Virgin*, based around 3500 B.C. during the ascendancy of patriarchy.

For ten years she partnered with a much younger woman, a special education teacher, who moved a mobile home on the property. The two of them purchased the surrounding acre from Adobe, sharing a love of hiking, tennis, camping and traveling throughout the southwest and northern Mexico in an RV. Glaucoma forced Hannah to give up tennis and driving, caused her to break a leg and made it difficult to read books or music. She found an ophthalmologist, who determined that a simple removal of cataracts would restore a great deal of her acute vision, even though the glaucoma had destroyed much of her peripheral vision. These difficulties, plus the return of some arthritis, highlighted the age difference with her partner and Hannah chose to free her by concentrating on the beloved kiva, some gardening and, of course, her writing, her composing and her dog Foxy.

During the last six years, Hannah has continued celebrating the pagan feasts, has started the Desert Women's Writers Group with Lois Lockhart and rewritten for a fourth time, her memoir, *That Strange Intimacy.* Hannah decided that as emotionally difficult as it would be to write it again, she should include those extremely difficult six years, since they definitely played a large part in her development.

Hannah received what she calls "the gift of her old age" when she met and partnered with a woman she describes as "the love of my life." Together they have faced the ravages of age and arthritis, including the need for Hannah to realize she could no longer live in the wonderful but somewhat primitive conditions of the kiva. The disappearance of Foxy on a trip in the mountains and adjusting to life in the city, albeit in a large mobile home with her beloved, have been most difficult for Hannah.

However, her life has brightened considerably with the sale of the kiva to a woman who appreciates and loves the kiva in much the same way Hannah does. Susan has the resources to upgrade the kiva as well as to maintain it and is also becoming a good friend.

It has seemed to Hannah that after an exhausting push to get *That Strange Intimacy* published, along with the forthcoming *Growing Tall in Colorado* (the story of her childhood) and *Self Portraits in the Nude*, consisting of essays, letters journal entries and poems from her later life, together represent an almost miraculous fruition of her life.

Margaret Moore
March, 2005

AIDS TO PROSPECTIVE SINGERS

IN THE CONVENT I was given the opportunity to study and sing Gregorian Chant, which I learned to love very much. One thing that appealed to me was that it grew up out of the language. Therefore, it does not introduce a strict beat to be used throughout a song. This seems logical to me since the spoken word of any language I know of does not follow the same rhythmic pattern throughout. While the *neums* (the symbols used in Gregorian chant to represent tones, comparable to our notes) do indicate differences in length of individual notes, they are not held to the same accuracy as our quarter notes, half notes etc. All this seems logical to me when setting words to a melody. Of course instrumental music is quite a different thing.

Since the poems I choose to put to melodies are not set to a recurring meter, (as in iambic pantemeter etc.) you will not find a time signature nor bar lines in the music. I use modern notes rather than neums, since musicians who have studied neums are somewhat rare. I choose the eighth note as the fundamental note, although it does not receive the value of one beat as our quarter note, but of a half beat, as it does in modern music.

Gregorian chant does elongate certain notes for emphasis, or to end a phrase and other reasons, so you will find quarter notes and half notes and the use of the dot in my music. But especially in long passages of eighth notes you follow the rhythm of the words and therefore the notes are not exactly equal in length.

It would be convenient to use the neums, because they are not set to a key signature or absolute pitch, but only give the pattern of whole and half steps, or relative pitch. This would enable the singer to easily adjust the melody to suit his or her own range. I hope you will feel free to do this anyway.

Tree

Words by Robert Lax

Music by Hannah Blue Heron

Love- ly in Thy light this light is Lord, touch- ing through

the trees in ear- ly morn- ing. Love- ly in Thy light this light Be-

lov - ed, Speak - ing through the trees, Thy word of love. How

Tree 2

Tree *3*

through all the sum- mer day.   When ca- ta- racts of light

pour through the tree, and touch to song the green and qui- et grow- ing.

What songs my heart sings this green tree   What songs the tree sings,

Tree 4

sings my heart to Thee.

Unanswerable Questions

Words and Music by Hannah Blue Heron

You've been here all a- long and I'm just see- ing you? You've al- ways

worn so ma- ny hues -of greens and blues? Why the blue- vio- let of the

black- ber- ry bush's bram- bles is glow- ing!

Is my see- ing you be- ing? Or is my see- ing be- ing you?

I lie face down to feel the pul- sing of the breath- ing, the breath- ing

of the moun- tain sides of trees! Through the earth I find I *am*

breath- ing with the trees!

Is my breath-ing you be- ing? Or is my breath- ing be- ing you?

Unanswerable questions 2

I hear your sing- ing ring- ing through the cos- mos. All round my

ears the sound waves are qua- ver- ing! With the pul- sing of my

breath- ing, I join in with the sing- ing!

Is my sing- ing you be- ing? Or is my sing- ing be- ing you?

Crossing a Creek

Words by Martha Courtot

Music by Hannah Blue Heron

C / Am / Am / G / C / Am / G
Cros- sing a creek re- quires three things A cer- tain se- re- ni- ty of mind,

Dm C / C / G / C
bare feet And a sure trust that the snake we know slides si- lent- ly

G / Dm / G / Am / Em
un- der water Just be- yond our vi- sion will choose to ig- nore the flesh

Dm / Dm / C / Dm C / AmG
that cuts through its ter- ri- to- ry and we will pass through. Some

Am / Am / Am C G / C Dm Em / G
peo- ple think that cros- sing a creek is ea- sy, but I say this All crossings

Em / Dm / Dm / A7 / Dm
are hard, whether creeks, moun- tains, or in- to o- ther lives And we must

C / C / Am / G / G / Am
al- ways be- lieve in the snakes at our feet Just out of our vision And we must

C / Eflat / Dm / AmG / Am G C
prac- tice be- liev- ing We will come through, we will come through

Under A Mushroom

Words by Martha Courtot

Music by Hannah Blue Heron

This is a new country women have en- tered Every where there are small

fires to be avoided Our feet kick the rubble, looking for things to save us

The muscles in the arms of women are changing All this cliff hanging changes

the body Insects nibble at the soft insides of our thighs Our eyes are smoky

like the sky Our men wander sleep walking, day dreaming Their eyes are

somewhere else They think we live in the same world But they do not see

the fires nor the cliffs we hang from For women the blast has already

happened We live in the holocaust, holding on Waiting for the new world.

Our faces are covered with ash.

Women of the Dream

Words by Martha Courtot

Music by Hannah Blue Heron

324

That Strange Intimacy

Women of the Dream 2

wail- ing our an- cient grief. Each spring then we will let them know the

dream was worth it. As their bones whi- ten the pu- rest al- le- lu- ias of

hope! Al- le- lu- ia! Al- le- lu- ia! Al- le- lu- ia!

At the end of the third alleluia, raise the cone of power*, at the same time rattling the maraca .

*Raise the cone of power by toning (not singing) from a low tone, gradually raising it to a high tone, at the same time raising your arms and ending with a whoop.

ISBN 1-41205803-1